Christmas ~ 2

*To   Our Ver
With*

Gaurce v Winston

DAILY DEVOTIONS
FROM THE PURITANS

I. D. E. THOMAS

© I.D.E. Thomas, 1995, 1997
First Published in 1995 by Hearthstone Publishing Ltd.,
Oklahoma City, Oklahoma, USA under the title,
Puritan Daily Devotional Chronicles
This edition published by Gwasg **Bryntirion** Press, 1997
ISBN 1 85049 130 5

All Scripture references are from the King James Version.

Cover design: burgum boorman ltd.

Typesetting: Go Graphics
The Cairn, Hill Top, Eggleston, Co. Durham, DL12 0AU

Published by the
Gwasg **Bryntirion** Press
(formerly Evangelical Press of Wales)
Bryntirion, Bridgend CF31 4DX, Wales, UK
Printed by Creative Print & Design (Wales) Ltd.
Ebbw Vale, Mon., Wales, UK

INTRODUCTION

Come, taste this food from the Puritan table! You will soon discover that there is nothing like it in all of literature. The Puritan has been maligned and vilified for too long. Gratefully, he is being rehabilitated. Modern, specialised research no longer considers him a negative, sour-faced kill-joy, but a man of monumental intellect and of profound acquaintance with God and his Word. He was learned in the whole sweep of divine revelation, and possessed an extraordinary skill in applying the Word to every department and category of life. His expertise in spiritual probing and discerning was second to none. As a seer of divine truth and surgeon of human souls, the Puritan remains peerless.

These selected samples, culled from the voluminous writings of the Puritans, supply us with a unique spiritual diet; and a germane and relevant diet. It is a totally false assessment to think of the Puritans as being involved in purely abstract and hypothetical doctrines. On the contrary, they were custodians of what can accurately be called 'practical divinity'. What motivated these highly learned and university-trained divines was a consummate desire to live a life that was well-pleasing to God. Nothing else mattered. As B. B. Warfield stated, 'Puritan thought was almost entirely occupied with loving study of the Holy Spirit, and found its highest expression in dogmatic-practical expositions of the several aspects of it.'

A case could be made that some of the derisive criticisms levelled at the Puritans were due to a smouldering resentment at their God-fearing and Christ-honouring lives. This trait in the Puritan makeup seems to disturb and agitate a society given over to pleasing 'the world, the flesh and the devil.'

To rekindle interest in the spiritual and the eternal, these daily readings should prove invaluable. They have a capacity of supplying a completely new dimension to our lives, where God becomes the all-important Person. To do what these readings urge upon us will bring us into God's own presence, and put us on speaking terms with him. To hear him, and to fear him, will be the most revolutionary experience we can ever encounter. Other fears vanish as we learn to fear him. It is in this vein that H. G. Wood described the Puritan as a man who had 'learned to fear God and found that he had nothing else to fear.'

It is my prayer that these readings from the Puritans will whet our appetite for more of this food. May it produce a hunger and a craving for the sources themselves, where we can feed not on samples but on full supplies. And our journey should not end with these sources of over three hundred years ago, but go back far beyond them to the great source himself. The Puritans would be the first to recommend that we go all the way back to the one who alone is the 'Bread of life', and who still holds out the promise that 'he that cometh to me shall never hunger.'

Unlike the so-called modern diets, this is not means for the reducing of our physical weight but for the stimulating of our spiritual growth. Having begun with the appetizers and samples, may we soon be heard saying: 'Give us more!'

JANUARY

Run man run

... let us lay aside every weight, and the sin which doth so easily beset us, and let us run with patience the race that is set before us, Looking unto Jesus ... (Heb. 12:1-2).

C onsider there is no way but this: you must either win or lose. If you win, then heaven, God, Christ, glory, ease, peace, life, yes, life eternal, is yours. You must be made equal to the angels in heaven. You shall sorrow no more, sigh no more, feel no more pain. You shall be out of the reach of sin, hell, death, the Devil, the grave, and whatever else may contribute to your hurt. Contrariwise, if you lose ... you procure eternal death, sorrow, pain, blackness and darkness, fellowship with devils, together with the everlasting damnation of your own soul.

Consider that this Devil, this hell, death and damnation, follow after you as hard as they can drive, and have their commission so to do by the law, against which you have sinned. Therefore, for the Lord's sake, make haste.

If they seize upon you before you get to the city of Refuge, they will put an everlasting stop to your journey. This also cries, Run for it.

Know also, that at this present time heaven's gates, the heart of Christ and his arms are wide open to receive you ...

Keep your eyes upon the prize. Be sure that your eyes be continually on the profit you are likely to get. The reason why men are so apt to faint in their race for heaven is either one of these two things: 1. They do not seriously consider the worth of the prize. 2. If they do, they are afraid it is too good for them ... I tell you, heaven is prepared for whosoever will accept it ... Consider, therefore, that as bad as you have got there. Thither went scrubbed, beggarly Lazarus ... Therefore take heart and run man, run.

— John Bunyan, *The Heavenly Footman*, pp. 30-33. (R.P.)

Time wise

So teach us to number our days, that we may apply our hearts unto wisdom (Ps. 90:12).

Every day is a little life, and our whole life is but a day repeated. This is why old Jacob numbered his life by days, and Moses desired to be taught this point of holy arithmetic, to number not his years but his days. Those, therefore, that dare lose a day are dangerously prodigal, those that dare to misspend a day desperate. All days are his who gave time a beginning and continuance; yet some he has made ours, not to command but to use. In none may we forget him: in some we must forget all besides him ...

Now, when sleep is rather driven away than leave me, my desire always is to awaken with God. My first thoughts are for him who has made the night for rest, and the day for travail; and as he gives, so he blesses both. If my heart is early seasoned with his presence, it will savour of him all day after ... That done, after some meditation, I walk up to my masters and companions, my books. Sitting down among them with the keenest anticipation, I dare not reach forth my hand to salute any of them, till I have first looked up to heaven ...

Sometimes I go for my learning to one of those ancients whom the Church has honoured with the name of Fathers, whose volumes I confess not to open without a secret reverence for their holiness and gravity; sometimes to those later Doctors, who want nothing but age to make them classical; always to God's book ...

Before my meals, therefore, and after, I let myself loose from all thoughts, and would forget that I ever studied. A full mind takes away the body's appetite, no less than a full body makes a dull and unwieldy mind.

— Joseph Hall, *Contemplations*, p. 20 (T.N.)

Time management

For I am now ready to be offered ... (2 Tim. 4:6).

Christians should so manage their time and the work which God has appointed them to do for his name in this world, that they may not have a part thereof to do when they are departing this world ... If so, dying will be a hard work for them, especially if God awakens them about their neglect of duty.

The way of God with his people is to visit their sins in this life; and the worst time for you to be visited, is when your life is struck down, as it were to the dust of death, when natural infirmities break in like flood upon you, sickness, fainting, pains, wearisomeness, and the like. Now I say, to be charged also with the neglect of duty, when in no capacity to do it ... will not this make your dying hard? Yes, when it seems both in your own eyes, as well as in the eyes of others, that you fall short of the Kingdom of heaven for this and other transgressions; will not this make your dying hard?

David found it hard, when he cried, 'O spare me, that I may recover strength, before I go hence, and be no more' (Ps. 39:13). David at this time was chastened for some iniquity; yes, brought for his folly to the doors of the shadow of death. But here he could not enter without great distress of mind; wherefore he cries out for respite and time to do the will of God, and the work allotted to him ...

Yes, this will make you cry, though you be as good as David. Wherefore learn by his sorrow, as he himself also learned, to serve his own generation by the will of God, before he fell asleep ... Let then these thoughts prevail with you, as a ransom of great weight to provoke you to study to manage your time in wisdom while you are in good health.

— John Bunyan, *Paul's Departure and Crown*, pp. 21-23 (R.P.)

God's two books

For the invisible things of him from the creation of the world are clearly seen, being understood by the things that are made, even his eternal power and Godhead; so that they are without excuse (Rom. 1:20).

S tudy God in the creatures as well as in the Scriptures. The primary use of the creatures, is to acknowledge God in them; they were made to be witnesses of himself and his goodness, and to be heralds of his glory, whose glory of God as Creator 'shall endure for ever' (Ps. 104:31) ...

As grace does not destroy nature, so the book of redemption does not blot out that of creation. Had he not shown himself in his creatures, he could have never shown himself in his Christ; the order of things required it. God must be read wherever he is legible; the creatures are one book, wherein he has written a part of the excellency of his name ... God's glory, like the filings of gold, is too precious to be lost wherever it drops; nothing is so vile and base in the world, but it carries in it an instruction for man, and drives in further the notion that creation speaks to man, every shrub in the field, every fly in the air, every limb in a body. 'Consider me, God disdains not to appear in me; he has discovered in me his being and a part of his skill, as well as in the highest ... '

We have indeed a more excellent way, a revelation setting him forth in a more excellent manner, a firmer object of dependence, a brighter object of love, raising our hearts from self-confidence to a confidence in him. Though the appearance of God in the one is clearer than in the other, yet neither is to be neglected. The Scriptures direct us to nature to view God; else it would have been in vain for the apostle to make use of arguments from nature. Nature is not contrary to Scripture, nor Scripture to nature; unless we should think God contrary to himself who is the author of both.

— Stephen Charnock, *The Existence and Attributes of God*,
Vol. 1, p. 86 (B.B.)

The cry of creation

For we know that the whole creation groaneth and travaileth in pain to-gether until now (Rom. 8:22).

What is it that the creation groans under? The fearful abuse it is subject to in serving the lusts of unsanctified men. And what is it that the creation groans for? For freedom and liberty from this abuse; for the creature is not willingly made subject to this bondage (Rom. 8:20-21). If the irrational and inanimate creatures had speech and reason, they would cry under it, as a bondage insufferable, to be abused by the ungodly, contrary to their natures and the ends that the great Creator made them for ...

There is not a creature, if it had reason to know how it is abused till a man be converted, but would groan against him. The land would groan to bear him, the air would groan to give him breath, their houses would groan to lodge them, their beds would groan to ease them, their food to nourish them and their clothes to cover them ...

I think this should be a terror to an unconverted soul, to think he is a burden to the creation. If inanimate creatures could but speak, your food would say, 'Lord, must I nourish such a wretch as this, and yield forth my strength for him, to dishonour thee? No, I will choke him rather, if thou wilt give commission.' The very air would say, 'Lord, must I give this man breath, to set his tongue against heaven, and scorn thy people ... No, if thou wilt but say the word, he shall be breathless for me.' His poor beast would say, 'Lord, must I carry him upon his wicked designs? No, I will break his bones, I will end his days rather, if I may have but leave from thee.'

A wicked man; the earth groans under him, and hell groans for him, till death satisfies both.

— Joseph Alleine, *An Alarm to the Unconverted*, pp. 89-90 (B.T.)

Atheistical babblings

The fool hath said in his heart, There is no God. They are corrupt, they have done abominable works, there is none that doeth good (Ps. 14:1).

Said in his heart; that is, he thinks, or he doubts, or he wishes. The thoughts of the heart are in the nature of words to God, though not to men ... he dares not to openly publish it, though he dares secretly to think it. He cannot erase the thoughts of a Deity, though he endeavours to blot them out in his soul. He has some doubts whether there is a God or not: he wishes there were not any, and sometimes hopes there is none at all. He cannot convince himself by valid arguments to demonstrate to others, but he tampers with his own heart to try and persuade himself and so smothers within him those evidences of a Deity. His thoughts are so contrary to nature, that such a man may well be called a fool ...

No man is exempted from some spice of atheism by the depravity of his nature, which the psalmist intimates, 'there is none that doeth good.' Though there are indelible convictions of the being of a God, that they cannot absolutely deny; yet there are some atheistical babblings in the hearts of men, which are evident in their actions. As the apostle says, 'They profess that they know God; but in works they deny him' (Titus 1:16). Evil works are the dust stirred up by an atheistical breath.

— Stephen Charnock, *The Existence and Attributes of God*,
Vol. 1, pp. 23-25 (B.B.)

Now, if according to the impiety of atheists, there is no God, why do they invoke him in their adversities? If there be, why do they deny him in their prosperity?

— William Bates

If there be no God — then what?

If the foundations be destroyed ... (Ps. 11:3).

I f you take away God, you take away conscience, and thereby all measures and rules of good and evil. And how can any law be made when the measure and standard of them are removed? All good laws are founded upon the dictates of conscience and reason, upon common sentiments in human nature, which spring from a sense of God; so that as the foundation is demolished, the whole superstructure must tumble down. A man then could be a thief, a murderer, an adulterer, and could not in a strict sense be considered an offender. The worst of actions could not be evil, if a man were a god to himself, a law to himself.

Nothing but evil deserves a censure, and nothing would be evil if there were no God—the Rector of the world against whom evil is actually committed. No man can make that morally evil that is not evil in itself. When there is just a faint sense of God, the heart is more strongly inclined to wickedness; but where there is no sense of God, the barriers are removed, the floodgates are opened for all wickedness to rush in upon mankind. Religion prevents men from abominable practices, and restrains them from being slaves to their own passions: an atheist's arms would be free to do anything.

— Stephen Charnock, *The Existence and Attributes of God*, Vol. 1,
p. 78 (B.B.)

There is a conscience in man; therefore there is a God in heaven.
— Ezekiel Hopkins

I am resolved

Then shall ye remember your own evil ways, and your doings that were not good, and shall loathe yourselves in your own sight ... (Ezek. 36:31).

Consider, is it not better to remember your sins on earth, than in hell? Before your physician, than before your judge? ... O wretch, that I am! Where was my understanding, when I played so boldly with the flames of hell, the wrath of God, the poison of sin! When God stood by, and yet I sinned! When conscience rebuked me, and yet I sinned! When heaven or hell were close at hand, and yet I sinned! When, to please my God and save my soul, I would not hold back a filthy lust, or forbidden vanity of no worth! When I would not be persuaded to a holy, heavenly, watchful life though all my hopes of heaven depended on it! I am ashamed of myself; I am confounded in the remembrance of my wilful, self-destroying folly! I loathe myself for all my abominations! O that I had lived in poverty and rags when I lived in sin! And O that I had lived with God in a prison, or in a wilderness, when I refused a holy, heavenly life, for the love of a deceitful world!

Will the Lord pardon what is past, I am resolved through his grace to do things no more. I will loathe that filth that I took for pleasure, and abhor that sin that I made my sport, and die to the glory and riches of the world, which I made my idol. I am resolved to live entirely to that God that I did so long ago and so unworthily neglect; and to seek that treasure, that kingdom, that delight, that will fully satisfy my expectation ... Holiness or nothing shall be my work and life, and heaven or nothing shall be my portion and felicity.

— Richard Baxter, *Twenty Centuries of Great Preaching*, Vol. 11, pp. 259, 265-266 (20C)

The five seasons

... the fruit of the Spirit is ... joy (Gal. 5:22).

J oy is sitting upon the top of a pinnacle—it is the cream of the sincere milk of the Word ...

Joy is so real a thing that it makes a sudden change in a person; and turns mourning into melody ... What are the seasons in which God usually gives divine joys to his people? There are the five seasons. The first: sometimes at the blessed Supper. The soul comes weeping after Christ in the sacrament, and God sends it away weeping for joy ... There are two grand results of the sacrament, the strengthening of faith, and the flourishing of joy ...

The second is before God calls his people to suffering. 'As the sufferings of Christ abound in us, so our consolation also aboundeth' (2 Cor. 1:5). This made the martyrs' flames beds of roses.

The third is after sore conflicts with Satan. He is the red dragon who troubles the waters ... As the sufferings of Christians evidence, yet he may cast such a mist before his eyes, that he cannot read it. When the soul has been bruised with temptations, God will comfort the bruised reed by giving joy ...

The fourth season is after desertion ... When the soul is in this condition, and ready to faint in despair, God shines upon it, and gives it some apprehension of his favour, and turns the shadow of death into the light of the morning. God keeps his cordials for a time of fainting. Joy after desertion is like a resurrection from the dead.

The fifth season is at the hour of death. Even those who have had no joy in their lifetime, God puts this sugar in the bottom of the cup, to make their's sweet. At the last hour, when all other comforts are gone, God sends the Comforter ...

— Thomas Watson, *A Body of Divinity*, pp. 186-187 (B.T.)

Soul and body

And fear not them which kill the body, but are not able to kill the soul: but rather fear him which is able to destroy both soul and body in hell (Matt. 10:28).

G od will not let the sharpness, nor keenness, nor venom of the arrows of the enemies of his people, reach so far as to destroy both body and soul at once. But he will preserve them, to his eternal kingdom and glory ...

The truth is, persecution of the godly was of God, and never intended for their destruction, but for their glory; to make them shine the more when they are beyond this valley of the shadow of death ...

The reason why, by God's ordinance the spirit is not to be touched in suffering is because it is that which is to sustain the infirmity of the sufferer. God therefore will have the spirit of his servants kept sound, and in good health (Prov. 18:14; Isa. 57:16).

The room therefore, and the ground that the enemy has to play upon, are the body and outward substance of the people of God. The spirit is reserved, for the reason hinted before, and also that it might be capable of maintaining communion with God. And how else could they obey that command that bids them rejoice in tribulation, and glorify God in the fires as it is.

But, I say, if they have not power to touch, much less have they the power to destroy, body and soul for ever. The body is God's, and he gives that to them to destroy; the spirit is God's, and he keeps that to himself; to show that he has both power to do so with us what he pleases, and that he will recover our body also out of their hand. For if the spirit lives, so must the body, when men have done what they can with it. This is the argument of our Lord Jesus Christ himself (Luke 20:37).

— John Bunyan, *Advice to Sufferers*, pp. 126-128 (A.B.P.)

Man

What is man, that thou art mindful of him? and the son of man, that thou visitest him? (Ps. 8:4).

B ut, O God! What a little lord has thou made over this great world? The least grain of sand is not so small to the whole earth, as man is to heaven. When I see the heavens, the sun, moon, and stars, O God, what is man? Who would think thou shouldest make all these creatures for one, and that one well-near the least of all?

Yet none but he can see what thou hast done; none but he can admire and adore thee in what he sees. How had he need to do nothing but this, since he alone must do it!

Certainly the price and virtue of all things consist not in the quantity: one diamond is worth more than many quarries of stone; one lodestone has more virtue than mountains of earth. It is lawful for us to praise thee in ourselves. All thy creation has not more wonder in it, than one of us:

- ◆ other creatures thou madest by a simple command; man, not without a divine consolation;
- ◆ others at once, man thou didst first form, then inspire;
- ◆ others in several shapes, like to none but themselves; man, after thine own image;
- ◆ man had his name from thee; they had their names from man.

— Joseph Hall, *Contemplations*, p. 4 (T.N.)

Paradise lost

Therefore the Lord God sent him forth from the garden of Eden ...
(Gen. 3:23).

And if he [Satan] was so cunning at the first, what shall we think of him now, after so many thousands of years' experience? Only thou, O God! and these angels that see thy face, are wiser than he. I do not ask why, when he left his goodness, thou didst not bereave him of his skill: still thou wouldst have him continue an angel, though an evil one; and thou knowest how to ordain his craft to thine own glory. I do not desire thee to reduce his subtlety, but to make me wise: let me beg it, without presumption, make me wiser than Adam. Even thine image which he bore, made him not wise enough to obey thee ... When he chose rather to be at Satan's feeding than thine, it was just of thee to throw him out of thy gates with a curse. Why shouldst thou feed a rebel at thine own board?

And yet we transgress daily, and thou shuttest not heaven against us: how is it that we find more mercy than our forefather? His strength is worthy of severity, our weakness finds pity. That God, from whose face he fled in the garden, now makes him with shame to flee out of the garden; those angels that should have kept him, now keep the gates of paradise against him ... The same cause that drove man from paradise has also withdrawn paradise from the world.

... Neither now do I care to seek where that paradise was which we lost: I know where that paradise is, which we must care to seek, and hope to find. As man was the image of God, so was that earthly paradise an image of heaven; both the images are defaced, both the first patterns are eternal.

— Joseph Hall, *Contemplations*, pp. 7-8 (T.N.)

When the enemy steals our weapon

Then saith Jesus unto him, Get thee hence, Satan: for it is written ...
(Matt. 4:10).

But what is this I see? Satan himself with a Bible under his arm, and a text in his mouth: 'It is written ...' Who could not but over-wonder at this, if he did not consider, that since the Devil dared to touch the sacred body of Christ with his hand, he may well touch the Scriptures of God with his tongue? Let no man henceforth marvel to hear heretics or hypocrites quote the Scriptures, when Satan himself has not spared to cite them ...

How many thousand souls are betrayed by the abuse of that Word, whose use is sovereign and saving! No devil is so dangerous as the religious devil ...

What can be a better act than to speak Scripture? It is a wonder if Satan does a good thing well. He cites Scripture but with mutilation and distortion; it comes out of his mouth maimed and perverted; one piece is left, all misapplied. Those that wrest or mangle Scripture for their own purpose, it is easy to see from what school they come. Let us take the Word from the author, not from the usurper ...

Is our Saviour distasted with Scripture, because Satan mislays it in his dish? Does he not rather snatch this sword out of that impure hand, and beat Satan with the very weapon which he abuses? 'It is written again, thou shalt not tempt the Lord thy God' (Matt. 4:7) ... All the devils in hell could not elude the force of this divine answer: and now Satan sees how vainly he tempts Christ to tempt God.

— Joseph Hall, *Contemplations*, pp. 431-432 (T.N.)

Satan is only God's master fencer to teach us to use our weapons.
— Samuel Rutherford

Civil war within

For the flesh lusteth against the Spirit, and the Spirit against the flesh ...
(Gal. 5:17).

There is flesh as well as spirit in the best of saints: and as the spirit of grace always introduces something that is good, so the flesh will continually introduce that which is evil.

Now, this is the reason why you find so often in the Scriptures warnings and cautions to Christians to look to their lives and conduct: as, 'Keep thy heart with all diligence' (Prov. 4:23); 'Watch ye, stand fast in the faith, quit you like men, be strong' (1 Cor. 16:13).

All works are not good that seem to be so. It is one thing for a man's ways to be right in his own eyes, but quite another thing for them to be right in God's eyes. Often 'that which is highly esteemed among men is abomination in the sight of God' (Luke 16:15).

Seeing corruption is not yet out of our natures, we are prone to build (even upon the right foundation) wood, hay, and stubble, instead of gold and silver, and precious stones. How was David the king, Nathan the prophet, and Uzza the priest, deceived, touching the good works! Peter also, in both defending his Master in the garden, and dissuading him from his sufferings, although both were done out of love and affection to his Master, yet was deceived regarding good works.

— John Bunyan, *Christian Behaviour*, pp. 20-22 (B.T.)

Sin goes in a disguise, and thence is welcome; like Judas, it kisses and kills; like Joab, it salutes and slays.

— George Swinnock

Enjoying God

... in thy presence is fulness of joy ... (Ps. 16:11).

Man's chief end is to enjoy God forever ... There is a twofold fruition or enjoying of God; the one is in this life, the other in the life to come.

1. The enjoyment of God in this life. It is a great matter to enjoy God's ordinances, but to enjoy God's presence in the ordinances is that which a gracious heart aspires after ... In the Word we hear God's voice, in the sacrament we have his kiss ... The godly have had, in ordinances, such divine raptures of joy, and soul transfigurations, that they have been carried above the world, and have despised all things here below ...

Let it be our great concern to enjoy God's sweet presence in his ordinances. Enjoying spiritual communion with God is a riddle and mystery to most people. Everyone that hangs about the court does not speak with the king. We may approach God in ordinances, and hang about the court of heaven, yet not enjoy communion with God. We may have the letter without the Spirit, the visible sign without the invisible grace ...

2. Let it be the chief end of our living to enjoy this chief good hereafter. Augustine enumerates 288 opinions from philosophers about happiness, but all were short of the mark. The highest elevation of a reasonable soul is to enjoy God forever. It is the enjoyment of God that makes heaven ...

You complain, Christian, that you don't enjoy yourself. In the day you cannot enjoy ease, in the night you cannot enjoy sleep ... Let this revive you, that shortly you shall enjoy God, and then shall have more than you can ask or think; you shall have angels' joy, glory without intermission or expiration. We shall never enjoy ourselves fully till we enjoy God eternally.

— Thomas Watson, *Body of Divinity*, pp. 15, 17-18 (B.T.)

Glory to the Trinity

Whoso offereth praise glorifieth me ... (Ps. 50:23).

Glorifying God has reference to all the persons in the Trinity; to God the Father, who gave us life; to God the Son, who lost his life for us; and to God the Holy Spirit, who produces a new life in us; we must bring glory to the whole Trinity ...

Creatures below us, and above us, bring glory to God; and do we think to sit rent free? Shall everything glorify God but man? ... Creatures below us glorify God: the inanimate creatures ... Creatures above us glorify God: the angels are ministering spirits. They are still waiting on God's throne, and bring revenues of glory to the exchequer of heaven. Surely man should be much more studious of God's glory than the angels; for God has honoured him more than the angels, in that Christ took man's nature upon him, and not the angels' ... He has married mankind to himself; the angels are Christ's friends, not his spouse ...

We glorify God, by praising him. Doxology, or praise, is a God-exalting work. 'Whoso offereth praise glorifieth me' (Ps. 50:23). David was called the sweet singer of Israel, and his praising God was called glorifying God. 'I will praise thee, O Lord my God, with all my heart: and I will glorify thy name' (Ps. 86:12). Though nothing can add to God's essential glory, yet praise exalts him in the eyes of others. When we praise God, we spread his fame and renown, we display the trophies of his excellency ... Praising God is one of the highest and purest acts of religion. In prayer we act like men; in praise we act like angels ...

— Thomas Watson, *Body of Divinity*, pp. 4, 7, 11 (B.T.)

Affliction: the good and the bad

... the prosperity of fools shall destroy them (Prov. 1:32).

Freedom from afflictions seems most desirable both to nature and grace. We naturally love our ease, and would have nothing befall us that is grievous to flesh and blood; and gracious persons pray and strive to prevent and remove afflictions. But yet the experience of all, good and bad, in all ages of the world, proclaims this upon the housetops, that more have got good by afflictions, than by being without them ...

There is more danger in freedom from affliction than we are willing to suspect; and it is more difficult to love, and fear, and trust God, when we have the world, than when we want it. Without serious godliness, it is impossible to withstand the insinuating and pleasing temptation of flattering prosperity; and unless our faith is active, we cannot deal with it.

Why, then! is an afflicted condition to be preferred? Some that have had experience of both, say that they have been afraid to be without their afflictions. Some sick persons have been afraid of health, though they desired it, lest what they got in their sickness they should lose in their health.

But yet the continuance of afflictions breaks the spirit, and hinders that cheerful serving and praising God which is, or should be, the life of a Christian. Though many are made better by afflictions, yet none are allowed to pray for afflictions, but against them, and use all good means to avoid or remove them. It is one thing that makes heaven desirable—to be done with all our afflictions.

— Samuel Annesley, *Puritan Sermons*, Vol. 3, p. 22 (P.S.)

Let the glory shine

Let your light so shine before men, that they may see your good works, and glorify your Father which is in heaven (Matt. 5:16).

I confess it is possible for trembling, troubled and distressed Christians to be saved. But O, that they knew what a scandal they are to unbelievers, and what a dishonour to God, whom their lives should glorify! What man will fall in love with terrors and unquietness of mind? If you would glorify God by your fears and tears, they must be such as are accompanied with faith and hope; and you must not only show men what would make you happy *if* you could obtain it, but also that it is attainable.

Happiness is every man's desire; and none will come to Christ, unless they believe that it tends to their happiness. They indulge in the present pleasures of the flesh, because they have no satisfying apprehensions of any better; and if no man shows them the firstfruits of any better here, they will hardy believe that they may have better hereafter. It is too hard a task to persuade a poor drunkard, fornicator, or a proud and covetous worldling, to believe that a poor, complaining, comfortless Christian is happier than he, and that so sad and sorry a life must be preferred before all his temporal contentments and delights. You must show him better, or the signs and fruits of better, before he will part with what he has. You must show him the bunch of grapes, if you will have him go for the Land of Promise.

— Richard Baxter, *Puritan Sermons*, Vol. 2, p. 468 (P.S.)

To see a wicked man merry, or a Christian sad, is alike uncomely.
— William Gurnall

Abated, not abolished

Who are kept by the power of God through faith unto salvation ...
(1 Pet. 1:5).

When I say, believers persevere, ... I grant that those that are not serious believers may fall away. 'Demas hath forsaken me' (2 Tim. 4:10). Blazing comets soon evaporate. A building on sand will fall. Seeming grace may be lost. It is not wonder to see a bough fall from a tree that is only tied on. Hypocrites are only tied on Christ by an external profession, they are not ingrafted ...

I grant that if believers were left to stand on their own legs, they might fall finally. Some of the angels, who were stars full of light and glory, actually lost their grace; and if those pure angels fell from grace, much more would the godly, who have so much sin to betray them, if they were not upheld by a superior power.

I grant that, although true believers do not fall away actually, and lose all their grace, yet their grace may fail in degree, and may make a great breach in their sanctification. Grace may be ... dying, but not dead ... Corruption may break forth lively and vigorous in the regenerate; they may fall into enormous sins. But though all this be granted, yet they do not ... fall away finally from grace. David did not quite lose his grace: for if so, why did he pray, 'take not thy holy spirit from me' (Ps. 51:11)? He had not quite lost the Spirit. As Eutychus, when he fell from a window ... and all thought he was dead: 'No,' says Paul, 'there is life in him.' So David fell foully, but there was still the life of grace in him. Though the saints may come to that pass that they have but little faith, yet it is not to have no faith. Though their grace may be drawn low, yet it is not drawn dry; though grace may be abated, it is not abolished ...

— Thomas Watson, *Body of Divinity*, pp. 194-196 (B.T.)

Temptation

Blessed is the man that endureth temptation ... (Jam. 1:12).

No sooner is Christ come out of the water of baptism, than he enters into the fire of temptation. No sooner is the Holy Spirit descended upon his head in the form of a dove, than he is led by the Spirit to be tempted. No sooner does God say, 'This is my Son,' than Satan says, 'If thou be the Son of God.' It is not in the power either of the gift or seals of grace to deliver us from the assaults of Satan; they may have the force to repel evil suggestions, they have none to prevent them. Yes, the more we are engaged to God by our public vows and pledges of favour, the more busy and violent will be the rage of that Evil One to encounter us ...

It is not the presenting of temptations that can hurt us, but their entertainment. Bad counsel is the fault of the giver, not the refuser. We cannot forbid lewd eyes form looking in through our windows, but we may shut our doors against their entrance. It is no less our praise to have resisted, than Satan's blame to have suggested evil. Yes, O blessed Saviour, how glorious it was for thee, how happy for us, that thou wert tempted ...

O God, how can I hope to escape the suggestions of that wicked one, when the Son of thy love cannot be free! When even grace itself draws on enmity, that enmity that spared not to strike at the head; will he forbear the weakest and remotest limb? Arm thou me, therefore, with an expectation of that evil I cannot avoid. Make thou me as strong as he is malicious. Say to my soul also, 'Thou art my Son,' and let Satan do his worst.

— Joseph Hall, *Contemplations*, pp. 426-427 (T.N.)

A black catalogue

... ye fathers, provoke not your children to wrath ... (Eph. 6:4).

I t has been, is, and may be, the lot of gracious parents to have unconverted, wicked children. Let me add, the best of parents can be afflicted with very wicked, yes, the worst of children.

Had not Adam an envious, murderous Cain? Noah a cursed Ham? Abraham a mocking, persecuting Ishmael? Lot a Moab and Ammon? ... Isaac a profane Esau? Eli's two sons, Hophni and Phinehas, both 'sons of Belial', prodigies of lust and wickedness? David an ambitious Adonijah, and incestuous Amnon, a murderous, traitorous, rebellious Absalom? ...

The wickedness of these unconverted children has been and is still, too often occasioned, yes, advanced, by the sinful severity or indulgence of their unwary, though gracious, parents.

Sinful severity: it betrays itself in and by the irregular passions, austere looks, bitter words, and rigid actions of those parents who abuse their parental power ... The severity of their punishment exceeds the greatness of the crime ...

Sinful indulgence: a sovereign antidote against that fatal pleurisy of fond affection, is to 'bring them up in the nurture and admonition of the Lord.' Children must be 'nurtured', though they may not be 'provoked'. Parents must not be cruel ostriches, and expose their young ones to harm and danger; nor yet must they be such fond apes, who are said to hug their cubs so closely that they kill them with their embraces ...

Sinful severity, with Saul, has slain its thousands; sinful indulgence, with David, its ten thousands.

— Thomas Lye, *Puritan Sermons*, Vol. 3, pp. 154, 156, 160, 164 (P.S.)

The sin of indulgence

And he said unto them, Why do ye such things? for I hear of your evil dealings by all this people (1 Sam. 2:23).

Eli had two sons: 'sons of Belial', a brace of hell-hounds, Hophni and Phinehas, whose names do almost stain the sacred writ. They were wretches that were as desperately lewd as Eli himself was eminently holy.

If the goodness of example, precept, education and profession could have been antidotes against the extremity of sin, these sons of so holy a father could not have been so hellishly wicked ... As to old Eli: did he know all this? It is true especially of great men, that they usually are the very last to be informed of the evil of their own house, but yet as to Eli, it could not very well be, because when all Israel rang of the lewdness of his sons, how could he be ignorant of it ...

But, to our amazement, hear what he says: 'He said unto them, Why do ye such things? for I hear of your evil dealings by all this people.' What an indulgence, to a prodigy, to the notorious crimes of his wicked sons! ... to punish the thefts, plunders, sacrileges, adulteries of his sons with a mere, 'Why do ye so?' This was no other than to shave the head that deserved the axe ... An easy reproof only encourages wickedness ... It is a breach of justice, not to proportion the punishment to the offence.

Observe, I beseech you, observe, indulgent citizens, we do not read of any sin that Eli was charged with, but with that which is epidemical, I fear, among you, and looked upon as a peccadillo, and if a sin, at most but venial ... God swears, that he 'will judge Eli's house', and that with beggary, with death, with desolation ...

— Thomas Lye, *Puritan Sermons*, Vol. 3, pp. 168, 170-173 (P.S.)

Sin in my own family

... Job said, It may be that my sons have sinned, and cursed God in their hearts ... (Job 1:5).

We ought to mourn the sins of our near and dear relatives to a greater degree than those of mere strangers. Natural affection, sanctified, is the strongest. As nature puts forth itself to nearest relatives in strong affection, so grace engages to a proportionable degree in spiritualsing that affection. How earnest and desirous was holy Paul for his 'kinsmen according to the flesh' (Rom. 9:3), 'that they might be saved' (Rom. 10:1). Job offered sacrifices and prayers and tears too, no doubt, for the very fear that his children might offend God. There is in the saints a 'natural affection: spiritualised': no godly man knows how to spare any one of his children for the Devil. It must trouble him greatly that they who are so near to him in this life, could be so distant in the next ... To see them poor in this world, is nothing compared to the fear that they will never be rich towards God ...

Near relations may also be a great danger to the residue of those that belong to our family: sin in one or two, though in a large family, may endanger and infect the whole. We always strive to quench those flames that destroy houses near to us; we are more fearful of them than of those at greater distance ...

We must be more troubled for the poisonous root of sin, than for the branches and fruits of suffering that spring from the root. We must mourn more for the sin of a child than for the sickness of a child; lay more to heart what our children have done, than what they have undergone; more for their impiety than for their poverty; more because they have left God, than because their trades or estates have left them; more for fear (that) they died in sin, than because they died.

— William Jenkyn, *Puritan Sermons*, Vol. 3, pp. 113-114 (P.S.)

The errors of holy zeal

And he gave unto Moses, when he had made an end of communing with him upon mount Sinai, two tables of testimony, tables of stone, written with the finger of God (Exod. 31:18).

There was never so precious a monument as the tables written with God's own hand. If we saw the stone on which Jacob's head rested, or on which the foot of Christ once trod, we would treat it with more than ordinary respect. With what eyes should we behold this stone, which was hewed, and written with the very finger of God? ...

Prophecies and evangelical discourses he has written by others; never did he write anything himself, but these tables of the law. The hand, the stone, the law, were all his. But the more precious the record, how much greater the fault of defacing it ... At the first, God engraved his image on the table of man's heart; Adam blurred the image, but, through God's mercy, saved the table. Now he writes his will on the tables of stone; Moses breaks the tables, and defaces the writing ...

He forgets the law written, when he sees the law broken. His zeal for God transported him from himself and his duty to the charge of God. He hated more the golden calf, wherein he saw engraven the idolatry of Israel, than he honoured the tables of stone, wherein God had engraven his commandments. He longed more to deface the idol, than he cared to preserve the tables. Yet that God, which so sharply revenged the breach of one law upon the Israelites, does not check Moses from breaking both the tables of the law. The law of God is spiritual. The internal breach of one law is so heinous, that, in comparison with it, God scarcely counts the breaking of the outward tables a breach of the law at all ...

The tables had not offended; the calf had, and Israel in it.

— Joseph Hall, *Contemplations*, pp. 61-62 (T.N.)

Provoked to holiness

... and holiness, without which no man shall see the Lord (Heb. 12:14).

I t is but reasonable that they that expect to live in heaven, should live accountably while on earth. They that hope to be perfectly holy there, should be as holy as they can here. It ill becomes them to lead sensual lives now, that look for spiritual enjoyment then; to live like beasts, or even like men now, that hope hereafter to live with God; and to neglect him at present, whom they hope to enjoy at last.

It is serious holiness which must maintain a Christian's faith. A man can only maintain his faith when his practice is answerable to it: 'Faith without works is dead' (Jam. 2:26). Faith respects commands, as well as promises; the conditions of the promise, as well as the mercy promised. Now, the promise made to holiness as well as to faith, is that man cannot have a true faith without holiness. He cannot believe that God will save him, if he does not walk in that way which God has promised to save him. Though men do not have their title to heaven by their holiness, yet they cannot be saved without it (Heb. 12:14). It is the qualification required in all that are saved; and no man can be assured of his salvation, if he is not in some measure qualified and fitted for it. It is certain that holiness is a condition, though not of justification, yet of salvation. Therefore faith ... provokes and stirs up a man to the exercise of holiness, as being the way in which he must, if ever, attain to happiness.

— Edward Veal, *Puritan Sermons*, Vol. 3, p. 46 (P.S.)

Beginning the day with God

... I shall be satisfied, when I awake, with thy likeness (Ps. 17:15).

Rise early in the morning (if you be not necessarily hindered) following the example of our Saviour Christ (John 8:2), and of the good matron in Proverbs (Prov. 31:15). For this will usually much conduce to the health of your body, and the prosperity, both of your temporal and spiritual state.

In the time between your awakening and rising ... it will be useful to think upon some of these: I must awake from the sleep of sin, to righteousness (Eph. 5:14, 1 Cor. 15:34), as well as out of bodily sleep, to labour in my calling. The night is far spent, the day is at hand, I must therefore cast off the works of darkness and put on the armour of light ...

It is also a good time to call to mind what rules are to be observed, that you may dress yourself as becomes one that professes godliness. Namely:

1. That your apparel, for matter of fashion, suits with your general and special calling (1 Tim. 2:9-10), and with your estate, sex and age ...
2. That your apparel is consistent with health and comeliness (1 Cor. 6:14-15) ...
3. That the fashion is neither strange, immodest, singular, nor ridiculous ...
4. That you are not over curious, or over long, taking up too much time in putting it on.
   — Henry Scudder, *The Christian's Daily Walk*, pp. 29-31 (S.P.)

Five helps in the Christian walk

And make straight paths for your feet ... (Heb. 12:13).

Regarding bodily illness we reckon that the wisest and best physician, is the one who has more regard for the health than the will of his patient. The carpenter squares his work by the rule, not the rule by his work ... Therefore, says our Saviour, strive to enter in at the straight gate (Luke 13:24); that is, strive to enter because the gate is straight ...

But many of God's children do not attain to this strictness, yet are saved. This is true; though all God's children travel to one country, yet they do not do so with equal speed ... There is some difference in the outward action, but none in their inward intention; some inequalities in the event, none in the affection. In the degree there is some disparity, none in truth and uprightness.

All that are regenerate are equally strict in these five things, at least.

♦ First, they have but one path or way in which they all walk (Isa. 35:8).
♦ Second, they have but one rule to guide them in that way which they all follow (Gal. 6:15-16).
♦ Third, all their eyes are upon this rule, so not to be willingly ignorant of any truth (2 Peter 3:5).
♦ Fourth, they all desire and endeavour to obey every truth (Luke 11:9).
♦ Fifthly, if they fall by temptation (Gal. 6:1), yet they are in pain till they are set right again. If they stumble, through infirmity (as sheep may slip into a puddle) yet they will not lie down, and wallow in the mire, which is the property of swine.

— Henry Scudder, *The Christian's Daily Walk*, pp. 18-19 (S.P.)

Holiness: an evangelistic tool

But now being made free from sin, and become servants to God, ye have your fruit unto holiness, and the end everlasting life (Rom. 6:22).

Holiness has a mighty influence upon others. When this appears with power in the lives of Christians, it works mightily upon the spirits of men; it stops the mouths of the ungodly, who are ready to reproach religion, and to throw the dirt of professors' sins on the face of the profession itself. They say that frogs will cease croaking when a light is brought near to them. The light of a holy life puts as it were a padlock on profane lips; yes, it forces them to acknowledge God in them ...

One reason why such shoals of souls came into the net of the Gospel in primitive times was, because at that time the divinity of the Gospel doctrine appeared in the divinity and holiness of Christians' lives. Justin Martyr, when converted, professed, 'That the holiness which shined in Christians' lives and patience, that triumphed over their enemies' cruelty at their deaths, made him conclude the doctrine of the Gospel was truth.'

Yes, Julian himself, vile wretch as he was, could say that the Christian religion came to be propagated so much because Christians were a people that 'did good to all, and hurt to none.'

I am sure we have found, by woeful experience, that in these debauched times, when religion is so bespattered with frequent scandals, yes, a general looseness of professors, it is hard to get any to come into the net of the Gospel ... If they were but holy and exemplary, they would be as a repetition of the preacher's sermon to the families and neighbours among whom they converse, and would keep the sound of his doctrine continually ringing in their ears.

— William Gurnall, *The Christian in Complete Armour*,
Vol. 1, pp. 423-424 (B.T.)

Reproof and reproach

Let the righteous smite me; it shall be a kindness: and let him reprove me; it shall be an excellent oil, which shall not break my head ... (Ps. 141:5).

Consider carefully the difference between a *reproof* and a *reproach*. They may both be false alike, and that in which we are reproved may have no more truth in it than that in which we are reproached. Yes, we may be honestly reproved for that which is false, and wickedly reproached with that which is true. Augustine stated this when he referred to the maid who confronted his mother about drinking wine, as a hard and unjust reproach, although the matter itself was true enough. But a reproach is an acting of the mind designing of and rejoicing in evil. Regarding a reproof it is essential that it springs from love. 'Whom I love, I rebuke,' is the absolute rule of these things. Let a man rebuke another, and though for something which indeed is false, if it is done in love, it is a reproof; but let him rebuke another, though for something which is true, if it be the product of a mind delighting in evil, it is a reproach ...

Reproofs, if there is not open malice and continued wickedness manifest in them, are to be interpreted as gracious providential warnings to watch lest at any time we should be actually overtaken with that which at present we are falsely charged with. We know little of the dangers that continually attend us, the temptations with which we may be surprised at unawares, nor how near on their account we may be to any sin or evil which we consider ourselves most remote from and least obnoxious to. Neither on the other hand can we readily understand the ways and means whereby the holy, wise God issues forth those hidden provisions of preventing grace which are continually administered for our preservation.

— John Owen, *Puritan Sermons*, Vol. 2, pp. 609-610 (P.S.)

Instruments that glorify God

My little children, let us not love in word, neither in tongue; but in deed and in truth (1 John 3:18).

B elieve it, it is a preacher whose matter and manner of preaching and living demonstrates a hearty love to God, love to godliness, and love to all his people's souls, that is the fit instrument to glorify God by convincing and converting sinners. God can work by what means he wills; by a scandalous, domineering, self-seeking preacher; but such is not his ordinary way. Foxes and wolves are not nature's instruments to generate sheep. I never knew much good done to souls by any pastors, but such as preached and lived in the power of love, working by a clear convincing light, and subject to a holy, lively seriousness ...

And what I say of ministers, I say of every Christian ... While men are all *for* themselves, and would draw all *to* themselves, to a genuine Christian, another's good makes him rejoice as if it were his own. But the scandalous, selfish hypocrite lives quietly, and sleeps easily, as long as he is well himself ... irrespective of how it goes with all his neighbours, with the church, or with the world ...

Ministers, and Christians all ... let not want of charity hinder you at any time from giving, though want of ability may hinder you, and prudence may restrain you, and must guide you. If you say, 'Alas! we don't have it to give'; I answer: (1) Do what you can. (2) Show by your compassion, that you would, if you could, take care of your poor brethren. (3) Beg of others on their behalf, and encourage those that can do it.

— Richard Baxter, *Puritan Sermons*, Vol. 2, pp. 470, 472-473 (P.S.)

Love never faileth

Judge not, that ye be not judged (Matt. 7:1).

May I not speak evil of another person when it is true?
1. *A man may be at fault in so doing.* The real secret faults of your neighbour ... you ought not unnecessarily to publish. And suppose there is no untruth nor injustice in it; yet there is uncharitableness, and unkindness in it; and that is a sin. You would not have all the truth said about yourself, nor all your real faults publicly slandered ...
2. *You may speak evil of another person when necessity requires it.* It may be necessary for his good; and so you may speak evil of him to those that can help him; as a man may acquaint parents with the misdeeds of their children, for their own amendment. Thus Joseph brought to his father the vile report of his brethren ... But for a man to do this unnecessarily and unprofitably—this is the sin I have been speaking of.
3. *If you will speak evil of other persons, do it the right way.* Christ has given us an excellent rule: 'If thy brother shall trespass against thee, go and tell him his fault between thee and him alone: if he shall hear thee, thou hast gained thy brother. But if he will not hear thee, then take with thee one or two more ... And if he shall neglect to hear them, tell it unto the church' (Matt. 18:15-17).
4. *In doubtful cases, silence is the safest way.* It is rarely men's duty to speak evil of men; and when it is not their duty to speak, it is not their sin to be silent. It is seldom that any one suffers by my silence, or concealment of his fault; but great hazards are run, and many persons are made sufferers, by my publication.

— Matthew Poole, *Puritan Sermons*, Vol. 2, pp. 455-456 (P.S.)

FEBRUARY

He is all things to me

... He hath done all things well ... (Mark 7:37).

Cast your eyes which way you will and you shall hardly look on anything but Christ. Jesus has taken the name of that thing upon himself.

Is it day? And do you behold the sun? He is called the Sun of Righteousness. Or is it night? And do you behold the stars? He is called a Star, 'There shall come a Star out of Jacob.' Or is it morning? And do you behold the morning star? He is called 'the bright Morning Star.' Or is it noon? And do you behold clear light all the world over? He is 'that Light that lighteth every man that cometh into the world.'

Come nearer: if you look upon the earth, and take a view of the creatures about you, do you see the sheep? 'As a sheep before her shearer is dumb ... ' Or do you see a lamb? 'Behold the Lamb of God.' Do you see a shepherd watching over his flock? 'I am the Good Shepherd.' Or do you see a tree good for food, or a flower? He is 'the Tree of Life', and 'the Lily of the Valley', and 'the Rose of Sharon.'

Are you adorning yourself, and viewing your garments? 'Put ye on the Lord Jesus Christ.' Are you eating food, and seeing what you have on the table? He is 'the Bread of God'; 'the true Bread from Heaven'; 'the Bread of Life.'

— Isaac Ambrose, *A Homiletic Encyclopedia*, p. 886 (H.E.)

Since he looked upon me my heart is not my own, he hath run away to heaven with it.

— Samuel Rutherford

From nature to grace to glory

A bruised reed shall he not break ... (Matt. 12:20).

T his bruising is required (1) *before conversion*, that the Spirit may make way for himself into the heart by levelling all proud, high thoughts, and that we may understand ourselves to be what indeed we are by nature.

(2) *After conversion* we need bruising, that reeds may know themselves to be reeds, and not oaks. Even reeds need bruising, by reason of the remainder of pride in our nature, and to let us see that we live by mercy. And (also) that weaker Christians may not be too much discouraged when they see stronger shaken and bruised. Thus Peter was bruised when he wept bitterly (Matt. 26:75). This reed, till he met with this bruise, had more wind in him than pith ...

The people of God cannot be without these examples. The heroic deeds of those great worthies do not comfort the church so much as their falls and bruises do. Thus David was bruised (Ps. 32:3-5), until he came to a free confession, without guile of spirit ... Thus Hezekiah complains that God had broken his bones as a lion (Isa. 38:13). Thus the chosen vessel St. Paul needed the messenger of Satan to buffet him, lest he should be lifted up above measure.

Hence we learn that we must not pass too harsh a judgement upon ourselves or others when God exercises us with bruising upon bruising. There must be conformity to our head, Christ, who 'was bruised for us,' that we may know how much we are bound to him ... It is no easy matter to bring a man from nature to grace, and from grace to glory ...

— Richard Sibbes, *The Bruised Reed and Smoking Flax*, p. 4 (B.T.)

God's method of weaning

But he knoweth the way that I take: when he hath tried me, I shall come forth as gold (Job 23:10).

Two lessons God would principally teach you by affliction: First: That your affections be taken off from earthly possessions. When Israel doted on Egypt as a palace, God made it an iron furnace to make them weary of it. The creature is our idol by nature, but infinite wisdom makes it our grief, that it may not be our God. When children fare well abroad, they are mindless of home; but when abused by strangers, they hasten to their parents. The world is therefore a purgatory, that it might not be our paradise. As soon as Laban frowned on Jacob, he talks of returning to his father's house ...

Second: That you choose the good part that shall never be taken from you. Man's heart will be fixed on something as its hope and happiness. God therefore puts out our candles, that we may look up to the sun. When we are delving in the earth to find treasure, he sends dampness purposely to make us call to be drawn upward. Till the prodigal met with a famine, he regarded not his father. If the waters be abated, the dove is apt to wander and defile herself; but when they cover the face of the earth and allow her no rest, then she returns to the ark.

— George Swinnock, *A Homiletic Encyclopedia*, p. 110 (H.E.)

We cast our eye, not upon the agent, God, but upon the instruments, his creatures, which cannot do us the least harm till they have a commission from him to do so.

— John King

Evaluate your friends

... and there is a friend that sticketh closer than a brother (Prov. 18:24).

I n the choice of a bosom friend, some respect ought to be had to his prudence. Some men, though holy, are indiscreet, and in point of secrets are like sieves. They can keep nothing committed to them, but let them all run through. A blab of secrets is a traitor to society, as one that causes much dissension. It is good to try him whom we intend for a bosom friend before we trust him ...

Many complain of the treachery of their friends, and say, as Queen Elizabeth, that in trust they have found treason ...

Too many are like the Dead Sea, in which nothing sinks to the bottom, but everything thrown into it swims at the top, and is in sight.

Companions of my secrets are like locks that belong to a house: whilst they are strong and close, they preserve me in safety; but weak and open, they expose me to danger, and make me a prey to others.

If you have found a man false once, beware of him the second time. He deserves to break his shins that stumbles twice at one stone. That proverb of the Italians is worthy of consideration: 'If a man deceives me once, it is his own fault; if a second time, it is my fault.' He has need to sit sure who backs that horse which once has cast his rider.

— George Swinnock, *A Homiletic Encyclopedia*, p. 2119 (H.E.)

Sycophancy

... a flattering mouth worketh ruin (Prov. 26:28).

Flattery: It is the basest counterfeit of friendship and justice. It seems to do you right as justice binds, but it is with a design to injure you. It seems to act with love and endeared affection, but only as the crocodile which weeps over the skull of the man he has devoured.

A flattery from others ... represents our good or evil very truly, by making the good seem better than it is, and making the evil seem less than it is, and deceitful in both for advantage ... He is deeply in love, who cannot live without what is loved. Thousands of great and rich people cannot live without extravagant, notorious and incredible falsities of these parasites ...

Solomon tells you in our text, that it (flattery) 'worketh ruin.' ... The Scriptures assure us that where it is not cured, it kills ... 'An open sepulchre' and a flattering tongue are inseparable (Ps. 5:9). If the glutton digs his own grave with his teeth, the designing flatterer digs other men's with his tongue.

If you want to be cured (of love and flattery) you must resolutely and decisively reject the friendship of man who turns due praises into flattery. Let such know that they please least when they praise most; and that you make their first offence an opportunity to inform them, but that the second such offence shall be unpardonably punished with loss of your friendship.

— Henry Hurst, *Puritan Sermons*, Vol. 3, pp. 187, 190-195 (P.S.)

He gives comfort

Blessed be God, even the Father of our Lord Jesus Christ, the Father of mercies, and the God of all comfort (2 Cor. 1:3).

We see in the body that if any member is hurt, thither immediately, runs the blood to comfort the wounded part. The man himself, eye, tongue and hand is altogether involved in that wounded member, as if he were forgetful of all the rest. So in the family, if one of the children is sick, all the care and kindness of the mother is concentrated on that sick child, to the extent that all the rest begin as it were to envy his sickness. If nature does thus, will not God, who is the author of nature, do much more? For if an earthly mother do thus to a sickly and suffering child, will not the Heavenly Father, who has an infinite, incredible and tender love for his people?

This is the difference between God and the world. The world runs after those that rejoice in prosperity, as the rivers run to the sea where there is water enough already. But God comforts us in our tribulations. His name and style is, he 'comforteth those that are cast down.' The world forsakes those that are in poverty, disgrace and want; but God promises most of his presence to them that holy, meekly and patiently bear the afflictions which he lays upon them. And one drop of this honey is enough to sweeten the bitterest cup that ever they drank of. If God be with us, if the power of Christ will rest upon us, then we may even glory in infirmities, as Paul did.

— Thomas Manton, *A Homiletic Encyclopedia*, p. 202 (H.E.)

Our comforts compete with the number of our sorrows, and win the game.

— Thomas Adams

What you are speaks louder ...

Walk in wisdom toward them that are without ... (Col. 4:5).

Individual Christians, walking 'in wisdom toward them that are without,' may be exceeding helpful to promote the reception of the gospel among them.

This they may do, and more; for they may be helpful to promote their conversion and salvation. To further the reception of the gospel among them, is but the means; to promote their conversion and salvation, is the end. And the means are for the end. Now it is expressly affirmed, that an individual believer may save an infidel: ' ... how knowest thou, O man, whether thou shalt save thy wife?' (1 Cor. 7:16). That is, the believing party may be induced to cohabit with the unbeliever upon a hopeful prospect, that it is possible to conquer them by love, to attract them to have an esteem for holiness by an exemplary conversation, and to obtain God's grace for them by ardent prayers, and so be the means of saving their souls.

The apostle Peter exhorts Christian women who were yoked with unbelievers, to become eminent for their modesty, chastity, humility and respectfulness to their husbands (1 Pet. 3:1-2). Christian graces, being so exercised that they may be seen in their proper lustre, are excellent orators, and have a mighty power to persuade. It is more to *live* virtue, than to *commend* it.

Let me have leave to say to 'women professing godliness,' as the apostle styles them—O, live to such an eminent pitch of holiness, that you may ... give them occasion to say, as it is reported that Libanius, a heathen philosopher, did, 'O, what excellent women have these Christians!'

— George Hammond, *Puritan Sermons*, Vol. 4, p. 412 (P.S.)

A glorious contradiction

And to know the love of Christ, which passeth knowledge, that ye might be filled with all the fulness of God (Eph. 3:19).

Here we meet a seeming contradiction ... to know what is unknowable. And to 'be filled with all the fulness of God.' What is that, but to comprehend what is incomprehensible? The narrow vessel of our heart can no more contain the boundless and bottomless ocean of the divine fullness, than our weak intellectual eye can drink in the glorious light of that knowledge.

And yet there are many such expressions in the holy Scriptures. Thus Moses saw him that was invisible (Heb. 11:27). He saw him by the eye of faith in the glass of revelation, whom he could not see by the eye of reason in the glass of creation. And thus we are instructed in the Gospel, how to approach that God who is unapproachable; to approach that God by Jesus Christ according to the terms of the new covenant ...

The words will be consistent, and without any appearance of self-contradiction if we take the following position ... Although there is much of the love of Christ which is beyond our present knowledge, yet there is enough of that love that may be known: enough to feed our knowledge, so that it does not starve in this life; and enough to whet the soul's appetite to know more in the life to come ... The love of Christ has depths wherein the daring soul may drown, and yet shallows wherein the humble soul may safely wade ...

In a word: as Moses could not see God's face, and live (Exod. 33:20); and yet Moses could not live except he saw God's face; so there is a measure, and degree, of knowledge of the love of Christ, which we cannot reach even if we died for it; and yet there is such a measure and degree of the knowledge of that love of Christ, which we must reach, or we die for it.

— Vincent Alsop, *Puritan Sermons*, Vol. 4, pp. 285, 287-288 (P.S.)

Love: divine and human

Herein is love, not that we loved God, but that he loved us ...
(1 John 4:10).

N ow ... there is resemblance between that mutual love of the Father and the saints wherein they hold communion. (But) there are sundry things wherein they differ:
1. The love of God is a love of *bounty*; our love to him is a love of *duty*. The love of the Father is a ... descending love; such a love carries him out to do good things to us, great things for us ... he loves us, and sends his Son to die for us; he loves us, and blesses us with all spiritual blessing ...

Our love to God is a love of *duty*, the love of a child. His love descends upon us in bounty and fruitfulness; our love ascends to him in duty and thankfulness. He adds to us by his love; we nothing to him by ours.
2. The love of the Father to us is an *antecedent* love; our love unto him is a *consequent* love ... His love goes before ours. The father loves the child, when the child knows not the father, much less loves him. Yes, we are by nature haters of God (Rom. 1:30). He is in his own nature a lover of men; and surely all mutual love between him and us must begin on his part ... Never did a creature turn his affections toward God, if the heart of God was not first set upon him ...

The saints do not love God for nothing, but for that excellency, loveliness, and desirableness that is in him. As the psalmist says, in one particular verse (Ps. 116:1), 'I love the Lord, *because*!' So may we in general say, we love the Lord, *because*!

— John Owen, *Communion With God*, pp. 28-29 (A.P.)

Gifts and graces

Though I speak with the tongues of men and of angels, and have not ....
(1 Cor. 13:1).

Though a man has many parts and gifts, yet if he has not grace with them, he may go to hell and perish to all eternity; for by his gifts he is not united to Jesus Christ, nor made the child of God, nor estated into the covenant of grace (Matt. 7:21-23). You see how it is with children playing in the day—when night comes, one child goes to his father, and the other to his father. It may be that during the day they are so alike that you cannot say, whose child is this, or that. But when night comes, the father comes to his child, and says, 'Come, my child, come indoors.' And if the other child offers to go in there, 'No, child, you must go home to your own father.'

While we are living, grace and gifts are mingled together. Some men have gifts, and some men have graces, and they look very much alike. But ah, when night comes, and when death comes, then says God to those that have grace, 'Come, my children, enter in'; but if those that have gifts only come, he sends them away.

If a man go to hell and perish, the more gifts he has the deeper will he sink into hell. As it is with a man that is in the water, sinking in the water, the more he is laden with gold the more he sinks, and as he is sinking, if he has any time to cry out, he says, 'Oh take away these bags of gold, these bags of gold will sink me, they will undo me.' So I say, these golden parts and golden gifts will undo men. When men come to hell, the more golden gifts they have had, the deeper they shall sink ...

— Isaac Ambrose, *A Homiletic Encylopedia*, p. 2216 (H.E.)

It un-devils but not un-mans

And the very God of peace sanctify you wholly .... (1 Thess. 5:23).

Christianity abolishes not affection, but rectifies it. It does not dry up the streams of sorrow, joy, hatred, etc., but only turns them into the right channel; it does not remove their being, but their ill-being.

Religion slays not, but sanctifies, affections. It does not un-*man* a man, but only un-*devil* him. Grace is like the percolating or draining of salt water through the earth; it only takes away the brackishness and unsavouriness of our affections and faculties. It kills not Isaac, but the ram. It doesn't break, but only tunes, the strings of nature. It destroys not, but advances, nature.

When you are godly, you have more innocent humanity than ever. You may exercise human affections and actions as much as you desire, but just don't damn yourselves. You may eat without being gluttons; drink without being drunk; buy and sell without making a sale of your good conscience. Grace gives leave to everything except your souls.

— William Jenkyn, *Puritan Sermons*, Vol. 3, p. 125 (P.S.)

The power of the Law is to 'unkennel sins and make them take hold on a man's soul.'

— Vavasor Powell

Lord, make me beautiful within

Favour is deceitful, and beauty is vain; but a woman that feareth the Lord, she shall be praised (Prov. 31:30).

Is it beauty that you are proud of? I have told you what sickness and death will do to that before. 'When thou with rebukes dost correct man for iniquity, thou makest his beauty to consume away like a moth: surely every man is vanity' (Ps. 39:11). And if your beauty would continue, how little good will it do you? And who but fools look at the skin of a rational creature, when they would assess its worth?

A fool, and a slave of lust, and Satan, may be beautiful. A sepulchre may be gilded that hath rottenness within. Will you choose the finest purse, or the fullest? Who but a child or a fool will value his book by the fineness of the cover, or the gilding of the leaves, and not by the worth of the matter within? Absalom was beautiful, and what better was he?

— Richard Baxter, *A Homiletic Encyclopedia*, p. 435 (H.E.)

The soul of man bears the image of God; so nothing can satisfy it but he whose image it bears.

— Thomas Gataker

The pursuit of happiness

Whom having not seen, ye love; in whom, though now ye see him not, yet believing, ye rejoice with joy unspeakable and full of glory (1 Pet. 1:8).

What comfort can a malefactor, that has myriads of indictments against him upon the file, the least of which is sufficient to take away his life, expect from a just and righteous judge? That case is yours and mine, but infinitely more dreadful than between a malefactor and a magistrate. My sins are innumerable, and the least is mortal; God is the judge, and hell is the prison; wrath, horror, fire, the worm, and all endless—that is the punishment. The judge is, and cannot be otherwise than, most true and righteous; what comfort can I hope to expect from God absolute, that is, without relation to Christ? Behold, instead of comfort, a devouring flame, and instead of joy, a consuming fire.

I speak thus because a large number of our people say, 'God is merciful', and they do their best. They hope that God will be their comfort and so they serve him: and all this time they don't as much as think of Jesus Christ. We are all natural Socinians: and although we may never have heard their names, and much less read their books, yet we live in their heretical and blasphemous principles.

O the amazing stupidity of the so-called Christian world, that we can smile, and laugh, and hug ourselves in false comfort upon the brink of hell! There can be no comfort to us, without the God of all comfort; and no comfort can come to us from God, but by the Lord Jesus; and no Jesus to us without faith. We rejoice in God, says the apostle; but how? By Jesus Christ. Why? By him we have received the atonement; he has made it by his blood and we receive it by faith.

— Christopher Fowler, *Puritan Sermons*, Vol. 2, p. 527 (P.S.)

One man, one woman

... let every man have his own wife, and let every woman have her own husband (1 Cor. 7:2).

Mutual fidelity, especially to the marriage bed, and also in each other's secrets ... is directed in this verse. By which rule, the thoughts, desires and actions of each of them are confined to their own lawful yoke-fellow, as the dearest, sweetest and best object in the world; and this by virtue of the covenant of their God. The least aberration in this (if it be not speedily and sincerely mortified) will strangely gain ground and fester in the soul, and never rest till it come to plain adultery. And then the comfort of their lives, the quiet of their consciences, and the credit of their families, will bleed; and without true repentance, their eternal happiness shipwrecked ... And though some greater shame and other inconveniences follow the unfaithfulness of the wife; yet man and wife being one flesh are equal; unless the wisdom and strength of the man make his fault the greater ... Sin is boundless, and nothing but grace and the grave can limit the desires of the heart.

The same faithfulness is necessary in the wise concealment of each other's secrets, whether natural, moral, or civil, unless in cases where a superior obligation releases them. For there cannot be a more unnatural treachery than when husband or wife make one another obnoxious to shame or harm: bad, when it is done unwittingly; worse, when in the heat of passion; worst of all, when it is through ill-will and malice.

— Richard Steele, *Puritan Sermons*, Vol. 2, pp. 276-277 (P.S.)

A gracious wife satisfieth a good husband, and silenceth a bad one.
— George Swinnock

Hold your peace to keep the peace

Nevertheless let every one of you in particular so love his wife even as himself; and the wife see that she reverence her husband (Eph. 5:33).

A married couple, therefore, must study and pray for a meek and quiet spirit; mortify pride, learn self-denial and sometimes wisely withdraw till the storm is over; and hold their peace, to keep the peace. They must consider, as holy Mr. Bolton says, that they are not two angels met together, but two sinful children of Adam, from whom little can be expected but weakness and waywardness.

They must reckon it to be the greatest worth and honour to be the first in overtures of peace, and never suffer those unnatural passions to ferment. What honour or comfort can any one have in falling out with himself? What prize in that victory? Let some lesser faults be winked at; and let the husband wait discreetly for the right season to admonish his wife, and the wife respectfully to acquaint the husband, of things amiss. And if the faulty person would conscientiously make an acknowledgement of his error to the other, and both beg pardon of God for it, it would be a good antidote against the like folly, and bring glory to God. This is certain, he or she that can injure the other without scruple, is not kept from wrongdoing others by any honest principle. And, lastly, let them consider that it is much better to give place to one another, than by nourishing anger to 'give place to the devil' (Eph. 4:27).

— Richard Steele, *Puritan Sermons*, Vol. 2, p. 278 (P.S.)

A prudent wife commands her husband by obeying him.

— John Trapp

Three yokes

And the Lord God said, It is not good that the man should be alone; I will make him a help meet for him (Gen. 2:18).

H ence they are called 'yoke-fellows ... ' There are three yokes which they must jointly carry:

1. *The yoke of cares.* This all people must expect to bear in a married condition, and, for the most part, that of labour also. These lying solely on one shoulder will overload; but when some help comes in, when the husband takes care without, and the wife takes care within; when the husband travels abroad, and the wife is busy at home; then the burden is easier. To this end, it is good for the wife to read often the last chapter of Proverbs, and the husband the rest of that book ...

2. *The yoke of crosses and troubles.* For those that are married, though they expect nothing but pleasure, yet they must 'have trouble in the flesh' (1 Cor. 7:28), losses in their estates, afflictions in their children, crosses both from friends and enemies ...

3. *The yoke of Jesus Christ.* They should live 'as being heirs together of the grace of life' (1 Pet. 3:7). And the highest goal of their relationship is to promote one another's everlasting happiness. The knowledge of the husband must help the wife, and the zeal of the wife must help the husband. When the sun shines, the moon retreats; when that is set, this appears.

— Richard Steele, *Puritan Sermons*, Vol. 2, p. 277 (P.S.)

Recovering our lost rib

This beginning of miracles did Jesus in Cana of Galilee ... (John 2:11).

Was this, then, thy first miracle, O Saviour, that thou didst in Cana of Galilee? Could there be a greater miracle than this, that having been thirty years upon the earth, thou didst no miracle till now? ...

O Saviour, none of thy miracles is more worthy of astonishment than thy not doing miracles! What thou didst in private, thy wisdom thought fit for secrecy: but if thy blessed mother had not been acquainted with some domestic wonders, she would not now expect a miracle away from home. The stars are not seen by day; the sun itself is not seen by night. As it is no small art to hide art, so it is no small glory to conceal glory.

Thy first public miracle graces a marriage. It is an ancient and laudable institution, that the rites of matrimony should not want a solemn celebration. When are feasts in season, if not at the recovery of our lost rib? If not at this main change of our estate, where they joy of obtaining, meets with the hope of further comforts? The Son of the virgin, and the mother of that Son, are both at a wedding ...

He that made the first marriage in paradise, performs his first miracle in a Galilean marriage. He that was the author of matrimony, and sanctified it, does, by his holy presence, honour the resemblance of his eternal union with his church.

Happy is that wedding where Christ is a guest! O Saviour ... thou makest marriages in heaven, thou blessest them from heaven.

— Joseph Hall, *Contemplations*, pp. 435-436 (T.N.)

Ad hominem

... being knit together in love ... (Col. 2:2).

W hat can most hopefully be attempted to allay animosities among Christians, so that our divisions may not be our ruin? We are too prone to ... dislike things, for the simple reason that we dislike the persons who practise them. Such a prevailing disaffection makes us inapt to understand one another, and precludes our entrance into one another's mind and sense. If only love inclined us more to consider the matters of difference themselves, than to imagine some hidden meaning and design in the persons expressing them, it is likely we would find ourselves much nearer to one another than we thought we were, and an easier step for the one side to go over to the other ...

I know, many are apt to justify themselves in their animosity and bitterness of spirit toward others, on the pretence that *they* have the same disaffected mind toward them. But besides being a manifest and indefensible injustice, if they charge the innocent or such as they are not sure are guilty ... they make their tainted, vicious imagination to create its object ... How contrary is this vindictive spirit to the rules and spirit of the Christian religion! Is this to love our enemies, to bless them that curse us and despitefully use us, etc.? How unlike the example of our blessed Lord, when, even in dying agonies, he breathed forth these words and his soul almost at once: 'Father, forgive them,' etc. Or of the holy martyr Stephen: 'Lord, lay not this sin to their charge!'

I hope it is integral to all our principles: that no man will say it is against his conscience to love his brother.

— John Howe, *Puritan Sermons*, Vol. 3, pp. 92, 105-106 (P.S.)

The embraces of Christ

And lest I should be exalted above measure through the abundance of the revelations, there was given to me a thorn in the flesh, the messenger of Satan to buffet me ... (2 Cor. 12:7).

The evil of temptation is overruled for good to the godly ... it abates the swelling of pride. The thorn in the flesh was to puncture the puffing up of pride. Better is that temptation which humbles me, than that duty which makes me proud. Rather than a Christian shall be haughty-minded, God will let him fall into the Devil's hands awhile, to be cured of his swelling ...

The Devil tempts, that he may deceive; but God suffers us to be tempted, to try us. Temptation is a trial of our sincerity ...

Temptations work for good, as God makes those who are tempted, fit to comfort others in that same distress. A Christian must himself be under the buffetings of Satan, before he can speak a word in due season to him that is weary. St. Paul was versed in temptations. 'We are not ignorant of his devices' (2 Cor. 2:11). Thus he was able to acquaint others with Satan's cursed wiles. A man that has ridden over a place where there are bogs and quicksands, is the fittest to guide others through that dangerous way. He that has felt the claws of the roaring lion and has lain bleeding under those wounds, is the fittest man to deal with one that is tempted. None can better discover Satan's sleights and policies, than those who have been long in the fencing school of temptation ...

When Satan puts the soul into a fever, God comes with a cordial; which made Luther say, that temptations are Christ's embraces ...

— Thomas Watson, *A Divine Cordial*, pp. 24-27 (S.G.)

Hope—the younger sister

My soul fainteth for thy salvation: but I hope in thy word (Ps. 119:81).

As faith and love are cooperative, so faith and hope are very near of kin. Only, hope is the younger sister as to operation, as waiting with patience for that good which faith lays claim to in the promise; and without this hope we can neither live nor die with comfort ...

God made a promise to Abraham of multiplying his seed; but neither he, nor yet Isaac nor Jacob, must live to see it fulfilled. But says Stephen, 'When the time of the promise drew nigh ... the people grew and multiplied in Egypt'; so that God's promises have their stated times and seasons, during which there is work for hope, or else the soul would swoon away ... Hope is a cordial against the soul's fainting fits.

Again: during this interspace between the promise and the accomplishment, you may meet with many tribulations, through which you must enter into the Kingdom of heaven—fightings without, and fears within. The watchmen may smite you, and the keepers of the walls may take away your veil, as if you were not a virgin, but a prostitute; you may meet with sad eclipses and the hiding of God's face; his wrath may be hard upon you, and all his waves afflict you. You may even meet sometimes with such a storm, that neither sun or stars may appear in many days; during which time, you may reel to and fro like a drunken man, and be at your wit's end ... In these and like cases, what will you do without casting the anchor of your hope ... ?

— William Hook, *Puritan Sermons*, Vol. 2, pp. 686-687 (P.S.)

Neighbours all

... And who is my neighbour? (Luke 10:29).

There are some well-known men in the world that will tell you, that 'in the language of the Old Testament, "neighbour" means "one of the same country and religion", and that it is the peculiarity of the Gospel, that every man is my neighbour.' But if we examine Scripture, we shall find this to be a gross mistake.

I need not go farther for its confutation than to the Decalogue itself: 'Thou shalt not bear false witness against thy neighbour' (Exod. 20:16). I suppose it will seem very farfetched to affirm that it is lawful to bear false witness against a stranger. So when God commands, 'Thou shalt not lie carnally with thy neighbour's wife' (Lev. 18:20), I presume these gentlemen would not allow themselves that liberty with the wife of a stranger. If God may be his own interpreter, this controversy will quickly be ended from Leviticus 19, where, if you compare two verses—verse 18 'Thou shalt love thy neighbour as thyself' with verse 34 'But the stranger that dwelleth with you shall be unto you as one born among you, and thou shalt love him as thyself'; you will not need the help of an expert to form this conclusion, that the stranger is, in God's account, and ought to be in my account, my neighbour ...

Most true therefore is that saying of St. Augustine: 'Every man is a neighbour to every other man ... ' And the scribe, of whom we read in Luke 10, knowing the mistakes of many of his brethren, asks our Saviour this question: 'Who is my neighbour?' And our Saviour gives him an answer, the sum of which is this, that even the Samaritan was to be looked upon as his 'neighbour'.

— Matthew Poole, *Puritan Sermons*, Vol. 2, pp. 444-445 (P.S.)

Revenge

... for it is written, Vengeance is mine; I will repay, saith the Lord
(Rom. 12:19).

C onsider, that though Cain was a murderer, yet God disallowed any man from meddling with him under the penalty that his revenge would return on his own head sevenfold ...

The reason is, because he persecuted his brother for righteousness' sake, and so espoused a quarrel against God. For he that persecutes another for righteousness' sake, sets himself against God, fights against God, and seeks to overthrow him. Such a one a Christian must leave well alone, so that God will have his full blow at him in his time. This is why he says to his saints, and to all who are anxious to revenge themselves: 'Give way, stand back, let me come, leave such a one to be handled by me.' 'Dearly beloved, avenge not yourselves' (Rom. 12:19).

It was because of this that the Lord set a mark upon Cain, lest any finding him should slay him. You must not, indeed you must not, avenge yourselves of your enemies. Yes, though it was lawful once so to do, it is not lawful now. 'Ye have heard that it hath been said, thou shalt love thy neighbour, and hate thine enemy. But I say unto you, love your enemies, bless them that curse you ... ' (Matt. 5:43-44).

I say, Where is your love to your enemy? Where is your joy under the cross? Where is your peace? ...

A Christian, when he sees trouble coming upon him, should not fly in the face of the *instrument* that brings it, but in the face of the *cause* of its coming. Now the cause is yourself, your base self, your sinful and your unworthy demeanour toward God in spite of all the mercy, patience and long-suffering that God has shown you and exercised towards you.

— John Bunyan, *Advice to Sufferers*, pp. 136-139 (A.B.P.)

The more excellent man

... Knowledge puffeth up, but charity edifieth (1 Cor. 8:1).

W e must know that, as faith united us to the head, so love unites us to all the members; and as we can have no faith or hope without charity, so, as any man increases in faith, so he is enlarged in his charity. The more true piety man has, doubtless the more charity still does that man have. 'We that did hate one another,' says Justin Martyr of the Christians, 'do now live most friendly and familiarly together, and pray for our enemies.' If we must err one way, it is safer for us to err by too much mildness, than by over-much rigour; for Almighty God, though he be wise and just, yet he is most emphatically called 'Love.' ...

If the things in question be any way necessary, God forbid that you should refuse them; if they be not, God forbid that you should urge them. It was King James' remark to Cardinal Perron: 'The next way to concord, is to distinguish between things that are *necessary*, and to endeavour to reach a full agreement in those; and things that are *not necessary*, and to allow a Christian liberty in these.'

In dissuading you from extremes, I would never want to commend lukewarmness or halting in the course that men have chosen. They should so govern their resolution by wisdom and charity, that they may not unnecessarily provoke, grieve, or exasperate others, who perhaps have as sound hearts, if not as clear heads, as themselves ... It was a great and wise man's motto, *mediocria firma*; and a true proverb among the vulgar: 'Too-too will break in two.'

— Richard Steele, *Puritan Sermons*, Vol. 4, pp. 249-250 (P.S.)

Three things best forgotten

By which also you are saved, if ye keep in memory what I preached unto you, unless ye have believed in vain (1 Cor. 15:2).

There is no complaint more common among religious people, than the weakness of their memories; thinking, perhaps, that the defect does imply least guilt; or, it may be, mistaking their carelessness for forgetfulness ...

'Ye are saved, if ye keep in memory ... ' Our salvation in some sort depends upon it: for without the Gospel, no salvation; without faith, no benefit of the Gospel; and without hearing and retaining what we hear, no saving faith ...

The soul of man is a subject of wonder; and nothing more wonderful than the memory. That such innumerable images of things should be lodged in a finite faculty and that what seems to be utterly lost in it, should be fully recovered; it is justly deemed by the learned to be a miraculous mercy. It has power to bring things that are absent and past, back to the present ...

Three things which we should forget:

1. *Things unprofitable.* There are a thousand needless and useless matters that cluster the memory, and keep out better things ...
2. *Things hurtful.* In other words, injuries. These usually stick in the memory, when better things slip out ... As one says, 'We can remember *old songs* and *old wrongs* long enough.' ... It is not wrong for a man to have a natural remembrance of an injury, so long as he does not have an angry remembrance of it.
3. *Things sinful.* Thus we can remember a filthy story seven years, when we forget a saving sermon in seven hours.

— Richard Steele, *Puritan Sermons*, Vol. 3, pp. 347-349 (P.S.)

Age and beauty

The hoary head is a crown of glory ... (Prov. 16:31).

... the beauty of old men is the grey head (Prov. 20:20).

T rue grace is the most excellent recipe for beautifying your face: 'Wisdom maketh his face to shine' (Eccl. 8:1). There is something in an unaffected gravity, and unforced modesty, in an ingenuous, affable deportment, free and natural, without starch and pedantry, that recommends and endears itself more to the acceptance of the judicious than all the curious mixtures of artificial colours ...

It is lawful by natural means to recover what preternatural accidents have taken away. If sickness has impaired your complexion and beauty, health with restore it. Let the physician do his part, and restore health; he can restore decayed comeliness better than the painter. The physician is God's agent primarily to preserve life and restore health, I know; but whose agent is the painter, employed for the restructuring of faded beauty, you'd better inquire of Jezebel; for I confess my ignorance ...

It seems to me that we should acquiesce in the devastations which time has made upon our bodies. At the same time, improved health in our declining years may make us more lively, active, cheerful and vigorous in God's work. 'The hoary head is a crown of glory' and 'the beauty of old men is the grey head.' And are we ashamed of our glory? Do we despise our crown? Will nothing serve but juvenile hairs on an aged head? Must we need experiments to bring back the spring in autumn? The former is indeed more pleasant but the latter more fruitful and profitable. Who would exchange the harvest for the seed-time?

— Vincent Alsop, *Puritan Sermons*, Vol. 3, pp. 502-503 (P.S.)

Foul falls of the false

But he that shall endure unto the end, the same shall be saved
(Matt. 24:13).

The Christian must keep on his way to heaven in the midst of all the scandals that are cast upon the ways of God by the apostasy and foul falls of false professors. There were ever such in the church, who by their sad miscarriages in judgement and practice have laid a stone of offence in the way of their profession. Weak Christians ready to make a stand, as they did at the bloody body of Asahel (2 Sam. 2:22), do not know whether they can venture any further in their profession, seeing such leaders, whose gifts they so much admired, lie before them, wallowing in the blood of their slain profession ... No more like the men they were some years past. They are like the vale of Sodom now a bog and quagmire compared to what it once was—a fruitful garden of the Lord.

We need a holy resolution to withstand such discouragements, and not to faint; as Joshua, who lived to see the whole camp of Israel (with very few excepted) revolting, and in their hearts turning back to Egypt, and yet with an undaunted spirit maintained his integrity, yes, he resolved though not a man would stand beside him, to serve the Lord.

— William Gurnall, *The Christian in Complete Armour*,
Vol. 1, pp. 14-15 (B.T.)

We may occasion other men's sins by example, and the more eminent the example, the more infectious it is. Great men cannot sin at a low rate because they are examples; the sins of commanders are commanding sins; the sins of rulers ruling sins; the sins of teachers teaching sins.

— Ralph Venning

When all others fall ...

Nevertheless the foundation of God standeth sure, having this seal, the Lord knoweth them that are his. And, Let every one that nameth the name of Christ depart from iniquity (2 Tim. 2:19).

T wo considerable persons, and probably highly accounted in the church, apostatised from the truth ... (but) these wretches did not perish alone, but 'overthrow the faith of some' (v. 18) ... When men on a field-battle see such fall who stood next to them, or were before them, their hearts are apt to alarm them, lest the next bullet should kill them also ...

To such the apostle accommodates these words ... Granting ... that some may fall away, and some who seemed so resolute have apostatised, yet 'the foundation of God standeth sure.' To prove, which the apostle offers a double security:

1. The election and foreknowledge of God. 'The Lord knoweth them that are his.' ... God not only *knows* his people, as he knows all other men ... but he has a special eye upon every one of his own, and a special care for them as well as love for them. This is, as it were, *the privy seal* which every child of God may take for his security.

2. A broad seal, their sanctification ... For as the apostle would not have the defection of others to cause anyone to despond; so he would not, by any means, have the security of others, upon any pretensions whatsoever, to cause them to presume. But as a wise physician, having prescribed so great a remedy against their fainting at the sight of other's falling, by telling them, that they who were of God's building should stand; he gives them direction how to use this remedy, lest, if unwarily taken, it might strengthen their disease.

— Peter Vinke, *Puritan Sermons*, Vol. 4, pp. 265-266 (P.S.)

Needed: a balanced outlook

For now we see through a glass, darkly; but then ... (1 Cor. 13:12).

In all our grievances let us look for something that may *comfort us, as well as discourage.* Look for that we enjoy, as well as that we want. As in prosperity God mingles some crosses to balance our diet, so in all crosses there is something to comfort us. As there is a vanity hid in the best worldly good, so there is a blessing hid in the worst worldly evil.

When we feel inferior to others God usually makes up for it with some advantage of another kind. Others may be in greater position, but they are also in a greater danger. Others are richer, and so their cares and snares are greater. The poor in the world may well be richer in faith than they are (Jam. 2:5). The soul can better adapt to, and master, a low estate than a prosperous one; with humiliation, they are less distance from God ... For one-half of our lives, the meanest are as happy and free from cares, as the greatest monarch, that is, while both sleep. And usually the sleep of the one is sweeter than the sleep of the other. What good is all that the earth gives us, if God denies us health? And this a man in the meanest condition may enjoy. The one thing that makes one man differ from another, is just a title, and that for only a little time; death levels all.

There is scarcely a man alive, but that the good he receives from God is more than the ill he feels, if our unthankful hearts would only admit it. Is not our health more than our sickness? Do we not enjoy more than we want, I mean, of the things that are necessary? Are not our good days more than our evil? But we would like to go to heaven upon a bed of roses, and so we pay more attention to one cross than to a hundred blessings. So unkindly do we deal towards God. Is God indebted to us? Does he owe us anything? Those that deserve nothing should be content with anything.

— Richard Sibbes, *The Soul Conflict*, pp. 166-167 (B.T.)

The soul

... and man became a living soul (Gen. 2:7).

I wonder whether these men believe that they breathe in summer as well as in winter. In summer they cannot see their own breath; but as cold comes on, it begins to appear. God's providence, and their own soul, are things of so subtle a nature that they cannot see them during the summer of their pleasures. But when the winter of judgement comes, this will show them a God in their just sufferings; and in that soul of their's, which they would not believe they had, they shall feel an unspeakable torment. Then shall their pained sense supply the want of their faith ...

The soul was not made for the body, as the lute is not made for the case, but the body for the soul, as box for the jewel ...

I do not approve the meanness of the soul which wrongs the body; but even worse it is to have the body wrong the soul. It is like Hagar dressed up in Sarah's garments, and sitting at the head of the table.

If a painted dude, that dotes on her own beauty, could only see how her soul is being used, she would soon realize that her cosmetic embellishments are as gross as applying perfume to a putrefied coffin ... For shame, let us put the soul first, and not set heaven lowest and earth uppermost.

— Thomas Adams, *A Homiletic Encyclopedia*,
pp. 4616, 4642-4643 (H.E.)

The real value of an object is that which one who knows its worth will give for it. He who made the soul knew its worth, and gave his life for it.

— Arthur Jackson

MARCH

Regeneration

... the washing of regeneration ... (Titus 3:5).

In regeneration nature is not ruined, but rectified. The convert is the same man, but new made. The faculties of his soul are not destroyed, but they are refined. The same viol, but newly tuned.

Christ gave not the blind man new eyes, but a new sight to the old ones. Christ did not give Lazarus a new body, but enlivened his old body. So God in conversion does not bestow a new understanding, but a new light to the old; not a new soul, but a new life to the old one. The powers of the man are like streams, not dried up, but turned into another channel.

The truth is that man by his fall from God is so exceedingly degenerated and polluted, that repairing and mending will not serve, he must be wholly and thoroughly new made. As a house infected with leprosy, scraping will not do, it must be pulled down, and set up anew But as when a house pulled down is newly set up, we may we use the same timber, stones, and materials, which were in it before, only now they are newly squared and polished. What is rotten or wrong in them is shaved off, and what is wanting ... is added. So when this new building of regeneration is erected, the Spirit of God makes use of the old substantial materials—the soul and its faculties, the body and its members which were in man before, only he now polishes and purifies them, and squares them according to the rule of God's Word.

God does not take away our beings, but the wickedness and crookedness of our beings, and adds a new gracious beauty which we did not have before. We put off the rags of the old man, and put on the robes of the new man, and continue in regard of substance the same man.

— George Swinnock, *A Homiletic Encyclopedia*, pp. 4066 (H.E.)

De profundis

O Lord, thou hast brought up my soul from the grave: thou hast kept me alive, that I should not go down to the pit (Ps. 30:3).

Is not this a strange speech for David, as though there were a grave of the soul, as there is of the body? For if there be not, how then is it true that God has brought up his soul from the grave?

Is it, perhaps, that he calls it the soul, which is but the cementing of the body and life together? Or that he calls it the grave of the soul, when it is in the lowest estate of vivifying the body? Whatever it be, it shows a great mercy in God, and a great power of that mercy, to raise him up that was brought so low, and to keep him from falling into the pit, that was fallen already to the pit's brink. The truth is that as sin is the death of the soul, so continuance in sin is the grave of the soul ...

Oh, how many there are that have bodies walking above ground, when their souls are lying in the grave? That are lusty and strong in the natural life, when in the spiritual life they are dead and buried? Yet so long as they lie not buried above four days, so long as they continue not in sin so long, till it has brought the soul into an absolute corruption, there is an example in Lazarus; and where there is an example there is hope they may be raised again to life, and be kept from falling into the pit of perdition.

And now, O my soul, though God has not lifted you up to as high a place, yet seeing he has lifted you up from as low a place as he did David, have you not a just cause as he to say, I will extol thee, O God, for thou hast lifted me up, and hast not suffered my enemies, sin and death, to triumph over me? ... Oh, therefore, *Sing unto the Lord, all ye saints of his; give thanks unto him at the remembrance of his holiness.*

— Sir Richard Baker, *Meditations and Disquisitions*, pp. 347-348 (S.P.)

God versus Dagon

... behold, Dagon was fallen upon his face to the earth before the ark of the Lord ... (1 Sam. 5:3).

Dagon had never so great a day, and so many sacrifices, now that he deemed to have taken the God of Israel prisoner. Where should the captive be kept, but in the custody of the victor? Is it not love, but insultation, that lodges the ark close beside Dagon. What a spectacle was this, to see uncircumcised Philistines laying their profane hands upon the testimony of God's presence! To see the glorious mercy seat under the roof of an idol!

O the deep and holy wisdom of the Almighty, which overreaches all the finite conceits of his creatures! While he seems most to neglect himself, he achieves most glory to his own name! He winks, and sits still, on purpose to see what men would do, and is content to suffer indignity from his creatures for a time, that he may be everlastingly magnified in his justice and power.

If the Israelites did put confidence in the ark, can we marvel that the Philistines did put confidence in that power, which, as they thought, had conquered the ark? The less is ever subject unto the greater ...

God will let them sleep in this confidence: in the morning they shall find how vainly they have dreamed ... Dagon has a house, when God has but a tabernacle ... Into this house the proud Philistines come the next morning, to congratulate their god on so great a captive, such divine spoils, and, in their early devotions, to fall down before him under whom the God of Israel was fallen. And lo! they find their god fallen down on the ground upon his face, before him whom they thought both his prisoner and theirs ... O ye foolish Philistines! Did you think that the same house would hold God and Dagon? Go, read your folly in the floor of your temple; and know that he, which cast your god so low, can cast you lower.

— Joseph Hall, *Contemplations*, pp. 158-159 (T.N.)

A disfigured Christ?

For we have not a high priest which cannot be touched with the feeling of our infirmities; but was in all points tempted like as we are, yet without sin (Heb. 4:15).

I love to play the child with little children, and have learned something by so doing. I have met with a child that has had a sore finger; yes, so sore as to be altogether at present useless; and not only so, but by reason of its infirmity, has been a hindrance to the use of all the fingers upon that hand. Then have I begun to commiserate with the child, and said, Alas! my poor boy, or girl, have you got a sore finger! Ah! answers the child, with water in its eyes, and comes to be pitied. Then I offered to touch the sore finger. O! says the child, pray do not hurt me. I then have replied, Can you do nothing with this finger? No, says the child, nor with this hand either. Then have I said, Shall we cut off this finger, and give my child a better, a brave golden finger? At this the child starts, stares in my face, goes back from me, and entertains a kind of indignation against me, and no more cares to be intimate with me.

Then have I begun to make some uses of that good sermon which this little child has preached to me; and thus have I gone on ... And turning all this over to Jesus Christ, instead of matter and corruption, there presently comes honey to me out of this child's sore finger ... And though I have told this tale upon so grave a truth, as is the membership of Christians with their Head, yet bear with me; no child can be so tender of its sore finger as is the Son of God of his afflicted members; he cannot but be touched with the feeling of our infirmities ...

Should he lose a member, he would be disfigured, maimed, dismembered, imperfect, next to monstrous. For his body is called his fullness, yes, the fullness of him that fills all in all.

— John Bunyan, *Prayer*, pp. 145-147 (B.T.)

A double deliverance

And deliver them who through fear of death were all their lifetime subject to bondage (Heb. 2:15).

There were diverse weighty reasons why he (Our Lord Jesus Christ) assumed our nature, and therein subjected himself to death. Two of them are told us in this context:

1. That he might destroy the Devil.
2. That he might deliver the elect people of God.

That he might destroy the Devil. He is described as one 'that had the power of death'; not the supreme, but subordinate, power of death; a power of death as God's executioner to inflict it, and frighten men with it; to make it terrible and formidable to them, by heightening their guilty fears, and representing to them its dreadful consequences ... him (the Devil) has Christ destroyed, that is, disarmed and disabled. Christ has not destroyed him as to his being and substance, but as to his power and authority over the children and chosen of God ...

That he might deliver the elect people of God. 'Through fear of death they were all their lifetime subject to bondage.' ... This is the condition of the elect of God, as they come into the world: they are not only 'subject unto death,' but unto 'the fear of death,' and unto 'bondage' by reason of it ...

Now from this 'fear of death' God's children are said to be delivered by Christ. There are many evils from which he redeems and delivers them: he delivers them from the bondage of sin and Satan, from the rigour and curse of the law, from everlasting punishment and wrath to come; and he delivers them from 'the fear of death.' ... He himself in his own person has suffered, or 'tasted' death for them ... he not only died in their nature, but in their room; not only for their good, but also in their stead.

— Richard Mayo, *Puritan Sermons*, pp. 253-257 (P.S.)

His last will and testament

Father, I will that they also, whom thou hast given me, be with me where I am ... (John 17:24).

I will: a singular manner ... of praying. We never read anything like it by any saint in the word. Some of them have been very familiar with God ... yet nothing of this *I will* is to be heard or read in their prayers. *I will* is too high for a supplicant at God's footstool. Abraham was a great intimate with God, the first believer honoured with the noble name of *the friend of God*; yet this great friend, when pleading for Sodom reveals great humility mixed with his confidence ... Nothing like this *I will* ... Moses, that great wrestler with God for Israel, though he expressed a holy resoluteness, yet nothing appears like this *I will* ... No believer ever did, or ought to speak so to God; they should all ask according to his will ... Yet Christ did say, *I will*, and might well say so ...

(Yet) there is nothing like this in all the accounts we have of Christ's prayers at other times ... When he prays in his agony, not a word of *I will*; but, 'Let this cup pass from me: nevertheless not as I will, but as thou wilt.' Christians, behold the amazing difference between Christ's way of praying against his own hell, and his praying for our heaven. When praying for himself, it is, 'Father, if it be thy will.' ... But when Christ is praying for his people's heaven, it is 'Father, I will that they may be with me where I am.' ...

Here also our Lord is making his will; and therefore *I will* is fitly put in. Christ is making his last will and testament, and praying it over to his father, which is sealed next day with his blood; and here he tells what he wills to his people, even *that they may be with him where he is*. And nothing greater or better can be willed for them.

— Robert Traill, *The Works of Robert Traill*, Vol. 2, pp. 9-14 (J.O.)

God's foreknowledge

Him, being delivered by the determinate counsel and foreknowledge of God ... (Acts 2:23).

It is (therefore) certain, that God does foreknow the free and voluntary acts of man. How could he else order his people to ask of him things to come, in order to deliver them, such things as depended on the will of man, if he did not foreknow the motions of their will beforehand (Isa. 45:11)?

1. He foreknew actions, good or indifferent, that depended on the liberty of man's will ... Several of these he foretold. Not only did he predict that a person would build up Jerusalem, but he predicted the name of that person, Cyrus (Isa. 44:28) ... Was not the destruction of the Babylonian empire foretold, which Cyrus undertook, not by compulsion, but by a free inclination and resolve of his own will? And was not the dismissal of the Jews to their own country a voluntary act in that conqueror? If you consider the liberty of man's will, might not Cyrus as well have continued their yoke ... It was in the power of Cyrus to choose one or the other; his interest invited him to continue their captivity, rather than grant their deliverance; yet God knew that he would willingly do this rather than the other ...

2. God foreknew the voluntary sinful motions of men's wills. God has foretold several of them. Were not all the minute sinful circumstances about the death of our blessed Redeemer, as the piercing him, giving him gall to drink, foretold? As well as the not breaking his bones, and parting his garments? What were those but the free actions of men, which they did willingly without any constraint? And those foretold by David, Isaiah, and other prophets; some above a thousand years, some eight hundred years, and some more, some fewer years before they came to pass. And the events punctually answered the prophecies.

— Stephen Charnock, *The Existence and Attributes of God,*
Vol. 1, pp. 441-443 (B.B.)

Providence and predetermination

For there are certain men crept in unawares, who were before of old ordained to this condemnation ... (Jude 4).

The salvation of some, the damnation of others, is acknowledged by all to be certain as to the event; and that there is no event in time but what was foreknown of God from eternity, is not denied by any that believe God to be God. And that these events cannot be without the providence of God, is most manifest.

It is true, God has a greater influence on the elect than on others: for God does not only support their powers and faculties, and by a physical ability enables them to perform what is natural in their moral actions; but moreover God does by his mighty power in infinite wisdom sweetly direct the elect to do what is morally good and savingly gracious. God does not do so much in those actions that are sinful and vicious: the moral corruption or crookedness that is in a sinful action is not of God; though what is natural in a sinful action has its origin and rise from God, yet what is moral and vicious is not from God. God does not physically and invincibly predetermine that man does what is sinful in any action; the sinfulness of an action has no higher being than the creature for its author.

However, though the sins of the damned are without a divine physical predetermination, yet they are not without a divine providence. There is no event without the providence of God: as all events are according to the foreknowledge of God, so they are by his providence. The destruction of Pharaoh in the Red Sea was according to the foreknowledge of God; and the hardness of his heart, the cause of his ruin, was by God's providence. This providence is somewhat more than a mere unconcerned permission, and yet much less than a physical predetermination.

— Stephen Lobb, *Puritan Sermons*, Vol. 3, p. 444 (P.S.)

Only two religions

But that no man is justified by the law in the sight of God, it is evident: for, the just shall live by faith (Gal. 3:11).

T he revelation in nature tells us that there is a God, that he is to be worshipped, that the soul is immortal, that there is a state of bliss in another world, and that there is the righteousness of Christ, (of which the whole creation is silent, and nature altogether ignorant, and even the angels did not know it until it was revealed to them) and a man's righteousness; so there are but two religions in the world; namely Christianity and nature.

Call religions by whatever names you like ... it is still but nature. The sea has many names from the countries and shores; but still it is the same sea. These two righteousnesses cannot be mixed in the business of justification in the sight of God. If it is of Christ, as the Scriptures say, it is no more of works; if it is of works, as nature says, it is no more of Christ. We cannot be justified in his sight partly by the righteousness of Christ's obedience, and partly by our own. 'The law is not of faith' (Gal. 3:12). 'As many as are of the works of the law are under the curse.' 'The just shall live by faith'; therefore, not by law, this is Paul's logic.

A man cannot be the son of two mothers: 'Cast out the bondwoman and her son: for the son of the bondwoman shall not be heir with the son of the freewoman' (Gal. 4:30). And a woman cannot be a wife to two husbands together (Rom. 7:3). There is but one straight gate, one door, one way, one name.

Paul is the most perfect instance in this great case: while he was alive to the law, he was dead to Christ; and when he was alive to Christ, he was dead to the law (Gal. 2:19) ... Before, he acted from himself, for himself; now, from Christ and for Christ.

— Christopher Fowler, *Puritan Sermons*, Vol. 2, p. 533 (P.S.)

Once only

For by one offering he hath perfected for ever them that are sanctified
(Heb. 10:14).

That this sacrifice once offered was sufficient, I prove in these three
ways:
1. *Because it was as often as God required.* 'This commandment,' says our Lord, 'have I received of my father, that I should lay down
my life for my sheep, and take it again' (John 10:15-18). Hence, it is certain, that his father would have him lay it down once, and then to take it
again. But was it his intent that he should take it again to lay it down
again? Not so; for then, since he has not yet come to die again, it would be
our duty to expect him a second time to die for us; but this we do not
expect ... Our Saviour puts us beyond all doubt inasmuch as he has told us,
he will die no more: 'I am he that liveth, and was dead; and, behold, I am
alive for evermore' (Rev. 1:18) ...
2. *Because it was as much as the law required.* The law which was to
Adam—that if thou eatest of the forbidden tree, thou shalt die the death
threatened (Gen. 2:17), was but once to be executed; and therefore Christ,
being the sinner's surety, could not be bound to pay more than the sinner's
debt. This is clearly and fully asserted by the apostle: 'As it is appointed'
(that is, by the law) 'unto men once to die, but after this the judgement: So
Christ was once offered to bear the sins of many' (Heb. 9:27-28).
3. *Because it was as much as the sinner needed ...* It is evident that by sin
the holy God was provoked to anger: and therefore the sinner wanted a
reconciliation, which this one sacrifice once offered has procured: Christ
has reconciled both (that is, Jew and Gentile) 'unto God in one body by
the cross' (Eph. 2:16).
— Thomas Wadsworth, *Puritan Sermons*, Vol. 6, pp. 511-512 (P.S.)

Paid in full

And every priest standeth daily ministering and offering oftentimes the same sacrifices, which can never take away sins: But this man, after he had offered one sacrifice for sins for ever, sat down on the right hand of God (Heb. 10:11-12).

T his sacrifice of Christ once offered was so perfectly efficacious, that it took away sins fully and forever ...
        I say, first, it was so efficacious as to take away all sins to the true believer, fully and completely; nor can the apostle mean anything less, when he says, 'Who shall lay any thing to the charge of God's elect? It is God that justifieth. Who is he that condemneth? It is Christ that died.' (Rom. 8:33-34). Certainly, if there is no judge to be found in heaven or earth that can justly condemn the believer, then there is no sin that the believer is guilty of, but has been pardoned completely. For if there was but one sin unpardoned, there would be plenty of judges to condemn him. But how is it that the believer is so secure? The apostle tells you the reason, and it is that, 'Christ hath died.' ... What it means is, that through the death of Christ you have the remission of all sins, from which you could never be freed by all the sacrifices of the law of Moses.

And not only so; for as his one sacrifice took away or procured the pardon of all sins to the believer, so it took those sins away forever. This it did by procuring the second covenant, which contains this promise: 'I will be merciful to their unrighteousness, and their sins and their iniquities will I remember no more' (Heb. 8:12). To remember them no more, means exactly what is said, 'They shall be everlastingly forgiven, so that not one of them shall ever rise up to the condemnation of the believer.' The conclusion is this, that if all sins are eternally pardoned to the believer upon the merit of this one sacrifice once offered, then this sacrifice is a most complete and efficacious sacrifice; nor does the believer stand in need of any other sacrifice, no, never, nor of the repetition of this very same sacrifice.

— Thomas Wadsworth, *Puritan Sermons*, Vol. 6, p. 513 (P.S.)

Jesus paid it all

In whom we have redemption through his blood ... (Eph. 1:7).

Hen the Lord Jesus Christ offered up himself as a sacrifice unto God the Father, and had our sins laid upon him, he did give more perfect satisfaction to divine justice for our sins than if you, and I, and all of us had been damned in hell to all eternity. For a creditor is more satisfied if his debt be paid him all down at once, than if it be paid by the week. A poor man that cannot pay all down, will pay a pound a week, or ten pounds a week; but it is more satisfaction to the creditor to have all paid at once.

Should we have been all damned, we should have been but paying the debt a little, and a little, and a little; but when Christ paid it, he paid it all down to God the Father. Had we gone to hell and been damned forever, we would always be satisfying God; yes, but God would never be satisfied: but now when Christ makes satisfaction, God is satisfied.

The creditor, if he be a merciful and good man, is more truly satisfied where the debtor is spared. He does not desire that the debtor should be cast into prison, and there lie and rot; but he is better satisfied with the sparing of the debtor. 'Let me have but my money, and so the debtor be spared.' ... How, if all we had been cast into everlasting burnings, indeed the debt would have been a-paying, but the debtor would have been lost ... but now when Christ comes and makes satisfaction to divine justice, ah! the poor man is redeemed; here is the debtor spared. And, therefore, the Lord is infinitely more satisfied by the satisfaction that Christ made upon the cross for our sins, than if we had gone to hell and been damned to all eternity.

— William Bridge, *A Homiletic Encyclopedia*, p. 377 (H.E.)

Debt compounded

Therefore, brethren, we are debtors ... (Rom. 8:12).

After all, obedience will not make amends for past crimes; for obedience is a debt due of itself, and a debt of itself cannot be a compensation for another. What is a compensation must be something that does not fall under the notion or relation of a debt due before, but contracted by the injury done. Obedience was due from man if he had not sinned, and therefore is a debt as much due after sin as before it. But a new debt cannot be satisfied by paying an old ...

(Supposing) a man rebels against a prince of whom he holds some land. Will the payment of his quit-rent be satisfactory for the crime of his rebellion? So obedience to the law in our whole course was a debt upon us by our creation; and this has relation to the preceptive part of the law, and to God as a sovereign. But upon sin a new debt of punishment was contracted, and the penalty of the law was to be satisfied by suffering, as well as the precepts of the law satisfied by observing them. And this was a debt relating to the justice of God, as well as the other to the sovereignty of God. The debts are different: the one is a debt of observance, the other a debt of suffering, and contracted in two different states—the debt of obedience in the state of creation, the debt of suffering in the state of corruption. The payment of what was due from us as creatures cannot satisfy for what was due from us as criminals.

— Stephen Charnock, *A Homiletic Encyclopedia*, p. 375 (H.E.)

It is our bounden duty to live in obedience, but it would prove our utter ruin to live on obedience.

— William Secker

Lay down your weapons

For in the hand of the Lord there is a cup (Ps. 75:8).

L abour to grow better under all your afflictions, lest your afflictions grow worse, lest God mingle them with more darkness, bitterness, and terror. As Joab said to David, if he ceased not his scandalous lamentation on the death of Absalom, all the people would leave him, and then he should find himself in a far worse condition than that which he bemoaned, or anything that had befallen him from his youth.

The same may be said to persons under their afflictions. If they are not improved in a due manner, that which is worse may—nay, in all probability will—befall them. Whenever God takes this way, and engages in afflicting, he commonly pursues his work until he has prevailed, and his design on the afflicted party be accomplished. He will not cease to thresh and break the bread-corn until it be meet for his use.

Lay down, then, the weapons of warfare against him; give up yourselves to his will; let go everything about which he contends with you; follow after that which he calls you to; and you will find light arising to you in the midst of darkness. Has he a cup of affliction in one hand? Lift up your eyes, and you will see a cup of consolation on the other. And if all stars withdraw their light whilst you are in the way of God, assure yourselves that the sun is ready to rise.

— John Owen, *A Homiletic Encyclopedia*, p. 147 (H.E.)

Whenever I am in the cellar of affliction, I look for the Lord's choicest wines.

— Samuel Rutherford

Cain and Abel

And the Lord had respect unto Abel and to his offering ... (Gen. 4:4).

I t is necessary that this be distinctly laid down, that a man must be righteous first, even before he does righteousness: the argument is plain from the order of nature: for a corrupt tree cannot bring forth good fruit: wherefore make the tree good, and so its fruit good: or the tree corrupt, and its fruit corrupt ...

Besides, God accepts not any work of a person who is not first accepted of him: 'The Lord had respect unto Abel and to his offering,' to Abel first, that is, before that Abel offered. But how could God have respect to Abel if Abel was not pleasing in his sight? And how could Abel be yet pleasing in his sight for the sake of his own righteousness, when it is plain that Abel had not yet done good works? He was therefore first made acceptable in the sight of God, by and for the sake of that righteousness which God of his grace had put upon him ...

Now Abel, being justified, and in possession of this holy principle, offers this sacrifice to God. Hence it is said that he offered by faith, by the faith which he had demonstrated previously to his offering; for, if through faith he offered, he had that faith before he offered, but for the sake of that righteousness which God had already put upon him, and by which he was made righteous ...

From all this it is manifest that the person must be accepted before the duty performed can be pleasing to God: and, if the person must first be accepted, it is evident that the person must first be righteous; but, if the person be righteous before he does good, then it follows that he is made righteous by a righteousness that is none of his own, in which he had no hand, except to receive it as the gracious gift of God.

— John Bunyan, *The Desire of the Righteous Granted*,
pp. 20-21 (G.A.M.)

The Mediator

... and one mediator between God and men, the man Christ Jesus
(1 Tim. 2:5).

G reat and long preparations bespeak the solemnity and greatness of the work for which they are designed. A man that had seen the heaps of gold, silver and brass which David amassed in his time for the building of the temple, might easily conclude, before one stone of it was laid, that it would be a magnificent structure. But lo, here is a design of God as far transcending that as the substance does the shadow. For, indeed, that glorious temple was but the type and figure of Jesus Christ (John 2:19,21), and a weak adumbration of that living spiritual temple which he was to build, that the great God might dwell and walk in it (2 Cor. 6:16). The preparations for that temple were for a few years, but the consultations and preparations for this were from eternity. And as there were preparations for this work before the world began; so it will be a matter of eternal admiration and praise when this world shall be dissolved. What this astonishing and glorious work is, this text informs you; it is the work of mediation between God and man; and you have here a description of Jesus the Mediator.

1. He is described by his work or office: mediator, a middle person. The word implies a fit and equal person, who comes between two persons that are at variance to compose the difference and make peace. Such a person is Christ ...

2. He is described by the singularity of his mediation—one Mediator, and but one. There are many mediators of reconciliation among men, but there is one only Mediator of reconciliation between God and man; and it is as needless and impious to make more mediators than one, as to make more gods than one.

— John Flavel, *The Fountain of Life*, pp. 87-89 (B.B.)

Why do we need a mediator?

Therefore being justified by faith, we have peace with God through our Lord Jesus Christ (Rom. 5:1).

Once there was a sweet league of amity between God and man. However, it was quickly dissolved by sin; the wrath of the Lord was kindled against man, pursuing him to destruction: 'Thou hatest all workers of iniquity' (Ps. 5:5). And man was filled with unnatural enmity against his God: 'haters of God' (Rom. 1:30).

It was upright perfect man, created in the image of God, that sinned: and he sinned when his mind was most bright, clear and apprehensive; his conscience pure and active; his will free, and able to withstand any temptation ...

He was a public as well as a perfect man, and well knew that the happiness or misery of his numberless offspring was involved in him. The condition he was placed in was exceedingly happy ... yes, he sinned while as yet his creation-mercy was fresh upon him: and in this sin was most horrible ingratitude; yes, as casting off the yoke of obedience almost as soon as God had put it on ...

The very design and end of this mediation was to make peace, by giving full satisfaction to the party that was wronged ...

And for any now to imagine to reconcile themselves to God by any thing but faith in the blood of this Mediator, is not only most vain in itself, and destructive to the soul, but most derogatory to the wisdom and grace of God ... Peace of conscience can be rationally settled on no other foundation but this; for God having made a law to govern man, and this law being violated by man, either the penalty must be levied on the delinquent, or satisfaction made by his surety. As well no law, as no penalty for disobedience; and as well no penalty, as no execution. He, therefore, that is to be a mediator of reconciliation between God and man, must pay a price adequate to the offence and wrong; and so did our Mediator.

— John Flavel, *The Fountain of Life*, pp. 89-91 (B.B.)

The death of the cross

The God of our fathers raised up Jesus, whom ye slew and hanged on a tree (Acts 5:30).

Our Lord, Jesus Christ was not only put to death, but to the worst of deaths, even the death of the cross ...

It was a violent death. Violent in itself, though voluntary. 'He was cut off out of the land of the living' (Isa. 53:8) ... I call his death violent, because he died not a natural death ... he was but in the flower and prime of life. And indeed, he must either die a violent death, or not die at all; partly, because there was no sin in him to open a door to natural death, as it does in all others ...

The death of the cross was a most painful death. Indeed, in this death were many deaths contrived in one. The cross was a rack as well as a gibbet. The pains which Christ suffered upon the cross are by the apostle emphatically styled 'the pains of death' (Acts 2:24); but properly they signify the pangs of travail ...

The death of the cross was a very slow and lingering death ... If a man must die a violent death, it is a favour to be despatched; as they that are pressed to death beg for more weight. On the contrary, to hang long in the midst of tortures, to have death coming upon us with a slow pace, that we may feel every tread of it as it approaches, is a misery ...

It was an unalleviated death. Sometimes they gave to malefactors, amidst their torments, vinegar and myrrh, to blunt, dull and stupefy their senses; and if they hung long, would break their bones to despatch them out of their pains. Christ had none of this favour. Instead of vinegar and myrrh, they gave him vinegar and gall to drink to aggravate his torments. And he died before they came to break his legs. For the Scriptures must be fulfilled, 'A bone of him shall not be broken.'

— John Flavel, *The Fountain of Life*, pp. 314-317 (B.B.)

The blood

And, having made peace through the blood of his cross, by him to reconcile all things unto himself; by him, I say, whether they be things in earth, or things in heaven (Col. 1:20).

That there is a sufficient efficacy in the blood of the cross to expiate and wash away the greatest sins, is manifest, for it is precious blood: 'Ye were not redeemed with corruptible things, as silver and gold ... But with the precious blood of Christ' (1 Pet. 1:18-19). This preciousness of the blood of Christ riseth from the union it has with that person, who is 'over all, God blessed forever.' And on that account it is styled the blood of God (Acts 20:28). On account of its invaluable preciousness, it becomes satisfying and reconciling blood to God. So the apostle speaks: 'And, having made peace through the blood of his cross, by him to reconcile all things unto himself; by him, I say, whether they be things in earth, or things in heaven' (Col. 1:20).

The same blood which is redemption to them that dwell on earth, is confirmation to them that dwell in heaven. Before the efficacy of this blood, guilt vanishes, and shrinks away as the shadow before the glorious sun ... It sprinkles us from all evil, that is, from an unquiet and accusing conscience (Heb. 10:22). For having enough in it to satisfy God, it must have enough in it to satisfy conscience ...

Such blood as this was shed, without doubt, for some weighty end; and who they are for whom it is intended, is plain enough from Acts 13:39: 'And by him all that believe are justified from all things, from which ye could not be justified by the law of Moses.' ...

Reader, the Word assures you, whatever you have been, or are, that sins of as deep a dye as yours have been washed away in this blood.

— John Flavel, *The Fountain of Life*, pp. 318-320 (B.B.)

Voluntarily imposed upon him

... the Lord hath laid on him the iniquity of us all (Isa. 53:6).

It was thy Father that laid upon thee the iniquity of us all. It was thine own mercy that caused thee to bear our sins upon the cross and to bear the cross with the curse annexed to it, for our sins.

How much more voluntary it must have been for thee, who requires things to be voluntarily undertaken by us! It was thy charge, 'If any man will come after me, let him deny himself and take up his cross, and follow me.' Thou didst not say, Let him bear his cross, as forcibly imposed by another; but, 'Let him take up his cross,' as his free burden; free in respect of his heart, not in respect of his hand: so free, that he shall willingly undergo it, when it is laid upon him; not so free as that he shall lay it upon himself unrequired.

O Saviour, thou didst not snatch the cross out of the soldier's hands, and cast it upon thy shoulder, but when they laid it upon thy neck, thou didst carry it. The constraint was theirs, the will was thine.

It was not so heavy to them, or to Simon, as it was to thee; they felt nothing but the wood, thou feltest it clogged with the load of the sins of the whole world ...

It is not out of compassion of thy misery, or care of thine ease, that Simon of Cyrene is forced to be the porter of thy cross; it was out of their own eagerness of thy dispatch; thy feeble paces were too slow for their purpose; their thirst after thy blood made them impatient of delay. If thou have wearily struggled with the burden of thy shame all along the streets of Jerusalem, when thou comest once past the gates, a helper shall be deputed to thee: the expedition of thy death was more sweet to them than the pain of a lingering passage. What thou saidst of Judas, they say to the executioner: 'What thou doest, do quickly.'

— Joseph Hall, *Contemplations*, pp. 582-583 (T.N.)

The glory of the cross

... and the Lord hath laid upon him the iniquity of us all (Isa. 53:6).

When Christ died, the sins of the whole church were laid upon the Head of the church. How many stings then had the death of Christ! 'All we like sheep have gone astray; we have turned every one to his own way; and the Lord hath laid upon him the iniquity of us all.'

And if *all* were laid upon him, *none* shall be laid to the charge of them who believe in him. But how was it that Christ did not sink under such a burden? The first sin of the first man was enough to sink all the world into hell. How could Christ bear up under all the sins of so great a multitude?

The reason is, because he is God; the blood of Christ is the blood of God. How loud does it cry for pardon and salvation, and how easily does it drown the cry of sin for vengeance! The blood and suffering of Christ, applied and relied on by faith, justify the sinner, silence Satan the accuser, purge the conscience from dead works, and open a way into the holiest of all.

By the cross of Christ we are to climb up to the throne of glory. The more the death of Christ is studied, the spirit will be more contrite, the heart more clean, the conscience more calm and quiet. The death of Christ puts the sin to death, but delivers the sinner from it.

— Nathanael Vincent, *Puritan Sermons*, Vol. 3, p. 300 (P.S.)

Death, to a pardoned sinner, is like arresting a man after the debt is paid.

— Thomas Watson

Lessons from the cross

... My God, my God, why hast thou forsaken me? (Mark 15:34).

When I see my Saviour hanging in so forlorn a fashion upon the cross: his head drooping down, his temples bleeding with thorns, his hands and feet with the nails, and his side with the spear; his enemies round about him, mocking at his shame and insulting over his impotence: how should I think otherwise of him, than, as himself complains forsaken of his father?

But, when again I turn mine eyes, and see the sun darkened, the earth quaking, the rocks rent, the graves opened, the thief confessing to give witness to his deity; and when I see so strong a guard of providence over him, that all his malicious enemies are not able so much as to break one bone of that body, which seemed carelessly neglected: I cannot but wonder at his glory and safety. God is ever near, though often unseen; and, if he wink at our distress, he sleeps not. The sense of others must not be judge of his presence and care; but our faith.

What care I, if the world give me up for miserable, as long as I am under his secret protection? O Lord, since, thou art strong in our weakness, and present in our senselessness, give but as much comfort in my sorrow, as thou givest me security, and at my worst I shall be well.

— Joseph Hall, *A Homiletic Encyclopedia*, p. 1651 (H.E.)

A heathen philosopher once asked: 'Where is God?' The Christian answered: 'Let me first ask you, where is he not?'

— John Arrowsmith

Life for the taking

But made himself of no reputation, and took upon him the form of a servant, and was made in the likeness of men (Phil. 2:7).

The terms of mercy are brought as low as possible to you. God has stooped as low to sinners as with honour he can. He will not be the author of sin, nor stain the glory of his holiness; and how could he come lower than he has, unless he should do this?

God does not impose anything unreasonable or impossible upon you, as a condition of life. Two things were necessary to be done, according to the tenor of the first covenant.

1. That we should satisfy the demands of justice for past offences.
2. That we should perform personally, perfectly and perpetually, the whole law for the time to come.

By our sins we have made our salvation impossible through either of these ways. But behold God's gracious provision in both. He does not insist upon satisfaction: he is content to take of the surety, and he of his own providing too, what he might have exacted from you ...

O consider the condescension of your God! Let me say to you, as Naaman's servant to him, 'My father, if the prophet had bid thee do some great thing, wouldest thou not have done it? how much rather then, when he saith to thee, wash and be clean?' If God demanded some terrible, some severe and rigorous thing of you, to escape eternal damnation, would you not have done it? ... If your offended Creator should have held you but one year upon the rack, and then bid you come and forsake your sins, accept Christ, and serve him a few years in self-denial or lie in this case forever and ever; do you think you should have hesitated at the offer, and disputed the terms, and have been unresolved whether to accept the proposal? O sinner, return and live; why should you die when life is to be had for the taking, when mercy entreats you to be saved?

— Joseph Alleine, *An Alarm to the Unconverted*, pp. 138-139 (B.T.)

Observing the ordinance

... this do in remembrance of me (1 Cor. 11:24).

I f any of you are offended at the outward lowliness of the ordinance, and are tempted to neglect its observance, I wish you to remember who they were that stumbled at Christ himself because of the poverty of his parents. 'Is not this,' they say, 'the carpenter's son?' This was the introduction to their rejecting of Christ, and to that great plague that followed, namely, their being rejected by Christ ...

I beseech you, consider whose command it is you break. It is the command of the Lord Jesus; to remember him in this supper is a debt you owe to him, your Saviour, Lord and Head. It is a command that carries the superscription of the most supreme authority in heaven or earth; and if by the sentence of Christ it was right to pay the tribute money to Caesar, because it bore his superscription, it is much more right for you to pay the tribute of obedience to this command, that bears the superscription of an authority greater than all the Caesars that ever were ...

Your neglect of this ordinance is a sin against the command, not only of 'the greatest', but of 'the best', Prince in heaven and earth. He is not only *maximus*, but *optimus* also ...

My brethren, in disobeying this command, you sin against Jesus the Just, and Jesus the Gracious; against him that is by position your Head, in love your Father, in openness of heart your Friend. You sin against him that emptied himself that he might fill you, that became poor that he might enrich you, that became an exile from his throne and Father's kingdom that he might bring you home to your Father's house, that became a curse that you might be blessed, that hung on a tree for you that you might sit on thrones with him ...

— Thomas Wadsworth, *Puritan Sermons*,
Vol. 2, pp. 128-129, 136 (P.S.)

The ransom

Being justified freely by his grace through the redemption that is in Christ Jesus (Rom. 3:24).

Redemption ... is the delivery of anyone from captivity and misery by the intervention of a price or ransom ... Only this spiritual redemption has some supereminent things in it, that are not to be found in other deliverances:

First, he that receives the ransom does also give it. Christ is a propitiation to appease and atone the Lord, but the Lord himself set him forth to be so, whence he himself is often said to redeem us. His love is the cause of the price in respect of its procurement, and his justice accepts the price of its merits; for Christ came down from heaven to do the will of him that sent him (John 6:38). It is otherwise in the redemption amongst men, where he that receives the ransom has no hand in the providing of it.

Second, the captive or prisoner is not so much freed from his power who detains him as brought into his favour. When a captive among men is redeemed, by the payment of a ransom, he is instantly set free from the power and authority of him that detained him; but in this spiritual redemption, upon the payment of the ransom for us, which is the blood of Jesus, we are not removed from God, but are 'made nigh' unto God (Eph. 2:13)— not delivered from his power, but restored to his favour.

Third, as the judge was to be satisfied, so the jailer was to be conquered; God, the judge giving him leave to fight for his dominion, which was wrongly usurped ... And he lost his power, as strong as he was, for striving to grasp more than he could hold; for the foundation of his kingdom being sin, assaulting Christ who did no sin, he lost his power over them that Christ came to redeem, having no part in him. So was the strong man bound, and his house spoiled.

— John Owen, *The Death of Death*, pp. 147-148 (B.T.)

Plenteous redemption

Let Israel hope in the Lord: for with the Lord there is mercy, and with him is plenteous redemption (Ps. 130:7).

He did not bid them hope in the Lord because they were the seed of Abraham, the peculiar people of God, made partakers of privileges above all the people in the world; much less because of their worthiness in themselves; but merely on account of mercy in God. The mercy of God, and the redemption that is with him, is the only ground to sinners for hope and confidence.

Two points should be noticed in this grace, the one expressed, the other implied. The fact is that it is *plenteous*, abundant. What principally discourages distressed souls from a comfortable waiting on God is their fears lest they should not obtain mercy from him, and that because their sins are so great and so many, or attended with such aggravations, that it is impossible they should find acceptance with God. This ground of despondency and unbelief the psalmist removes by representing the fullness, the plenty, the boundless plenty of the mercy of God. It is such as will suit the condition of the greatest sinners in their greatest depths; the stores of its treasures are inexhaustible.

The second is the implication in the word itself, of the relation which the goodness and grace of God have to *the blood of Christ*; whence it is called redemption. This has respect to a price; the price whereby we are bought, that is, the blood of Christ. This is that whereby a way is made for the exercise of mercy towards sinners; redemption, which properly denotes actual deliverance, is said to be with God, or in him, as the effect in cause. The causes of it are his own grace, and the blood of Christ, prepared for the redeeming of believers from sin and trouble to his own glory. And herein lies the encouragement ... nothing but God himself can give us confidence to go to him.

— John Owen, *The Forgiveness of Sin*, pp. 424-425 (B.B.)

Frustrating God's grace

I do not frustrate the grace of God: for if righteousness come by the law, then Christ is dead in vain (Gal. 2:21).

This sin of frustrating the grace of God is directly against man's salvation, and tends directly to damnation. All sin against the law tends to damnation deservedly; every sin merits hell. Every sin against the law of God rightly invokes wrath; but sin against the Gospel invokes wrath in a special way, and there is a great difference between these two. A man that commits a sin against the law, commits a sin that deserves death; but he that sins against the grace of the Gospel, in that very sin he invokes his own death. Other sins expose a man to the wrath of God as a judge, but this sin is like self-murder, the man executes the law upon himself. Every man by nature is under a sentence of condemnation, but rejecting the grace of God, leaves and binds a man under that condemnation. There is no other remedy for it, but only the grace of God through Christ; therefore rejecting that, is rejecting the only remedy.

I would issue a strong warning against this sin to ... moral, civil, well-natured people, good-livers, as we call them. Through the mercy of God, some are born with a better nature, as we call it, than others; of a sweet, easy temper ... Now, when this virtuous, natural disposition has the advantage of a godly education, these sort of people come quickly to look very well; and, therefore, they ought to take great care ...

There are some people so ill-natured, and of so bad a disposition, that they need, as we used to say, a great deal of the grace of God to save them. But are there any that do not need the grace of God? The Lord save any of you from thinking so! He is a woeful case indeed, if he thinks he does not need the grace of God. Moral, civil people are in great danger of this sin: they think they have sufficient assets of their own and therefore, they do not borrow from Christ.

— Robert Traill, *The Works of Robert Traill*, Vol. 4, pp. 181-183 (J.O.)

Through the valley

Forasmuch then as the children are partakers of flesh and blood, he also himself likewise took part of the same; that through death he might destroy him that had the power of death, that is, the devil (Heb. 2:14).

A dying time, is a time when the devil is very busy. He delivers at that time his last stroke on saints, and on sinners. He does his utmost to secure the damnation of sinners, that he may not lose them at the last. The devil's death-hold on a dying sinner is a strong one. He also does his utmost against believers, if not to ruin their salvation, yet to hinder their consolation. The devil's parting blow has been dreadful to many a saint.

It is a weighty word (Heb. 2:14), where he is said to *have the power of death*. It is true, but it is also said, that *Christ overcame him*, and *that by death*. Death is properly and strictly a part of the devil's dominions. Sin and death are properly the devil's though the Lord wisely orders both. God permits sin, and inflicts death; and death lies near the devil's great prison, hell. Most fall into the pit; others are brought through safe and sound, by the skill and mercy of their blessed guide, Christ ...

It is a great mystery of faith, and a great trial of faith, that the way to eternal life should lie through the midst of this dark valley of death. Our Lord Jesus Christ bought eternal life for us, by the price of his blood; he went through death to take possession of his kingdom and glory: and his people must go through death to take possession of the gift of eternal life ... through death must all the heirs of glory pass ...

This is the blessedness of believers, which this grace allows them a right to, and gives them a possession of. Therefore we should come to the throne of grace for it. Then you are happy Christians, when serious thoughts of death breed serious joy.

— Robert Traill, *The Works of Robert Traill*, Vol. 1, pp. 214-218 (J.O.)

The four causes of salvation

Moreover whom he did predestinate, them he also called: and whom he called, them he also justified: and whom he justified, them he also glorified (Rom. 8:30).

In election we behold God the Father in choosing; in vocation, God the Son teaching; in justification, God the Holy Ghost sealing; in salvation, the whole Deity crowning. God chooses of his love; Christ calls by his word; the Spirit seals by his grace. Now the fruit of all this, of God's love choosing, of Christ's word calling, of the Spirit's grace sanctifying, is our eternal glory and blessedness in heaven.

In election God bestows on us his love; in calling he grants the blessing of his world; in justifying he communicates to us the sweetness of his Spirit; in glorifying he does wholly give us himself ...

The gradation of assurance is sweetly contracted by St. Paul: 'Whom he did predestinate, them he also called: and whom he called, them he also justified: and whom he justified, them he also glorified.' Wherein the Fathers have found the four causes of our salvation. In predestinating, the efficient cause, which is God's love. In calling, the material cause, which is Christ's death, delivered in his word that calls us. In justifying there is the formal cause, a lively faith. In glorifying there is a final cause, that is, everlasting life ...

Conclude, then, faithfully to your own soul:

- ♦ I believe, therefore I am justified;
- ♦ I am justified, therefore I am sanctified;
- ♦ I am sanctified, therefore I am called;
- ♦ I am called, therefore I am elected;
- ♦ I am elected, therefore I shall be saved.

Oh! settled comfort of joy, which ten thousand devils shall never make void!

— Thomas Adams, *A Homiletic Encyclopedia*, p. 1777 (H.E.)

Yea and amen

... Jesus the mediator of the new covenant ... (Heb. 12:24).

In this covenant, pardoning mercy, renewing grace, and eternal glory are promised. Earth and heaven, the creature and the creator himself, by himself, belong to believers. You must know that all their promises are 'yea and Amen' in Christ (2 Cor. 1:20). The covenant was made for his sake: it was ratified and confirmed by his death. His blood is called 'the blood of the everlasting covenant' (Heb. 13:20). His blood being shed, the covenant stands good to all eternity.

Here is a vast encouragement to lay hold on the promises. If you come to God, and ask: 'Lord! hast thou not made promises of pardon to the penitent and believing? Promises of grace to the humble? Promises of satisfaction to the hungry souls? Promises of joy and comfort to the mourners?' In his word, God answers, 'Yes.' If you further add: 'Lord, let these promises be accomplished for thy Christ's sake'; the answer is, 'Amen, it shall be so: they shall be all fulfilled.'

— Nathanael Vincent, *Puritan Sermons*, Vol. 3, p. 303 (P.S.)

It is better to be as low as hell with a promise, than in paradise without one.

— John Flavel

Grace, grace for ever!

Wherein ye greatly rejoice, though now for a season, if need be, ye are in heaviness through manifold temptations (1 Pet. 1:6).

D o not marvel, if some are so foolish as to seek your hurt, and to afflict you, because your works are so good. For there is need that you should sometimes be in manifold temptations, in spite of your good and innocent life. For some of the graces of God that are already in you are not able to show themselves, nor their excellency, nor their power, nor their potential, except when you are in a state of suffering.

Why then do you think that our innocent lives should exempt us from suffering, or that no troubles should harm us? In truth, it is for our present and future good that our God sends them our way. I conclude, therefore, that such things are necessary for the health of our souls, just as bodily pains and labour are for the body. People who live high, and in idleness, bring diseases upon the body; and they who live in all the fullness of Gospel blessings, but are not exercised with trials grow gross, are diseased and full of bad emotions in their souls. And though this may seem strange to some, yet our day has provided such an experimental proof of this truth, as has not been known for some ages past.

Alas! We need those bitter pills, at which we wince and grimace so much: and it will be well if finally we are purged and healed by them. I am sure we are only a little better as yet, although the physician has been treating us for a long time. Before long, some of these bad emotions will be driven out of us, but, for the present, the disease is so acute that some professors are more afraid that the treatment will empty their purses than that their souls be made better.

I see that we still need these trials; and if God by these, will judge me as he judges his saints, that I may not be condemned with the world, I will cry, 'Grace, grace for ever!'

— John Bunyan, *Advice to Sufferers*, pp. 4-5 (A.B.P.)

APRIL

The game for souls

For the enemy hath persecuted my soul; he hath smitten my life down to the ground; he hath made me to dwell in darkness, as those that have been long dead ... Deliver me, O Lord, from mine enemies: I flee unto thee to hide me (Ps. 143:3,9).

All this the enemy has done to me; but what enemy? Is it not the enemy of all mankind, who has singled me out, as it were, to a duel? And can I resist him myself alone, when the whole army of mankind cannot? But is he not the enemy of thyself, O God, and who is but my enemy because I am thy servant? And wilt thou see thy servants persecuted ... and not protect them? ...

Alas, O Lord, if they were but some light evils that were inflicted upon me, I would bear them without complaining ... but they are the three greatest miseries that can be thought of: the greatest persecution, the greatest overthrow, and the greatest captivity. For what persecution is so grievous as to be persecuted in my soul; for he plays no less a game than for souls ...

And he strikes no light blows, for he has stricken my life down to the ground ... and being himself the prince of darkness, has kept me in darkness ... And it is no ordinary darkness that he has made me to dwell in, but even the darkness of dead men, and that in the ultimate degree as those that have been dead a long time. They that have been dead but a little while, are yet remembered sometimes, and sometimes talked of; but they that have been long dead are as forgotten as if they never had been ... Deliver me from my enemies, O God. And if it should be so, have we not then just cause to love our enemies, just cause to embrace our persecutors, seeing it is they that often made us lift up our souls, and flee to God ...

— Sir Richard Baker, *Meditations and Disquisitions*, pp. 277-278, 289 (S.P.)

Qualities of a waiter

I wait for the Lord, my soul doth wait ... (Ps. 130:5).

If there were not mercy with God, to what purpose should I wait upon him? For after all the service I could do, to the uttermost of my power, if one small error at the end might, for want of mercy, obliterate it all. But God is no such master, for there is mercy with him, and specially towards his servants that wait upon him. He will ignore faults in a servant that he would never bear in a stranger. It is reason enough for God to pardon my faults, because I am his servant and wait upon him. And yet I not only wait upon him but I wait for him ...

And now, O my soul, what do I live for, but only to wait upon God, and to wait for God? To wait upon him, to do him service, and to wait for him, so as to do him better service. To wait upon him, as being Lord of all; and to wait for him, as being the rewarder of all. To wait upon him whose service is better than any other command, and to wait for him whose expectation is better than any other possession.

Let others, therefore, wait upon the world, for the world; I, O God, will wait upon thee, for thee, seeing I find more true contentment in this waiting than all the world can give me in enjoying. How can I doubt of receiving a reward by my waiting for thee when my waiting for thee is itself the reward of my waiting upon thee? And therefore my soul waits ...

Alas, my frail body is very unfit to make a waiter: it rather needs to be waited upon itself. My body must have so much rest, so must leave to be excused from waiting, so that if God should have no other waiters than bodies, he would be often left to wait upon himself. But my soul is a portion of the divine breath, endued with all the qualities fit for a waiter ...

— Sir Richard Baker, *Meditations and Disquisitions*, pp. 263-264 (S.P.)

Camp of angels

The angel of the Lord encampeth round about them that fear him, and delivereth them (Ps. 34:7).

We think little that we have a continual guard about us, and think less that we have a whole camp for our guard, but think least of all that it is a camp of angels. Oh how safe should we be if this were so ... !

But how can we think there are angels to guard us when we scarcely think that there are any angels? For if there are, they must be creatures of God, and then certainly creatures of a most excellent nature ...

But we may think, perhaps, there are none because we can see none, as though we can see a thing that is invisible. Shall we therefore think we have no souls because we cannot see our souls? We live now by faith, and not by sight, and therefore can neither see souls nor angels. We shall then see both, when we shall live by sight, and not by faith. Alas! if we believe no more than we see, we seem not to live by faith neither, for faith believes that which it cannot see. Oh, therefore, my soul, in order to make it appear that you live, and that you live by faith, let this be an article of your creed, that the angels encamp and pitch their tents about you ...

But if there are angels to attend the godly, why do they not defend them? Why do they suffer them to be so molested, so afflicted as they are? For who are in such troubles, who groan under such afflictions as the godly? ... O my soul, you little consider the infinite benefits that the godly receive by the ministry of angels. If perhaps they suffer troubles of the body, do they not escape the far greater troubles of the soul? If they endure perhaps some momentary afflictions, do they not avoid afflictions that would be everlasting? Is there not an army of malignant spirits to assault them, and could they be safe from being torn in pieces if there were not a camp of angels to assist them?

— Sir Richard Baker, *Meditations and Disquisitions*, pp. 367-368 (S.P.)

There is no rest until ...

Let us labour therefore to enter into that rest (Heb. 4:11).

Strive to know heaven as the only happiness, and also as your happiness. We may confess that heaven is the best condition, though we despair of enjoying it; and we may desire and seek it, if we see heaven to be probable and hopeful: but we can never delightfully rejoice in it, till we are persuaded that we have the title to it.

What comfort is it to a man that has nothing to put in his mouth, to see a feast which he must not taste of? What delight has a man that has no house to put his head in, to see the sumptuous buildings of others? Would not all this rather increase his anguish, and make him even more sensible of his own misery? So for a man to know the excellences of heaven, and not to know whether he shall ever enjoy them, may well raise his desire, and provoke him to seek it, but it will give him but little joy and contentment.

Who will set his heart on another man's possessions? If your house, your goods, your cattle, were not your own, you would care less for them, and delight less in them. Oh, therefore, Christian, rest not till you can call this rest your own. Sit not down without this assurance.

— Richard Baxter, *A Homiletic Encyclopedia*, p. 315 (H.E.)

All saints shall enjoy a heaven when they leave this earth; some saints enjoy a heaven while they are here on earth.

— Joseph Caryl

Easter Sunday

But thanks be to God, which giveth us the victory through out Lord Jesus Christ (1 Cor. 15:57).

Surely, even the angels in heaven keep these Easter solemnities with joy. The glory of that victorious Lion who has triumphed over death and hell is even to them a matter of rejoicing. It is the Sabbath of the new world; our Passover from everlasting death to life; our true jubilee; the first day of our week; and the chief in our calendar ...

Christ, like the sun eclipsed by the moon, got himself out by his resurrection; and, as the sun by the moon, he was darkened by them to whom he gave light. His death did justify us, his resurrection did justify his death. He buried the law with himself, and both with glory. His resurrection was the first stone of the foundation ('In Christ shall all be made alive'), and the last stone of the roof, for God assures us that he shall come to judgement, by this token, that he raised him up from the dead (Acts 17:31). Satan danced on his grave for joy; when he had him there once, he thought him sure enough; but he rose again and trampled on the devil's throne with triumph. This is the faith peculiar to Christians ...

Him, that this day rose from the clouds, we expect from the clouds, to raise our bodies, to perform his promises, to finish our faith, to perfect our glory, and to draw us to himself. I do not say, come, see the place where they laid him, that is empty; but, come, see the place where he is. Here is the Lord. I say not with Mary, they have taken away the Lord, and I know not where they have laid him. He is personally in heaven; he is mystically, sacramentally, yes, in a spiritual sense, he is really here ... Christ had his Easter-day by himself; there shall be one general Easter-day for us all ...

— Thomas Adams, *A Homiletic Encyclopedia*, p. 4354 (H.E.)

The power of the resurrection

And what is the exceeding greatness of his power to us-ward who believe, according to the working of his mighty power, which he wrought in Christ, when he raised him from the dead, and set him at his own right hand in the heavenly places (Eph. 1:19-20).

Believers under the New Testament though they hear much of the power of God set forth in the letter of the word, and though they experience the efficacy of this power in their own hearts, yet that which puts the matter beyond any doubt with them, is the undeniable instance of divine power in the resurrection of Christ.

Abraham wanted this: though he knew much of the power of God toward him, in calling him alone from his father's house, and greatly increasing him afterwards, when he became 'two bands' (Gen. 32:10); and in giving him a son in his old age, etc; yet the greatest proof of God's power to Abraham, was the inward efficacy of it upon his own heart, that he should be brought to believe a resurrection. And when there was never any instance of such a thing in the world before. It is a sign he was satisfied in the almighty power of God; 'Accounting that God was able to raise him up,' though 'he received him in a figure' (Heb. 11:19). Isaac was not really slain; therefore Abraham's faith was more remarkable, that he should believe that God could raise his son from the dead; and that he would do it, rather than break his promise. He resolved to obey God for the present, and to trust him for the future.

All that we believe now is but the consequence of Christ's resurrection, and follows upon it: the Head being risen, the members will also rise, everyone in his own order; not only by a bodily resurrection at the last day, but by a spiritual resurrection in their souls here, when the time of their conversion and regeneration comes.

— Thomas Cole, *Puritan Sermons*, Vol. 4, pp. 333-334 (P.S.)

Gone the sting

O death, where is thy sting? O grave, where is thy victory? (1 Cor. 15:55).

Did Christ die the cursed death of the cross for believers? Then though there be much of pain, there is nothing of curse in the death of the saints. It still wears its dart, by which it strikes; but has lost its sting, by which it hurts and destroys. Death poured out all its poison, and lost its sting in Christ, when he became a curse for us.

But what speak I of the harmlessness of death to believers? It is their friend and benefactor. As there is no curse, so there are many blessings in it. Death is yours (1 Cor. 3:22). Yours as a special privilege and favour. Christ has not only conquered it, but is more than a conqueror; for he has made it beneficial, and very serviceable to the saints. When Christ was nailed to the tree, then he said, as it were, to death, which came to grapple with him there, 'O death, I will be thy plagues; O grave, I will be thy destruction': and so he was, for he swallowed up death in victory, spoiled it of its power. So that, though it may now frighten some weak believers, yet it cannot hurt them at all.

If Christ died the cursed death of the cross for us, how cheerfully should we submit to and bear any cross for Jesus Christ? He had his cross, and we have ours; but what are ours compared with his? His cross was a heavy cross indeed, yet how patiently and meekly did he support it! He endured his cross; we cannot endure or bear ours, though they cannot be compared with his.

— John Flavel, *The Fountain of Life*, p. 321 (B.B.)

God on any terms

But thanks be to God, which giveth us the victory through our Lord Jesus Christ (1 Cor. 15:57).

If God be such an immense reward, then see how little cause the saints have to fear death. Are men afraid to receive rewards?

There is no way to live but by dying. Christians want to be clothed with glory, but are loath to be unclothed. They pray, 'Thy kingdom come'; and when God leads them thither, they are afraid to go. What makes us desirous to stay here? There is more in the world to wean us than to tempt us. Is it not a valley of tears? And do we weep to leave it? Are we not in a wilderness among fiery serpents? And are we loath to leave their company? Is there a better friend we can go to than God? Are there any sweeter smiles, or softer embraces, than his? Sure, those who know that 'when they die they go to receive their reward, should neither be fond of life nor fearful of death' (Menander): the pangs of death to believers are but the pangs of travail by which they are born into glory ...

We may know that God is our reward by our choosing him. Religion is not a matter of chance, but choice (Ps. 119:30). Have we weighed things in the balance, and, upon mature deliberation, made an election: 'We will have God upon any terms?'

— Thomas Watson, *Puritan Sermons*, Vol. 3, pp. 73-75 (P.S.)

Be of good cheer, brother, I feel the bottom.

— John Bunyan

The consort of the soul

... we shall not be found naked (2 Cor. 5:3).

The body shall be awakened out of its deep sleep, and quickened into a glorious immortal life. The soul and body are the essential parts of man; and though the inequality is great in their operations regarding holiness, yet their concourse is necessary.

Good actions are designed by the counsel and resolution of the spirit, but performed by the ministry of the flesh. Every grace expresses itself in visible actions by the body. In the sorrows of repentance it supplies tears, in fasting its appetites are restrained, in thanksgivings the tongue breaks forth into the joyful praises of God. All the victories over sensible pleasure and pain are obtained by the soul in conjuction with the body.

Now it is most becoming the divine goodness not to deal so differently, that the soul should be everlastingly happy, and the body lost in forgetfulness; the one glorified in heaven, the other remain in the dust. From the cradle to the grave they ran the same race, and shall enjoy the same reward. Here the body is the consort of the soul in obedience and sufferings, hereafter in fruition. When the crown of purity or palm of martyrdom shall be given by the great Judge in view of all, they shall both partake in the honour. Of this we have an earnest in the resurrection of Christ in his true body, who is 'the firstfruits of them that slept.'

— William Bates, *A Homiletic Encyclopedia*, p. 4334 (H.E.)

We are more sure to arise out of our graves than out of our beds.

— Thomas Watson

The resurrection of the body

Blessed and holy is he that hath part in the first resurrection: on such the second death hath no power ... (Rev. 20:6).

I f you are regenerated, born in a new nature to God, you are 'begotten ... again unto a lively hope by the resurrection of Jesus Christ from the dead.' Christ's resurrection is the groundwork of our hope, and the new birth is our title or evidence of our interest in it. So that until our souls are partakers of the spiritual resurrection from the death of sin, we can have no assurance that our bodies shall be partakers of that blessed resurrection to life ...

Let no unregenerate souls expect a comfortable meeting with their bodies again. Rise they shall, by God's terrible citation, at the sound of the last trump, but not to the same end that the saints arise. They, and they only, who are sanctified by the Spirit, shall have a joyful resurrection.

If you be dead with Christ, you shall live again by the life of Christ. 'If we have been planted together in the likeness of his death, we shall be also in the likeness of his resurrection' (Rom. 6:5) ...

If your hearts and affections be now with Christ in heaven, your bodies in due time shall be there also, and conformed to his glorious body. 'For our conversation is in heaven; from whence also we look for the Saviour, the Lord Jesus Christ: Who shall change our vile body, that it may be fashioned like unto his glorious body' (Phil. 3:20-21). The body is here called vile, or the body of our vileness! Not as God made it, but as sin has marred it. Not absolutely, and in itself, but relatively, and in comparison with what it will be at the resurrection. Then those scattered bones and dispersed dust, like pieces of old broken, battered silver, will be new cast, and wrought in the best and newest fashion, even like to Christ's glorious body.

— John Flavel, *The Fountain of Life*, pp. 492-493 (B.B.)

A better resurrection

... and others were tortured, not accepting deliverance; that they might obtain a better resurrection (Heb. 11:35).

Christ and his resurrection have such a potent influence upon the resurrection of the saints. But it is the duty, and will be the wisdom of the people of God, so to govern, dispose, and employ their bodies, as becomes those that understand what glory is prepared for them at the resurrection of the just. Particularly ...

Be not fondly tender of them, but employ them for God. How many good duties are lost and spoiled by sinful indulgence to our bodies. Alas, we are generally more solicitous to live long than to live usefully. How many Christians have active, vigorous bodies, yet God has little service for them. If your bodies were animated by some other souls that love God more than you do, and burn with holy zeal in his service, more work would be done for God in a day, than is now done in a month. To have an able, healthy body, and not use it for God, is as if one should give you a strong and stately horse, upon condition you must not work or ride him. Wherein is the mercy of having a body, except it be employed for God? ...

Let not the indulgence of your bodies draw your souls into snares, and bring them under the power of temptations to sin. This is a very common case. Oh, how many thousands of precious souls perish eternally for the satisfaction of a vile body for a moment! Their souls must suffer, because the body must be indulged. It is recorded to the immortal honour of those worthies, Hebrews 11:32-35, that they accepted not deliverance, 'that they might obtain a better resurrection.' ... They were made of as tender flesh as we, but such was their care of their souls, and hope of a better resurrection, that they listened not to the complaints of their bodies. Oh that we all had the same resolution.

— John Flavel, *The Fountain of Life*, pp. 489-491 (B.B.)

Joy in the morning

... weeping may endure for a night, but joy cometh in the morning
(Ps. 30:5).

What is the evening but the end of a day? And what is the evening of our life but the end of our days? And in this evening indeed there is commonly heaviness—weeping for parting of friends that have lived together; but this heaviness is removed as soon as morning comes; for what is the morning but when the sun rises again? And what is our morning but when we shall rise again? And as when this morning comes there will be a day that shall have no more evening, so when this joy comes all tears shall be wiped from our eyes, and there shall be no more weeping.

Indeed, all our great joys have always come in the morning. It was a joy that came in the morning at the birth of Christ; it was a joy that came in the morning at the resurrection of Christ; it was a joy that came in the morning at the descending of the Holy Ghost upon the apostles; and these joys were then so great that they have made us feasts ever since (our Christmas, our Easter, our Whitsuntide);

Yet these joys had their heaviness preceding: the joy of Christ's birth had the heaviness of his mother's flight; the joy of Christ's resurrection had the heaviness of his passion; the joy of the descending of the Holy Ghost, the heaviness of Christ's departing. But these heavinesses were so presently followed with joys that it has made this aphorism to be still true, heaviness may endure for a night, but joy cometh in the morning.

And now, O my soul, why should it trouble you to have heaviness in the evening, so long as you are sure to have joy in the morning? Why should it trouble you to be weeping for a time, when you are sure of rejoicing when time shall be no more?

— Sir Richard Baker, *Meditations and Disquisitions*, p. 349 (S.P.)

Registered in the calendar of heaven

Precious in the sight of the Lord is the death of his saints (Ps. 116:15).

T hat which is precious is commonly desired. Does God then desire the death of his saints? He desires, no doubt, that death of his saints which is to die to sin, but for any other death of his saints, it is said to be precious in his sight, because he lays it up with greater carefulness. This is why there are several mansions in God's house, that to them whose death is precious in his sight, he may assign the most glorious mansions. This indeed is the reward of martyrdom; and the encouragement of martyrs, though their sufferings be most insufferable, their tortures most intolerable, yet this makes amends for all, that precious in the sight of the Lord is the death of his saints. If it is so great a happiness to be acceptable in his sight, how much greater a happiness it must be to be precious in his sight?

When God at the creation looked upon all his works, it is said he saw them to be exceeding good; but it is not said that any of them were precious in his sight ...

O my soul, this is one of the miracles of his saints, and perhaps one of those which Christ meant when he said to his apostles that greater miracles than he did, they should do themselves. And what greater miracle than this, that death, which of itself is a thing most vile in the sight of God, yet once embraced by his saints, becomes precious in his sight? To alter a thing from being vile to being precious, is it not a greater miracle than to turn water into wine? Indeed so it is. Death does not damnify his saints, but his saints do dignify death ... When all monuments of the world shall be utterly defaced, and all records razed out, the death of his saints shall stand registered still, in fair red letters, in the calendar of heaven. For if there by glory laid up for them that die in the Lord, much more shall they be glorified that die for the Lord.

— Sir Richard Baker, *Meditations and Disquisitions*,
pp. 427-428 (S.P.)

Beyond love and life and fear of death

... I am ready not to be bound only, but also to die at Jerusalem for the name of the Lord Jesus (Acts 21:13).

Love made Christ suffer for us; love was the chain that fastened him to the cross; so if we love God, we shall be willing to suffer for him. Love has a strange quality, it is the least suffering grace, and yet it is the most suffering grace. It is the least suffering grace in one sense; it will not suffer known sin to lie in the soul unrepented of, it will not suffer abuses and dishonours done to God; thus it is the least suffering grace. Yet it is the most suffering grace; it will suffer reproaches, bonds, and imprisonments for Christ's sake ...

Love will carry men out above their own strength. Tertullian observes how much the heathen suffered for love to their country. If the spring-head of nature rises so high, surely grace will rise higher. If love to their country will make men suffer, much more should love to Christ. 'Love endureth all things.' Basil speaks of a virgin condemned to the fire, who having her life and estate offered her if she would fall down to the idol, answered, 'Let life and money go, welcome Christ.'

It was a noble and zealous speech of Ignatius, 'Let me be ground with the teeth of wild beasts, if I may be God's pure wheat.'

How did divine affection carry the early saints above the love of life, and the fear of death! St. Stephen was stoned, St. Luke hanged on an olive tree, St. Peter crucified with his head downward. These divine heroes were willing to suffer, rather than by their cowardice to make the name of God suffer. How did St. Paul prize his chain that he wore for Christ! He glorified in it as a woman that is proud of her jewels, says Chrysostom. And holy Ignatius wore his fetter as a bracelet of diamonds. 'Not accepting deliverance' (Heb. 11:35). They refused to come out of prison on sinful terms, they preferred their innocencey before their liberty.

— Thomas Watson, *A Divine Cordial*, pp. 62-63 (S.G.)

Best friend next to Jesus

... ye shall receive a crown of glory that fadeth not away (1 Pet. 5:4).

Here is a short fight, but an eternal triumph. A short race, but an imperishable crown of glory. A short term, but an eternal harbour. Who would not almost be covetous and ambitious of suffering upon such gainful terms? How much more this 'ever with the Lord?' There is no proportion between a Christian's cross and his crown ... Compare a mole-hill with a mountain, a glow-worm with the sun, a drop with the ocean, and more disproportionable are a saint's sufferings with his glory ...

'Ever with the Lord': this puts lilies and roses into the ghastly face of death, and makes the king of terrors to outshine Solomon in all his glory ...

Then tremble not, believer, at the approach of death, but go forth and meet him with this friendly salutation: Come in, thou blessed of the Lord; are you come to fetch me to my father? Welcome death! Thou art my best friend next to Jesus Christ. Death is my passage into a blessed eternity.

Death is Joseph's chariot, not to carry the saints down to Egypt, but up to Canaan; and how quickly he carries a believer thither! It is but winking, and he is at home. As soon as the eye of the body is closed here, the eye of the soul is open there! O blessed vision! to behold at once all the glories of eternity!

— Thomas Case, 'Mount Pisgah', *The Select Works of Thomas Case*, pp. 211, 214-215 (S.D.G.)

A plea for zeal

... ye should earnestly contend for the faith which was once delivered unto the saints (Jude 3).

The contention to which Jude exhorts these Christians is an eminent and extraordinary one: the word contend means, to strive, to fight, to labour fervently ...
It is for the faith that we must contend, and that vigorously, fervently, and with all our might (2 Tim. 4:5-7). A lazy, slender, slight contention will not serve the purpose. Lukewarmness neither pleases our Captain, nor prevails over our adversary. Holy fervour is never so seemly as in contending for a holy faith. Indifference better becomes our worldly contentions between man and man, than spiritual contentions between men and devils ...

We must contend for the faith constantly. We must never give over our conflict as long as one enemy is left. We must be faithful to the death if we expect a crown of life. Moderation is not always commendable ...

A Christian should be best when the times are worst. Cursed be that patience that can see error and say nothing ... If there be damnable heresies, I see not but there may be a damnable silence in those who should oppose them. Everyone must give account for his idle words, and for his idle silence ...

This faith is 'once delivered' that is firmly, irrevocably delivered. It shall ever be, it shall never be quite taken away from the church, it endures forever. The doctrine of faith shall never cease in the world.

— William Jenkyn, *Jude*, pp. 20-21 (B.T.M.)

Maranatha

Henceforth there is laid up for me a crown of righteousness, which the Lord, the righteous judge, shall give me at that day: and not to me only, but unto all them also that love his appearing (2 Tim. 4:8).

Another fruit of love is to long for Christ's appearing. Love desires union; Aristotle gives the reason, because joy flows upon union. When our union with Christ is perfect in glory, then our joy will be full. He that loves Christ loves his appearing. Christ's appearing will be a happy appearing to the saints. His appearing now is very comforting, when he appears for us as an advocate (Heb. 9:24); but the other appearing will be infinitely more so, when he shall appear for us as our husband.

He will at that day bestow two jewels upon us. His love; a love so great and astonishing, that it is better felt than expressed. And his likeness: 'When he shall appear, we shall be like him' (1 John 3:2). And from both these, love and likeness, infinite joy will flow into the soul. No wonder then that he who loves Christ longs for his appearance. 'The Spirit and the bride say, come ... even so, come, Lord Jesus' (Rev. 22:17, 20).

By this let us test our love to Christ. A wicked man who is self-condemned, is afraid of Christ's appearing, and wishes he would never appear but such as love Christ, are joyful to think of his coming in the clouds. They shall then be delivered from all their sins and fears; they shall be acquitted before men and angels; and shall be forever translated into the paradise of God ...

These are fruits of love to God. Happy are they who can find these fruits so foreign to their natures, growing in their souls.

— Thomas Watson, *A Divine Cordial*, pp. 63-64 (S.G.)

The omnipotency of a worm

Only fear the Lord, and serve him in truth with all your heart; for consider how great things he hath done for you (1 Sam. 12:24).

To attend upon the Lord without distraction is our duty ... Perfection herein I assert not; but that we may attain it in the substance and sincerity thereof, is proved.

1. From the *precept of God*. The wise and merciful God commands nothing, but he finds or makes it possible; his commands are not snares, but rules and helps. When a master commands, power and assistance wait not on his commands; the servant's strength must perform the master's will: but here are the commands of a father, which when they outstrip his child's strength, are still accompanied with his own assistance ...

2. With regard to *the power of God* it is possible. Ours is the duty, but his is the strength. God and his servant can do anything. When you look on a hard task, and your heart fails you, raise your eye of faith, and you will find God the strength of your heart; 'I can do all things through Christ which strengtheneth me' (Phil. 4:13). Lo here the omnipotency of a worm! If all things, that is, all my duty, then this among the rest ... His power is at your service, and therefore serve yourselves of it.

3. With regard to *the promise of God*, this is possible. To every command there is a promise. The command finds us work, the promise finds us strength.

— Richard Steele, *A Remedy for Wandering Thoughts in the Worship of God*, pp. 21-24 (S.P.)

Promises, though they be for a time seemingly delayed, cannot be finally frustrated ... the heart of God is not turned though his face be hid; and prayers are not flung back, though they be not instantly answered.

— Timothy Cruso

Earth and heaven

For I am in a straight betwixt two, having a desire to depart, and to be with Christ; which is far better: Nevertheless to abide in the flesh is more needful for you (Phil. 1:23-24).

W e have greater work to do here than merely securing our own salvation. We are members of the world and Church, and we must labour to do good to many. We are trusted with our Master's talents ... to do our best ... to propagate his truth, grace and Church; to bring home souls, honour his cause, edify his flock and further the salvation of as many as we can. All this is to be done on earth, if we are to secure our goal in heaven.

It is then an error, though it is but a few that are guilty of it, to think that religion only concerns the life to come ... All true Christians must seriously consider both the end and the means ... If they don't take care of the end, they will never be faithful in the use of means. If they mind not and use not, diligently, the means, they will never obtain the end. No one can use earth well that prefers not heaven, and none can come to heaven, at any age, that are not prepared by well using earth. Heaven must have the deepest esteem, and also habitual love, desire and joy; but earth must have more of our daily thoughts for present practice.

— Richard Baxter, *A Homiletic Encyclopedia*, p. 4137 (H.E.)

Deliver me from sudden death; not from sudden death in respect to itself, for I care not how short my passage be, so it be safe ... but let it not be sudden in respect of me. Make me always ready to receive death. Thus no guest comes unawares to him who keeps a constant table.

— Thomas Fuller

My Lord, what a morning!

But as it is written, eye hath not seen, nor ear heard, neither have entered into the heart of man, the things which God hath prepared for them that love him (1 Cor. 2:9).

To see Jesus clearly with the eye of faith, is to see the deep opening a way from Egypt's to freedom's shore; is to see the water gush, full and sparkling from the desert rock; is to see the serpent gleaming on its pole over a dying camp; is to see the lifeboat coming when our bark is thumping on the bank, or ground on rocks by foaming breakers; is to see a pardon when the noose is round our neck, and our foot is on the drop.

No sight in the wide world like Jesus Christ, with forgiveness on his lips, and a crown in his blessed hand! This is worth labouring for; praying for; living for; suffering for; dying for. You remember how the prophet's servant climbed the steps of Carmel. Three years, and never a cloud had dappled the burning sky—three long years, and never a dewdrop had glistened on the grass, or wet lips of a dying flower. But the cloud came at last. No bigger than a man's hand, it rose from the sea; it spread; and as he saw the first lightnings flash, and heard the first thunders roll, how he forgot all his toils! He would have climbed the hill, not seven, but seventy times seven, to hail that welcome sight!

It is so with sinners as soon as their eyes are gladdened with a believing sight of Christ; when they have got Christ; and with him peace. Be it that you have to climb the hill of prayer, not seven, but seven thousand times, such a sight shall more than reward all your toil.

— William Guthrie, *A Homiletic Encyclopedia*, p. 963 (H.E.)

Lessons learned in bankruptcy

... And the word of the Lord was precious in those days (1 Sam. 3:1).

B y chastisements God teaches us how to prize our outward mercies and comforts more, and to dote upon them less. To be more thankful for them, and yet less ensnared by them. This is indeed a mystery to nature, a paradox to the world; for naturally we are very prone either to slight, or to surfeit. It is sad to consider that we can make a shift to do both at once; we can undervalue our mercies even while we glut ourselves with them, and despise them even when we are surfeiting on them.

Witness that caution inculcated by Moses and Joshua: 'When thou hast eaten and art full ... Beware that thou forget not the Lord thy God' (Deut. 8:10-11). While men fill themselves with the mercies of God, they can neglect the God of their mercies. When God is most liberal in remembering us, we are most ungrateful to forget God ...

The prodigal, while yet at home, could despise the rich and well-furnished table of his father, but when God sent him to school to the swine-trough, he could value the bread that the servants did eat; 'How many hired servants of my father's have bread enough and to spare ... ' (Luke 15:17).

I do not believe that David ever slighted the ordinances, yet he never knew so well how to estimate them, as when he was banished from them ... The remembrance of the company of saints, the beauty of the ordinances, and the presence of God brought tears from his eyes, and groans from his heart, in his sorrowful exile. 'When I remember these things, I pour out my soul in me' (Ps. 42:40) ...

'And the word of the Lord was precious in those days.' When was it not precious? It was always precious in the worth of it: now it was precious for the want of it.

— Thomas Case, 'The Rod and the Word', *The Select Works of Thomas Case*, pp. 19-21 (S.D.G.)

Heaven

... an inheritance incorruptible, and undefiled, and that fadeth not away, reserved in heaven for you (1 Pet. 1:4).

There is a great deal of difference between the desire of heaven in a sanctified man and an unsanctified. The believer prizes it above earth, and had rather be with God than here. But to the ungodly, there is nothing that seems more desirable than this world; and therefore he only chooses heaven before hell, but not before earth. Therefore he shall not have it upon such a choice.

We hear of gold and silver mines in the Indies. If you offer a golden mountain there to an Englishman that has an estate and family here that are dear to him, perhaps he will say, 'I am uncertain whether their golden mountains be not mere fictions to deceive men; and if it be true that there are such things, yet it is a great way thither, and the seas are perilous ... I will stay at home as long as I can.' But if this man is about to be banished out of England, and had his choice whether to go to the golden islands, or to dig in a coal pit, or to live in a wilderness, he would rather choose the better than the worse.

So it is with an ungodly man's desire, in respect to this world and that to come. If he could stay here, in fleshy pleasures forever, he would; because he looks at heaven as uncertain and a great way off, and the passage seems to him more troublesome and dangerous than it is, and he is where he would be already. But when he sees that there is no staying here forever, but death will take him away, he would rather go to heaven than to hell, and therefore will be religious, as far as the flesh and the world will give him leave, lest he should be cast into hell when he is taken from the earth.

— Richard Baxter, *A Homiletic Encyclopedia*, p. 2783 (H.E.)

Hell

... and the fire is not quenched (Mark 9:44).

Some of the upper parts of the earth are to us *terra incognita*, an unknown land; but all of the lowest parts of hell are to us an unknown land. Many thousands have travelled thither, but none have returned from thence, to make reports, or write books of their travels. That piece of geography is very imperfect ...

When a curious inquisitor asked Augustine what God did before he created the world, Augustine told him he was making hell for such curious inquirers into God's secrets! Such handsome jerks are the best answers to men of curious minds. It concerns us but little to know where hell is. Certainly they are the best and wisest of men, who spend most of their thoughts, and time, and pains on how to keep out of it, rather than exercise themselves with disputes about it ...

Oh, sirs, were all the water in the sea ink, and every pile of grass a pen, and every hair on all the men's heads in the world the hand of a ready writer; all would be too short graphically to delineate the nature of this dungeon, where all lost souls must lodge forever ... If all the fires that ever were, or shall be in the world, were contracted into one fire, yet such a fire would be but as a painted fire upon the wall, to the fire of hell! ... Infernal fire is neither tolerable nor terminable. Impenitent sinners in hell shall have end without end, death without death, night without day, mourning without mirth, sorrow without solace, and bondage without liberty. The damned shall live as long in hell as God himself shall live in heaven.

— Thomas Brooks, *A Homiletic Encyclopedia*, p. 2974, 2803 (H.E.)

Heaven is aptly compared to a hill, hell to a hole.

— John Trapp

The glories to be

... when he shall appear, we shall be like him ... (1 John 3:2).

T o see Jesus Christ then, to see him as he is, to see him as he is in glory, is a sight that is worth going from family and out of the body, and through the jaws of death to see. This is to see him head over all, to see him possessed of heaven for his church, to see him preparing mansion-houses for those of his poor ones, that are now by his enemies kicked to and fro like footballs in the world; and is not this a blessed sight?

Second, I have a desire to be with him, to see myself with him. This is more blessed still; for a man to see himself in glory, this is a sight worth seeing. Sometimes I look upon myself and say, Where am I now? and do quickly return answer to myself again, Why I am in an evil world, a great way from heaven, in a sinful body, among devils and wicked men; sometimes benighted, sometimes beguiled, sometimes fearing, sometimes hoping, sometimes breathing, sometimes dying, and the like. But then I turn the tables and say, But where shall I be shortly? Where shall I see myself soon, after a few times more have passed over me? And then I can but answer this question thus, I shall see myself with Jesus Christ; this yields glory, even glory to one's spirit now. No marvel then if the righteous desire to be with Christ.

Third, I have a desire to be with Christ; there the spirits of the just are perfected; there the spirits of the righteous are as full as they can hold. A sight of Jesus in the word, can change us from glory to glory; but how we shall be changed and filled when we shall see him as he is!

— John Bunyan, *The Desire of the Righteous Granted,*
pp. 44-45 (G.A.M.)

Pre-eminence to him

Blessed be the God and Father of our Lord Jesus Christ, who hath blessed us with all spiritual blessings in heavenly places in Christ (Eph. 1:3).

C hrist was chosen before all worlds to be the head of the elect. He was predestinated and ordained by God. As we are ordained to salvation, so Christ is ordained to be the head of all that shall be saved. He was chosen eternally, and chosen in time. He was singled out to the work by God; and all others that are chosen are chosen in him. There has been no choosing of men but in him; for God saw us so defiled, lying in our filth, that he could not look upon us but in his Son. He chose him, and us in him ...

God chose him first, and then he chose us. God singled him out to be the Saviour, the second Adam, and he calls us in Christ.

God justified Christ from our sins, being our surety, taking our sins upon him. We are justified, because he by his resurrection quit himself from the guilt of our sins, as having paid the debt.

Christ is the firstfruits of them that rise again (1 Cor. 15:20). We rise again because he is risen. Christ first ascended; we ascend in Christ. Christ is first loved; we are loved in the beloved. Christ is first blessed; we are blessed with all spiritual blessings in Jesus Christ (Eph. 1:3). So, whatsoever is in us, we have it second hand. We have the Spirit in us, but he is first in Christ; God has put the Spirit for us all. He is first in all things; Christ must have the pre-eminence. He has the pre-eminence in all, both before time, in time, and after time; in election, in whatsoever is done here in this world, and in glorification. All is first in Christ, and then in us. He is the elder brother.

— Richard Sibbes, 'A Description of Christ', *Works of Richard Sibbes*, pp. 9, 18 (B.T.)

Salvation by grace

... by grace ye are saved (Eph. 2:5).

Let us then inquire what is meant by 'grace' here. In verse 4 of this chapter the mercy and love of God were stated to be the cause of salvation. But here in verse 5 he brings grace in as a cause distinct in some way from mercy and love. In Exodus 34:6 we read: 'The Lord God, merciful and gracious.' Grace is a distinct thing from mercy. Grace is the same thing for substance with love and mercy, yet it holds forth something more eminently than both; this expression 'grace' is more than mercy and love, it superadds to them.

Grace denotes not simply love but the love of a sovereign, transcendently superior one, that may do what he will, that may wholly choose whether he will love or not. There may be love between equals, and an inferior may love a superior; but love in a superior, and so superior as he may do what he will, in such a one love is called grace: and therefore grace is attributed to princes. Princes are said to be gracious to their subjects, whereas subjects cannot be gracious to princes. Now God, who is an infinite sovereign, who might have chosen whether ever he would love us or not, for him to love us, this is grace ...

Grace notes the greatest freeness. God is not necessitated to love any, and when he loves, he loves freely—that is, his love is not caused or motivated by anything in the creature. Therefore where the apostle uses the word 'grace' or 'graciously', our translators often render the word, to 'give us freely.'

— Thomas Goodwin, *Comments on Ephesians 2* (B.T.M.)

125

For ever and ever

... and so shall we ever be with the Lord (1 Thess. 4:17).

This is to be forever. The greatest blessing has the longest duration; if duration were a proper word to use of eternity, which is justly called a *perpetual now*. Christ's presence now where we are, is a choice blessing. Believers wish for it, when they are without it; and would wish to have more of it. But they cannot always have his presence when they would; nor can they always keep it, when they have got it. It may please him to *awake and leave them* (Canticles 3:5, 8:4) even when they are best pleased with his company ...

Christ's sweetest visits to his people *where they are*, are often embittered with the thoughts and fears of his withdrawing. 'Now,' says the believer, 'I have a clear sky; but how soon may the weather change, and clouds return again!' But in the state of glory above, when we *shall be with him where he is*, no fears, no ground, or suspicion of any such thing, shall ever enter into the heart of any of the glorified.

The state of grace is a sure state, of God's making. No vessel of grace and mercy shall ever be emptied of it. But it is not a sure state to every believer's thinking; for there may be fears of not making it where no real danger is. But the state of glory is not only sure and unchangeable, because it is of God's gracious making, but it is so to every glorified person's thinking. No pillars in the upper house can shake (Rev. 3:12). Pillars in the lower house may shake, but never are removed. But in heaven, there is no danger, no fear, nor any cause of either, to eternity. *We shall be ever with the Lord.*

— Robert Traill, *The Works of Robert Traill*, Vol. 2, pp. 72-73 (J.O.)

New revelations

And he said unto him, If they hear not Moses and the prophets, neither will they be persuaded, though one rose from the dead (Luke 16:31).

None of us should tempt God in hankering after new revelations or extraordinary discoveries; but adhere to the ordinary means which God has appointed to us for our conversion and confirmation. It is true, as a great man has well observed, that all religions depend, or are presumed to depend, upon revelations from above. 'Flesh and blood,' says Christ, 'hath not revealed it ... but my father which is in heaven' (Matt. 16:17). When this is consigned in a sufficient and clear canon, completely attested, with the exclusion of all additionals, under dreadful plagues (Rev. 22:18), we should rest satisfied, and not be reaching after novelties ...

We should be well contented with the proposals that God himself makes in his unerring word, and not expect to have our curiosities gratified with strange revelations from the dead. If the house of God is built upon the foundation of the 'apostles and prophets' (Eph. 2:20), then we shall not ask God to send any angel to us. As Martin Luther did write, 'I am wont to pray God daily, that he may not send any angel to me, for any cause. If any should be offered, I would not hear; unless he should signify what to cheer us up in civil matters. And yet I know not whether even in such case I would hearken to him and believe him. But in spiritual things we do not desire angels.'

The ordinary means of grace ... as ordained by God, will make us know what he would have us do, and what he will do for us. It is that which the Holy Spirit manifests himself in. This is usually far more effectual than prodigious and physical alarms, which uneasy souls desire to pry into.

— Richard Adams, *Puritan Sermons*, Vol. 4, p. 329 (P.S.)

The will of the Lord be done

And when he would not be persuaded, we ceased, saying, the will of the Lord be done (Acts 21:14).

Our sufferings are ordered and disposed by God, so that when you come into trouble for his name, you might not stagger, nor be at a loss; but be stayed, composed, and settled in your minds, and say, The will of the Lord be done ...

Three things the people of God should learn from this:

♦ *Learn to pity and bewail the condition of the enemy.* I know you cannot alter the counsel of God. Appointed they are, established they are for their work, and do it they must and shall. But yet it becomes you ... to pray for them. For who knows whether it is determined that they should remain implacable to the end, as Herod? Or whether they may through grace obtain repentance for their doings, with Saul? ...

♦ *Never grudge them their present advantages* ... Wish them no ill with what they get of yours; it is their wages for their work, and it will appear to them before long, that they have earned it dearly ...

♦ *Bless God that your lot fell on the other side.* Namely, to be one that should know the truth, profess it, suffer for it, and have grace to bear up under it, to God's glory, and your eternal comfort ... Do this, I say, though they get all, and leave you nothing but the shirt on your back, the skin on your bones, or a hole in the ground to be put in (Heb. 11:23-26).

— John Bunyan, *Advice To Sufferers*, pp. 94-96 (A.B.P.)

The making of a martyr

Wherefore let them that suffer according to the will of God commit the keeping of their souls to him in well doing ... (1 Pet. 4:19).

He that keeps the word of God, is one that has regard to both the *matter* and the *manner* thereof. The matter is the truth, the doctrine contained in it; the manner is that comely, godly, humble faithful way of doing it ... First, here is the will of God to be done; and secondly, to be done according to his will ...

That which makes a martyr, is suffering for the Word of God after a right manner. And that is when he suffers, not only for righteousness, but for righteousness' sake; not only for truth but of love to truth; not only for God's word, but according to it; namely, in that holy, humble, meek manner that the Word of God requires. A man may give his body to be burned for God's truth, and yet be none of God's martyrs (1 Cor. 13:1-3). Yes, a man may suffer with a great deal of patience, and yet be none of God's martyrs (1 Pet. 2:20). The one, because he lacks that grace that should poise his heart, and make him right in the manner of doing: the other, because he lacks that Word of the Holy One that alone can make his cause good as to matter. It is therefore matter and manner that make the martyr ...

I have often thought that the best Christians are found in the worst of times. And I have thought again, that one reason why we are no better, is that God purges us no more (John 15). I know these things are against the grain of the flesh, but they are not against the graces of the Spirit. Noah and Lot, who so holy as they, in the day of their afflictions? Noah and Lot, who so idle as they in the day of their prosperity?

— John Bunyan, *Advice To Sufferers*, pp. 38-56 (A.B.P.)

MAY

The five points of adoption

Beloved, now are we the sons of God ... (1 John 3:2).

The privileges we enjoy by Christ are great and innumerable ... I shall consider them only in the head, the spring and fountain whence they all arise and flow—this is *our adoption* ...

Now, adoption is the authoritative translation of a believer, by Jesus Christ, from the family of the world and Satan into the family of God, with his investiture in all the privileges and advantages of that family. To the complete adoption of any person, these five things are required:

1. That he be *actually*, and of his own right, of another family than that whereunto he is adopted.

2. That there be a *family* into which he has himself no right, into which he is to be grafted.

3. That there be an *authoritative, legal translation* of him, by someone who has the power to do so, from one family into another. By the *law* of old, it was not in the power of particular persons to adopt when and whom they would. It was to be done by the authority of the sovereign power.

4. That the adopted person be freed from all the obligations that were upon him in the family from whence he was translated; otherwise he could in no way be useful or serviceable to the family whereunto he is engrafted. He cannot serve two masters, much less *two fathers*.

5. That, by virtue of his adoption, he is invested in all the rights, privileges, advantages and title to the whole inheritance, of the family into which he is adopted.

— John Owen, *Communion with God*, pp. 207-208 (A.P.)

131

God's day

This is the day which the Lord hath made; we will rejoice and be glad in it (Ps. 118:24).

T he same sun arises on this day, and enlightens it: yet, because the Sun of Righteousness arose upon it, and gave a new life to the world in it; and drew the strength of God's moral precept into it; therefore we justly sing with the psalmist, 'This is the day which the Lord hath made.'

On this day, I forget the world, and in a way myself; and deal with my usual thoughts, as great men do, who during their time of privacy, forbid access to all visitors. Prayer, meditation, reading, hearing, preaching, singing, good conference, are the business of this day, which I dare not spend on any work or pleasure, but heavenly. I hate superstition on one hand, and laxity on the other; but I find it hard to offend in too much devotion, easy in profaneness. The whole week is sanctified by this day; and according to my use of this day, is my blessing on the rest.

— Joseph Hall, *Contemplations*, p. 21 (T.N.)

For notwithstanding this rest and cessation from labour which is required on the Lord's day, yet three sorts of works may and ought to be performed ... these are works of piety, works of necessity and works of charity.

— Ezekiel Hopkins

Church attendance

Not forsaking the assembling of ourselves together, as the manner of some is ... (Heb. 10:25).

In the sanctuary you have the openings of the Gospel treasury: there are the golden candlesticks, which bear the burning, shining tapers, whose light and heat diffuse themselves through all within their reach who are receptive of them; the gifts and graces, the affections and experiences, of Gospel ministers are in their communicative exercises. There God the Father sets and keeps his heart and eye; there the Lord-Redeemer walks by and amongst his commissioned officers and representatives, dispensing warmth and vigour through their ministry to hearts presented to him at his altar; there does the Holy Spirit fill heads with knowledge, hearts with grace, and all our faculties and Christian principles with vigour.

There mysteries are unfolded, precepts explained and enforced, promises fulfilled, souls improved ... And there, through the Angel-of-the-Covenant's moving upon the waters of the sanctuary, are soul-distempers and consumptions healed. And there you are informed, acquainted with, and confirmed in, what may instruct you in, and encourage you unto ...

There all is known, obtained and exercised. There you may fill your heads with knowledge, your hearts with grace, your mouths with arguments, your lives with fruitfulness, your consciences with consolations, and your whole selves with those experiences of divine regards to soul concerns ...

Keep, then, to these assemblies; that you may duly know whom, what, why to love; and how to suit yourselves, in spirit, speech and practice toward God, yourselves and toward each other ...

— Matthew Sylvester, *Puritan Sermons*, Vol. 4, pp. 469-470 (P.S.)

Three house churches

Likewise greet the church that is in their house .... (Rom. 16:5).

C hristian families are, or ought to be, domestic churches. Therefore they ought to pray together. In a church, conjunct prayers are made to God. But what kind of church would that be in which there is never any joint praying?

There are three families in the Scriptures renowned with the names of a 'church', and have this honourable title applied to them by God himself:

1. The family of Aquila and Priscilla: 'greet the church that is in their house' (Rom. 16:5).

2. The family of Nymphas: 'and Nymphas, and the church which is in his house' (Col. 4:15).

3. The family of Philemon: 'and to the church in thy house' (Phin. 2).

... Their houses were called 'churches', because of the religious duties performed in them, such as the reading of the Scriptures, praying to God together, and singing of psalms.

Aquila and Priscilla by occupation were tent-makers: yet though they laboured in this calling, and worked with their hands, they found time for family worship and joint religious duties. In this they are eminent and exemplary believers; and they are prominent in the scriptural record as a worthy pattern for all Christian families to imitate. Here is a plain proof. So did the other godly families in primitive times, and they are approved by God. What they did in their houses and families was pleasing to God, and had this honourable name of a 'church' given to them by God's Holy Spirit.

— Thomas Doolittle, *Puritan Sermons*, Vol. 2, pp. 220-221 (P.S.)

Union and communion

Nevertheless, whereto we have already attained, let us walk by the same rule, let us mind the same thing (Phil. 3:16).

As unity and peace may consist with the ignorance of many truths, and with the holding of some errors, so *it must consist with* (and cannot consist without) *the believing and practising of those things which are necessary to salvation and church communion.* And they are: Believing that Christ the Son of God died for the sins of men; that whoever believes ought to be baptized; essential to this communion is a holy and blameless lifestyle ...

In these three things, faith, baptism and holy life, all churches must agree and unite ... If the churches are wanting in them, it will destroy their being. But let no one think when I say that believing in these three things are essential to salvation and church communion, that I am excluding all other articles of the Christian creed as unnecessary ... rather, I understand this great article of believing that the Son of God died for the sins of men as comprehensive of all others. It is from this article that all other articles may be easily inferred.

And here again, I would not be mistaken, as though I held there was nothing else for Christians to practise, when I say this is all that is requisite to church communion. For I very well know that Christ requires many other things of us, after we are members of his body, which if we knowingly or maliciously refuse, may be the cause, not only of excommunication, but damnation. But yet those are such things as relate to the *well-being* and not to the *being* of churches ...

Consider, how pernicious a thing it is to make every doctrine (though true) the bond of communion. This is that which destroys unity ... The unity of the church is a unity of love and affection, and not a bare *uniformity* of practice and opinion.

— John Bunyan, *Exhortation to Unity and Peace*, pp. 6-15 (R.P.)

Make an appointment

... let him call for the elders of the church ... (Jam. 5:14).

I f you cannot see the sincerity of your hearts, go to your faithful, able guides, and open the case to them, and let not passion prevail against the Scripture and reason which they bring ... Though (their judgement) cannot give you full assurance, it may justly help to silence much of your self-accusations, and give you the comfort of probability.

If a physician that feels not what you feel, shall yet, upon your speeches and other evidences, tell you that he is confident your disease is not mortal, nor contains any cause of fear, you may rationally be much encouraged by his judgement, though it gives you no certainty of life. As wicked men through contempt, so many godly people through melancholy, do lose much of the fruit of the office of the ministry, which lies much in this assisting men to judge of the life or death of their souls. 'Alas!' say they, 'he feels not what I feel: he is used to judge charitably, and he knows me not as well as I know myself.' But when you have told him faithfully, as you do your physician, what it is that you know by yourself, he is able to pass a far sounder judgement of your life or death than yourselves can do, for all your feeling: for he knows better what those symptoms signify ...

Be not, then, so proud or wilful as to refuse the judgement of your faithful pastors, about the state of your souls, in a confidence on your own.

— Richard Baxter, *A Homiletic Encyclopedia*, p. 326 (H.E.)

God cannot endure that in his fields which he suffers in the wilderness.

— John Flavel

Three eyes

But the natural man receiveth not the things of the Spirit of God: for they are foolishness unto him: neither can he know them, because they are spiritually discerned (1 Cor. 2:14).

A faithful man has three eyes: the first, sense, common to him with brute creatures. Second, of reason, common to all men. Third, of faith, proper to his profession. Each looks beyond the other; and none of them meddles with the other's objects. For, neither does the eye of sense reach to intelligible things and matters of discourse, nor the eye of reason to those things which are supernatural and spiritual; neither does faith look down to things that may be sensibly seen.

If you discourse to a brute beast about the depths of philosophy ever so plainly, he understands not: because they are beyond the view of his eye which is only of sense. Or to a mere carnal man, of divine things; he perceives not the things of God, neither indeed can he do, because they are spiritually discerned. Therefore, it is no wonder if those things seem unlikely, incredible, impossible to him, whilst to the faithful man, having a proportionable means of apprehension, they are as plainly seen as any sensible thing ...

What a thick mist, yes what a palpable and more than Egyptian darkness, does the natural man live in! What a world is there that he does not see at all! And how little does he see in this, which is his proper element! There is no bodily thing, but that the brute creatures see as well as he; and some of them better. As for his eye of reason, how dim is it in those things which are best fitted to it. What one thing is there in nature which he does perfectly know? ... But for those things which concern the best world, he does not so much as confusedly see them; neither knows whether they exist ... He comprehends nothing of the beauty, majesty, power and mercy of the Saviour of the world, sitting in the Humanity at his Father's right hand.

— Joseph Hall, *A Homiletic Encyclopedia*, p. 1087 (H.E.)

Can I be sure?

The Spirit itself beareth witness with our spirit, that we are the children of God (Rom. 8:16).

If it be demanded how a believer may be assured that the Spirit does certainly witness with our spirits; I answer: he may be assured by two things: First, by that special distinguishing light that accompanies the testimony of the Spirit, which manifests itself so as to overcome all doubts and disputes both about our spiritual estate and about the testimony itself. Just as the light of the sun does not only discover other things, and reveal them; but manifests itself by its self-evidencing property, which is able to convince every beholder. Secondly, by the harmony and agreement that is between the testimony of the Spirit of God and our spirits; just as we know the testimony of our spirits to be certain and true by its agreement with the word.

Except all three agree in one, there can be no full certainty: but a believer's assurance is always confirmed by the concurring testimony of three things: (1) of the word, (2) of conscience, and (3) of the Spirit—all witnessing one and the same thing: (1) The sure word of God lays down certain signs and marks of true grace, and witnesses these signs to be good evidences. (2) Then conscience, or our own spirit, witnesses that these signs are sound in a believer. (3) Then God super-adds the witness of his own Spirit, which enables us yet more fully to know the things which are freely given us of God. And now what doubts can remain?

— Richard Fairclough, *Puritan Sermons*, Vol. 6, pp. 404-405 (P.S.)

Let the saints know that unless the devil can pluck Christ out of heaven, he cannot pull a true believer out of Christ.

— John Bunyan

Good works

Ye shall know them by their fruits ... (Matt. 7:16).

Whing hen I write of justification before God, from the dreadful curse of the law, then I must speak of nothing but grace, Christ, the promise, and faith. But when I speak of our justification before men, then I must join to those, good works. For grace, Christ and faith are things invisible, and so not to be seen by another, otherwise than through a life so blessed of the gospel as to declare to us the remission of his sins for the sake of Jesus Christ.

He then that would have forgiveness of sins, and so be delivered from the curse of God, must believe in the righteousness and blood of Christ: but he that would show to his neighbours that he has truly received this mercy of God, must do it by good works ...

Not that works make a man good; for the fruit makes not a good tree; it is the principle that it is faith that makes a man good, and his works that show him to be so (Matt. 7:16; Luke 6:44) ...

Not that faith needs good works as a help to justification before God. For in this matter, faith will be ignorant of all good works, except those done by the person of Christ. Here then the good man 'worketh not, but believeth' (Rom. 4:5), for he is not now to carry to God, but to receive from God the matter of his justification by faith. Nor is the matter of his justification before God ought else but the good deeds of another man, namely, Christ Jesus ...

However, good works are necessary, though God needs them not; nor does God need them for our justification with God, but is that faith worth a rush, that abides alone, or without them.

— John Bunyan, *A Holy Life*, pp. 3-4 (R.P.)

139

A fractured blessing

... Art thou he that troubleth Israel? (1 Kings 18:17).

That the peace of the church is beyond expression desirable, no Christian should deny it. Those that are the greatest troublers of the church's peace, do usually proclaim their friendship to it, calling their affection to a party, 'love to the church', and the welfare of their party, 'the peace of the church' ...

Outward prosperity was so much the blessing of the old covenant, that some confine it to that; but others upon better grounds expect more under the gospel; for this was the end of Christ's coming into the world, to 'deliver us out of the hands of our' worldly 'enemies, to serve him, without' affrightening 'fears' of men ... But here, as we used to say of pleasant weather, 'It is pity fair weather should do any harm'; so it is a pity the church's prosperity should do any harm.

But alas! The church of Christ can as little bear continual prosperity, as long adversity: a calm is sometimes as dangerous as a storm. Many are the temptations and snares of a prosperous condition: it breeds hypocrites; errors and heresies spring up like weeds in rank ground; professors are apt to grow remiss and careless, wanton and secure; to be too fond of the present, and to hanker after more temporal happiness than God judges good for them. How hardly were the very apostles awakened from dreaming of Christ's temporal kingdom, and the very best of them from suing the great office at court! O the division among brethren, when pride makes them quarrelsome!

— Samuel Annesley, *Puritan Sermons*, Vol. 3, p. 23 (P.S.)

The sword of the Spirit

... and the sword of the Spirit, which is the Word of God (Eph. 6:17).

The sword was always esteemed a most necessary part of the soldier's equipment, and therefore has obtained a more general use in all ages, and among all nations, than any other weapon. Most nations have some particular weapons or arms proper to themselves; but few or none come into the field without a sword. A pilot without his chart, a scholar without his book, and a soldier without his sword are alike ridiculous. But, above all these things, it is absurd for one to think of being a Christian, with knowledge of the Word of God and some skill to use this weapon ...

It is a weapon that is both defensive and offensive. Such is the sword. All the rest in the apostle's armoury are set out by defensive arms: girdle, breastplate, shield and helmet—such as are of use to defend and save the soldier form his enemy's stroke. But the sword both defends him and serves to wound his enemy also ...

It is for defence. Easily might the soldier be disarmed of all his other equipment, however so glistering and glorious, had he not a sword in his hand to lift up against his enemies' assaults. And with as little ado would the Christian be stripped of all his graces, had he not this sword to defend them and himself, too, from Satan's fury ... Let Christ but say, 'It is written', and the foul fiend runs away with more confusion and terror than Caligula at a crack of thunder ...

It is for offence. The sword, as it defends the soldier, so it offends his enemy. Thus the Word of God is, as a keeping, so a killing sword. It not only keeps and restrains him from yielding to the force of temptations without, but also by it he kills and mortifies his lusts within, and this makes the victory complete.

— William Gurnall, *The Christian in Complete Armour*,
Vol. 2, pp. 194-195 (B.T.)

Music of the spheres

*Speaking to yourselves in psalms and hymns and spiritual songs, singing
and making melody in your heart to the Lord* (Eph. 5:19).

H ere in the text the apostle teaches us a more refined way of rejoicing, namely, to tune the heart in psalms, to raise the heart in hymns,
and to vent the heart in spiritual songs; nay, to make the heart a
choir where spiritual music may be chanted ...

In the ordinance of singing, we must not make noise, but music; and
the heart must make melody to the Lord. Augustine complained of some
in his time, that 'they minded more the tune than the truth; more the manner than the matter; more the governing of the voice, than the uplifting of
the mind'; and this was a great offence to him. Singing of psalms should
be joyous breathing of an elevated soul; and here the cleanness of the
heart is more important than the clearness of the voice. In this service we
must study more to act the Christian than the musician. Many in their
singing of psalms are like organs, whose pipes are filled only with wind.
The apostle tells us, we must sing with our hearts (Col. 3:16) ...

If we are not in Christ, we are certainly out of tune. The singing of a
sinner is natural, like the singing of a bird. But the singing of a saint is
musical, like the singing of a child ... Christ must put his stamp of ap-
proval upon this as well as others; here the altar must sanctify the gift.
Christ perfumes the prayers of the saints (Rev. 5:8); and he must articulate
the singing of the saints. Indeed, he alone can turn our tune into melody ...

Let us be in him; and then our steps shall be metrical, our pauses musical, and our very cadences seraphical; our singing of psalms shall be the
music of the spheres.

— John Wells, *Puritan Sermons*, Vol. 2, pp. 72, 74, 88 (P.S.)

Whispering in church?

Let thine eyes look right on, and let thine eyelids look straight before thee (Prov. 4:25).

I t is said, 'The eyes of a fool are in the ends of the earth' (Prov. 17:24). Any new face that comes in, any strange garb, any noise, any head that moves, any leaf that stirs, commands the eyes and heart of a fool.

It is a precept among the rabbis, that if a Jew be at prayer, though a serpent come and bite him, yet he must not stir till he has done his duty. Satan, that old serpent, will be nibbling at your heel with one vain suggestion or other; but go through with your business, and let God alone with him ...

In hearing of God's Word, let the eye be chained to the preacher with the greatest attention and reverence; as if you saw an angel in the pulpit, or Christ himself ... 'The eyes of all them that were in the synagogue were fastened on him' (Luke 4:20) ...

And here I cannot but digress a little, but it is to cure a more criminal digression, which is, that frequent abuse of whispering and talking to one another in their service of God ... This is a sin in a high degree, and that, because it brings a guilt and distraction upon two persons at once. If a vain thought in church is so evil as you have heard, how criminal, then, is this, that involves you both, yes, perhaps occasions a distraction to twenty more that observe you ... Your heart testifies to God's face that you despise his presence ... And who but a practical atheist would be whispering with his neighbour about anything, while the King of heaven and earth is pleading with him about eternity? ...

There is even more offence in it. An offence to the preacher ... to the congregation ... to the angels ... to your own souls.

— Richard Steele, *A Remedy for Wandering Thoughts*,
pp. 184-188 (S.P.)

On God's right hand

... who is even at the right hand of God ... (Rom. 8:34).

C hrist's sitting at God's right hand in heaven, shows the advancement of Christ's human nature to the highest honour, even to be the object of adoration to angels and men. For it is properly his human nature that is the subject of all his honour and advancement; and being advanced to the right of Majesty, it is become an object of worship and adoration. Not simply as it is flesh and blood, but as it is personally united to the second Person and enthroned in the supreme glory of heaven.

Oh, here is the mystery, that flesh and blood should ever be advanced to the highest throne of Majesty, and that being there installed in glory, we may now direct our worship to him as God-man ... 'The Father ... hath committed all judgement unto the Son: That all men should honour the Son, even as they honour the Father.' And the Father will accept of no honour separate from his honour. Therefore it is added, 'He that honoureth not the Son honoureth not the Father which hath sent him' (John 5:22-23).

It signifies the sovereignty and supremacy of Christ over all, the investiture of Christ with authority over the empire of both worlds; all this belongs to him that sits upon his throne. When the Father said to him, 'Sit thou at my right hand,' he thereby delivered to him the dispensation and economy of the kingdom. He put the awful sceptre of government into his hand. So the apostle interprets it: 'He must reign, till he hath put all enemies under his feet' (1 Cor. 15:25) ... He is over the spiritual kingdom, the church, absolute Lord (Matt. 28:18-20). He is also Lord over the providential kingdom, the whole world (Ps. 110:2); and this providential for the advantage and benefit of the spiritual.

— John Flavel, *The Fountain of Life*, pp. 510-511 (B.B.)

Providences and promises

... wait for the promise of the Father ... (Acts 1:4).

The providences of God are sometimes dark, and our eyes dim, and we can hardly tell what to make of them. But when we cannot unriddle providence, believe it shall work together for the good of the elect (Rom. 8:28) ...

God is to be trusted when his providences seem to run contrary to his promises. God promised David to give him the crown, to make him king; but providence runs contrary to his promise. David was pursued by Saul, was in danger of his life; but all this while it was David's duty to trust God.

The Lord does oftentimes, by cross providence, bring to pass his promise. God promised Paul the lives of all that were with him in the ship; but now the providence of God seems to run quite contrary to his promise. The winds blow, the ship splits and breaks into pieces; and thus God fulfilled his promise. Upon the broken pieces of the ship, they all come safe to shore.

Trust God when providences seem to run quite contrary to promises.

— Thomas Watson, *A Homiletic Encyclopedia*, pp. 4051-4053 (H.E.)

A word of caution ...

For the most part we live upon successes, not promises:—unless we see and feel the print of victories, we will not believe.

— John Owen

The ascension

And when he had spoken these things, while they beheld, he was taken up; and a cloud received him out of their sight (Acts 1:9).

I t was not thy purpose, O Saviour, to ascend immediately from thy grave into heaven: thou meanest to take the earth in thy way, not for a sudden passage, but for a leisurely conversation. Upon thine Easter-day, thou spakest of thine ascension; but thou would have forty days between them. Hadst thou merely respected thine own glory, thou hadst instantly changed thy grave for thy Paradise: for so much the sooner hadst thou been possessed of thy Father's joy. We would not continue in a dungeon, when we might be in a palace; but thou, who for our sakes condescends to descend from heaven to earth, wouldst now, in the upshot, have a gracious regard to us in thy return ...

Whither then, O blessed Jesus! whither didst thou ascend? From the mountain wert thou taken up, and what but heaven is above the hills? ...

Already hadst thou approved thyself the Lord and commander of earth, of sea, of hell. The earth confessed thee her Lord, when at they voice she rendered thee thy Lazarus; when she shook at thy passion, and gave up her dead saints. The sea acknowledged thee, in that it became a pavement to thy feet, and, at thy command, to the feet of thy disciple; in that it became thy treasury for thy tribute money. Hell found and acknowledged thee, in that thou conqueredst all the powers of darkness; even him that had the power of death, the devil. It now only remained, that, as the Lord of the air, thou shouldst pass through all the regions of that yielding element; and as Lord of heaven, thou shouldst pass through all the glorious neighbourhoods thereof, so that every knee might bow to thee, both in heaven, and in earth, and under the earth.

— Joseph Hall, *Contemplations*, pp. 598-599 (T.N.)

God comes for fruit

Then said he unto the dresser of his vineyard, behold, these three years I come seeking fruit on this fig tree, and find none: cut it down ...
(Luke 13:7).

The day of grace ends with some men before God takes them out of the world. I shall give you some instances:

Cain was an angry professor; Ishmael, a mocking one; Esau, a lustful physical one. Three symptoms of a barren professor. For he that can be angry, and that can mock, and that can indulge his lusts, cannot bring forth fruit to God.

The day of grace ended with these professors at the time when they committed some grievous sin. Cain's, when he killed his brother; Ishmael's when he mocked at Isaac; and Esau's when out of love to his lusts, despised, and sold his birthright. Beware, barren professor; you may do in a few minutes, that evil from which you may not be delivered forever and ever ...

How then is a man to know that the day of grace is ended, or near to ending? God says to the dresser of the vineyard, 'Cut it down.' The barren professor has stood out against God, and has withstood all those means for fruit that God had used for the making of him a fruitful tree in the garden ... This indeed is the sum of the parable: the fig tree outstood, withstood, overstood, all that the husbandman did ... 'Cut it down.' ...

Well, sinner, well, barren fig tree ... God comes for fruit. 'What have I here?' says God. 'What fig tree is this, that has stood this year in my vineyard, and brought me forth no fruit? I will cry unto him, Professor, barren fig tree, be fruitful! I look for fruit, I expect fruit, I must have fruit.' At this the professor pauses: 'But these are words, not blows.' When God comes the second year, he finds him still as he was, a barren fruitless tree just taking up space ... When God comes the third year, he cries out ...'I have looked for fruit in vain, cut it down.'

— John Bunyan, *The Barren Fig Tree*, pp. 53, 57-59 (R.P.)

The Trinity

For there are three that bear record in heaven, the Father, the Word and the Holy Ghost: and these three are one (1 John 5:7).

Father, Son and Holy Ghost: three persons, but one God; or in Leo's expression—*one God without division in a Trinity of persons, and three persons without confusion in an unity of essence.* It is a discovery altogether supernatural.

Nature is so far from discovering the nature of the Trinity; that even now after Scripture has revealed it, she still cannot, with all the help of art, comprehend it. Grammar itself is unable to express it; logic cannot demonstratively prove it; and rhetoric has not apt illustrations to clarify such a mysterious truth ...

Of the similitudes usually employed to illustrate it, the judgement of Hilary is most valid: 'They may gratify the understanding of man, but none of them exactly suit with the nature of God.' For example, not that of a root, a trunk, and a branch, with the trunk proceeding from the root, the branch from both, yet but one tree. However, a root may sometimes be without a trunk, and a trunk without a branch; but God the Father never was without his Son, nor the Father and Son without their co-eternal Spirit.

Another illustration is that of a crystal ball held in a river on a sunny day. There is the sun in the firmament, begetting another sun on the crystal ball, and a third sun proceeding from both the former, appearing on the surface of the water—and yet, only one sun on all. However, even in this comparison two of the suns are purely imaginary; none real save that in heaven. But the Father, Word and Spirit are distinct persons indeed, but each one of them is truly and really God ...

The Trinity is a mystery which my faith embraces as revealed in the Word, but my reason cannot fathom.

— John Arrowsmith, *A Homiletic Encyclopedia*, p. 4811 (H.E.)

Watchfulness

Watch and pray, that ye enter not into temptation: the spirit indeed is willing, but the flesh is weak (Matt. 26:41).

The neglect of watchfulness *before* holy duties causes distractions; and that is, by not heeding the order of affairs with discretion for God's service ... Endeavour to time your affairs, and especially your duties. It is the character of a good man that he orders 'his affairs with discretion' (Ps. 112:5), and renders everything beautiful in its time.

Neglect of watchfulness *in* holy duties. Our hearts, so far as unregenerate, are forced into holy duties, as a pressed soldier into the field: he is brought in against his will, and has no principle of courage, or love to his country: he had rather be digging or idling at home ... It is just so with our naughty hearts ... It is said, the nightingale in her sweetest notes is apt to fall asleep; to prevent which she settles herself on a bough, with a thorn at her breast, that when she begins to nod that sharp monitor may awake her. The holiest saint is apt to nod, and steal away in the midst of his most solemn duties, if God's Spirit does not quicken his watch. Christ's own disciples, even just after a sacrament, were overtaken for want of this. 'What, could ye not watch with me one hour?' (Matt. 26:40).

Neglect of watchfulness *after* duties causes distractions ... People generally let loose their hearts when the duty ends, and unlace themselves for ease; and then their thoughts take liberty ...

The remedy against this neglect, is to be thoroughly convinced of the absolute necessity of constant watchfulness ... Be persuaded that watchfulness is as necessary as prayer. You think, without prayer you shall go to hell, and I aver that without watchfulness you cannot go to heaven ...

— Richard Steele, *A Remedy for Wandering Thoughts*,
pp. 101-106 (S.P.)

Free—in prison

Finally, my brethren, be strong in the Lord, and in the power of his might (Eph. 6:10).

P aul was now in bonds, yet not so close kept as to be denied pen and paper. God, it seems, gave him some favour in the sight of his enemies: Paul was Nero's prisoner, but Nero was much more God's. And while God had work for Paul, he found him friends both in court and prison ...

But how does this great apostle spend time in prison? Not in publishing invectives against those, though the worst of men, who had turned him in ... nor in political counsels, how he might manoeuvre himself out of his trouble, by sordid flattery of, or sinful compliance with, the great ones of the time. Some would have used any picklock to have opened a passage to their liberty and not scrupled, to escape, whether they got out at the door or window. But this holy man was not so fond of liberty or life, as to purchase them at the least hazard to the gospel. He knew too much of another world, to bid so high for the enjoying of this; and therefore he is regardless of what his enemies can do with him, well knowing he should go to heaven whether they would or no. No, the great care which lay upon him, was for the churches of Christ ...

The devil had as good have left Paul alone, for he no sooner comes into prison but he starts preaching, at which the gates of Satan's prisons fly open, and poor sinners come forth ... Nay, he does not only preach in prison, but that he may do the devil all the mischief he can, he sends his epistles to the churches so that tasting his spirit in his afflictions, and reading his faith, now ready to be offered up, they might much more be confirmed; amongst which Ephesus was not least in his thoughts ...

— William Gurnall, *The Christian in Complete Armour*,
Vol. 1, pp. 9-10 (B.T.)

Shattering the shackles

... and where the Spirit of the Lord is, there is liberty (2 Cor. 3:17).

To know the way to heaven, sometimes to cast a longing eye in that direction, and by fit and start to make a feeble effort heavenwards, can end in nothing. Man must get the Spirit of God. Thus only can we be freed of the shackles that bind the soul to earth, the flesh and sin.

I have seen a captive eagle, caged far from its distant home, as he sat mournful-like on his perch, turn his eye sometimes heavenwards; there he would sit in silence, like one wrapt in thought, gazing through the bars of his cage up into the blue sky. After awhile, as if noble but sleeping instincts had suddenly awakened, he would start and spread out his broad sails, and lead upward, revealing an iron chain that, usually covered by his plumage, drew him back again to his place. But though this bird of heaven knew the way to soar aloft, and sometimes, under the influence of old instincts, decayed but not altogether dead, felt the thirst of freedom, freedom was not for him, till a power greater than his own proclaimed liberty to the captive, and shattered the shackles that bound him to his perch. Nor is there freedom for us till the Holy Spirit sets us free, and, by the lightning force of truth, breaks the chains that bind us to sin.

— William Guthrie, *A Homiletic Encyclopedia*, p. 2871 (H.E.)

... **We are ready to turn into any house, stay and play with everything in our way, and sit down on every green bank, and much ado there is to get us home.**

— Richard Baxter

Paul: robber of churches!

I robbed other churches, taking wages of them, to do you service (2 Cor. 11:8).

Take notice, that it stands as a blot in the reputation of the Corinthians, that they were altogether for a gospel that should cost them nothing. Corinth was the most convenient, and so the most frequented, port of trade in all Greece. The inhabitants are said to have been very wealthy, proud, and voluptuous. They had abundance to spend upon themselves, but could find nothing for Paul, while he resided among them, and preached the gospel to them. For this the apostle makes a very mild, but a very keen, reflection upon them; enough to make their consciences to start, if they had any spiritual life and sense, and their faces to blush, if they retained any sparks of intelligence in them.

It is a sad word, but too frequently experienced, that a faithful minister of Christ may labour, and yet live in want, in a wealthy city. And I think it can be rationally supposed, that such as suffer those to want who labour among them, will be very forward with their purses to assist them who preach the gospel to infidels, in the remote parts of the world.

Under this head, give me leave to say this ... My city outshines Corinth in trade. God grant that it may still flourish in wealth, and yet be preserved from those vices which are the usual attendants of it! May my city ever have the Corinthians' advantages, and the Philippians' spirit!

— George Hammond, *Puritan Sermons*, Vol. 4, p. 421 (P.S.)

... We read not that Christ ever exercised force but once, and that was to drive profane ones out of his temple, and not to force them in.

— John Milton

Theologically knowing and spiritually ignorant

Moreover, brethren, I would not that ye should be ignorant ...
(1 Cor. 10:1).

A man may be theologically knowing and spiritually ignorant. Nicodemus was not of the lowest sect, being a Pharisee, nor of the lowest form among them, being a ruler; he had knowledge of the law above the vulgar, yet he was ignorant of the design of the Messiah, and the mystery of the new birth. A man may be excellent in the grammar of Scripture, yet not understand the spiritual sense of it. A man may have so much Latin as to construe a physician's bill, and tell the names of the plants mentioned in it, yet understand nothing of the particular virtues of those plants, or have any pleasure in the contemplation of them; so we may discourse of God, and the perfections of God ... without a sense of them. Though this be a good preparatory to a spiritual knowledge, it is insufficient of itself without further addition. It does not heal the soul's eye, nor chase away the spiritual darkness ...

The highest rational knowledge of God cannot profit without the knowledge of faith. This general and common knowledge of Christ is but a knowing after the flesh, not in the power of his Spirit. It can be of no more advantage to us than it was to the Jews knowing him, or to Judas living with him. In the Scriptures, Christians are not called knowing persons, but believers.

— Stephen Charnock, *A Homiletic Encyclopedia*, pp. 3119-3120 (H.E.)

Many a man's knowledge is a torch to light him to hell. You who have knowledge of God's will, but don't do it, in what way do you excel a hypocrite?

— Thomas Watson

Choosing a minister

For it hath been declared unto me of you, my brethren, by them which are of the house of Chloe, that there are contentions among you. Now this I say, that every one of you saith, I am of Paul; and I of Apollos; and I of Cephas; and I of Christ. Is Christ divided? ... (1 Cor. 1:11-13).

When we choose a minister to be, under Christ, the special guide of our souls, how shall we avoid preferring one before another? How may we escape that partiality which is one of the great sins of the age—to cry up some, and decry others; to overvalue some, and to undervalue others?

'*I am of Paul.*' He had an extraordinary call to the apostolic office: there is none who preaches free grace like him. He withstood Peter to the face, because he was to be blamed ...

'*I am for Apollos.*' He is a powerful preacher, an eloquent man, mighty in the Scriptures, fervent in spirit, diligent in the things of the Lord ... Paul is nothing to him for a preacher: Paul's bodily presence is weak, and his speech contemptible (2 Cor. 10:10) ...

'*I am for Cephas.*' He was the chief apostle. Christ gave him a special charge to feed his sheep and his lambs; and therefore I will be of his flock.

'*I am for Christ.*' All these others have their imperfections, but Christ has none; and therefore I will expect the immediate teaching of Christ by his Spirit. I am not for the teachings of men.

How may this disease be prevented or cured? Keep up your esteem of Jesus Christ, as your great Shepherd, and all faithful ministers as his under-officers ... It is impossible to overvalue Christ ... but do not expect from Christ that which he will not do. He will not teach you without the ministry of man, where he approves it. Christ has the words of eternal life, but he commits to the ushers of his school 'the word of reconciliation ... '

— Samuel Annesley, *Puritan Sermons*, Vol. 4, pp. 191-192 (P.S.)

Led by the Spirit

For as many as are led by the Spirit of God, they are the sons of God (Rom. 8:14).

The special leading of the Spirit is extraordinary or ordinary. The former was confined to some persons and to some times; and was not to extend to all saints, nor to continue in all ages. Thus the holy prophets and the apostles, were 'led by the Spirit'; as they were immediately inspired, guided and moved by him in the discharge of their extraordinary work and office. These, in the phraseology of the holy scriptures, and in all that they revealed from God, were acted upon and 'moved by the Holy Ghost' (2 Pet. 1:21). In this they were infallible in what they revealed. But this was extraordinary, and thus limited and temporary.

The other leading of the Spirit, therefore, must be the one which is referred to here, and which appertains to all God's children and at all times. Did the apostle, when he says 'As many as are led by the Spirit of God, they are the sons of God,' mean, that as many as have extraordinary visions, revelations, inspirations, impulses, from the Spirit of God, are thus related to God and none other? Surely, not. Should it mean this, then, we should exclude all but the forementioned prophets and apostles from being God's children; which would be both sad, and also false ...

There is the *having* of the Spirit, and there is the *leading* of the Spirit ... Now, although these two are associated and inseparable, yet there are distinct things. To have the Spirit, is to be made a possessor of him in his indwelling in us; to be led by the Spirit, is our partaking of his directive influence, after we are made possessors of him.

— Thomas Jacombe, *Puritan Sermons*, Vol. 3, pp. 588-593 (P.S.)

Holy zeal

... be zealous ... (Rev. 3:19).

Zeal has been little practised, less studied. Zeal is everywhere spoken against; it has many enemies and few friends. The world can no more abide it, than beasts can the elementary fire ... He is a zealot whose affections are passionately disposed; his love is ever fervent, his desires eager, his delights ravishing, his hatred deadly, and his grief deep. This being the nature of zeal in general, Christian zeal differs from carnal and worldly chiefly in its causes and objects. It is a spiritual heat wrought in the heart of man by the Holy Ghost, improving the good affections of love, joy, etc., for the furtherance of God's glory, his word, his house, his saints, and salvation of souls; directing the contrary of hatred, anger, grief, etc., towards God's enemies, the devil, his angels, sin, the world, with the lusts thereof.

A zealot, like David has zeal in every affection (Ps. 119). *Love*—'How love I thy law.' *Hatred*—'[Thine enemies] I hate ... with a perfect hatred.' *Joy*—'Thy testimonies ... are my delight.' *Grief*—'Rivers of waters run down mine eyes, because they keep not thy law.'

The fervency of the true zealot is in the spirit, not in show; for God, not himself; guided by the Word, not by his humours; such a man's worth cannot be set forth with the tongues of men and of angels.

— Samuel Ward, *A Plea for Zeal*, Vol. 1, p. 15 (B.T.M.)

The sin of sins

... but unto him that blasphemeth against the Holy Ghost it shall not be forgiven (Luke 12:10).

I t is the office of the Holy Ghost to be an advocate for us, and a comforter to us; in which respect, not absolutely, he is thus sent authoritatively by the Father and the Son ... And on this authoritative mission of the Spirit depends the right apprehension of many mysteries in the Gospel, and the ordering of our hearts in communion with him.

Because of this, the sin against the Holy Spirit (what it is I do not now discuss) is unpardonable, and has that adjunct of rebellion associated with it that no other sin has—namely, because he comes not and he acts not, in his own name only, though in his own also, but in the name and authority of the Father and Son, from and by whom he is sent. Therefore to sin against him is to sin against all the authority of God, against all the love of the Trinity, and against the utmost condescension of each person to the work of our salvation. It is, I say, because of the authoritative mission of the Spirit that the sin against him is peculiarly unpardonable; it is a sin against the recapitulation of the love of the Father, Son and Spirit.

And it is from this consideration, were that our present business, that we should investigate the true nature of the sin against the Holy Ghost. Certainly it must consist in the contempt of some of his operations, when he acts in the name and authority of the whole Trinity, and that in their ineffable condescension to the work of grace.

— John Owen, *Communion With God*, p. 229 (A.P.)

Sin against the Holy Ghost

... but unto him that blasphemeth against the Holy Ghost it shall not be forgiven (Luke 12:10).

T here are still some, who having heard that there is a sin against the Holy Ghost, and that it is unpardonable, are full of fears that they have committed that sin ...

All sin against knowledge and conscience is not this sin (1 Kings 15:5; 2 Sam. 11:4,6,10,15,25). Nor yet all wilful sinning. It is not any one sin against the law nor yet the direct breach of the whole law, nor every malicious opposing of the gospel if it is of ignorance; neither is it blasphemy, persecution of the gospel or falling into gross sins of diverse sorts, though done against knowledge and conscience. This sin against the Holy Ghost contains all these and more. It is a sin against the gospel, and the free offer of grace and salvation by Christ, through the Spirit ... It is called the sin against the Holy Ghost, and becomes unpardonable, because it is against the office of the Holy Ghost, and against the gracious operations of the Holy Ghost, and therein against the whole blessed Trinity, all of whose works ... are perfected in the work of the Holy Ghost. Moreover, know that it is unpardonable, not in respect of God's power, but in respect of his will ...

But to clear it of all doubt ... I would ask you, you who think you have committed the sin against the Holy Ghost, these questions:

♦ Does it grieve you that you have committed it?
♦ Could you wish that you had not committed it?
♦ Are you troubled that you cannot bring your heart to desire pardon and grace?

If you can say yes, then although the sin or sins which trouble you may be some fearful sin, of which you must be exhorted speedily to repent, yet certainly it is not the sin against the Holy Ghost ...

— Henry Scudder, *The Christian's Daily Walk*, pp. 238-241 (S.P.)

Is your day of grace past?

For it is impossible for those who were once enlightened, and have tasted of the heavenly gift, and were made partakers of the Holy Ghost, and have tasted the good work of God, and the powers of the world to come, if they shall fall away, to renew them again unto repentance (Heb. 6:4-6).

Are you crossed, disappointed and waylaid and overthrown in all your foolish ways and doings? This is a sign God has not quite left you ... Take it as a call to turn to him: for, by his thus doing, he shows he has a mind to give you a better portion. For usually, when God gives up men, and resolves to let them alone in the broad way, he gives them rope, and lets them have their desires in all hurtful things ...

Have you any enticing touches of the Word of God upon your mind? Does some holy word of God glance upon you, cast a smile upon you, let fall, though it be but one drop of its savour upon your spirit? If it does, and if it stays but one moment with you then the day of grace is not past! The gate of heaven is not shut! ... Take heed, therefore, that you make much of the heavenly gift, and of that good word of God which he has made you taste. Beware, I say, and take heed; there may be a falling away for all this; but I say, as yet God has not left you, as yet he has not cast you off.

With respect to your desires, what are they? Would you be saved? Would you be saved with a thorough salvation? ... Would you be the servant of your Saviour? Are you indeed weary of the service of your old master the devil, sin, and the world? And have these desires put your soul to flight? Have you, through desires, taken to your heels? Do you fly to him that is a Saviour from the wrath to come? If these be your desires ... fear not! You are one of those runaways which God has commanded our Lord to receive and not to send back to the devil again, but to give you a place in his house ...

— John Bunyan, *The Jerusalem Sinner Saved*, Vol. 1, p. 101 (R.P.)

Better not to have been born

For it had been better for them not to have known the way of righteousness, than, after they have known it, to turn from the holy commandment delivered unto them (2 Pet. 2:21).

What then will become of them that some time ago were running post-haste to heaven, insomuch that they seemed to outstrip many, but now are running as fast back again? Do you think that these will ever come to heaven?

What, to run back again, back again to sin, to the world, to the devil, back again to the lusts of the flesh? O! 'It had been better for them not to have known the way of righteousness, than, after they had known it, to turn' back again, 'from the holy commandment.' Those men shall not only be damned for sin, but for professing to all the world that sin is better than Christ. The man that runs back again, does as good as say, 'I have tried Christ, and I have tried sin, and I do not find so much profit in Christ as in sin.' I say, this man declares this, even by his running back again.

O sad! What a doom they will have, who were almost at heaven-gates, and then run back again. 'If any man draw back,' says Christ (by his apostle), 'my soul shall have no pleasure in him' (Heb. 10:38). Again, 'No man, having put his hand to the plough', that is, set forward, in the ways of God, 'and looking back', turning back again, 'is fit for the kingdom of God' (Luke 9:62). And if not fit for the kingdom of heaven then for certain he is fit for the fire of hell. Therefore, says the apostle, those that bring forth these apostatising fruits will be rejected as briars and thorns are rejected, and 'whose end is to be burned' (Heb. 6:8).

— John Bunyan, *The Heavenly Footman*, pp. 39-40 (R.P.)

A sin unto death

... There is a sin unto death: I do not say that he shall pray for it (1 John 5:16).

No man can know of a certainty, and ought not to conclude, concerning himself or others, that as long as they live, that the season of grace is quite over with them. We do not know of any rule that God has revealed on this matter ... It is thus to no purpose, and can be of no use to speculate. There being no such revelation ... who can tell what an arbitrary, sovereign, free agent will do, if he does not declare his own purpose himself?

And why should God make it known? To the person himself who is involved, it would clearly be of no benefit ... If God made it evident to a man that he was finally rejected, the man would be obliged to believe it. But shall it ever be said, that God has made anything to be a man's duty which was inconsistent with his felicity ... And so the case stands, i.e. man's perdition is directly connected with his sin, and not with his duty. If it were directly connected with his duty, he would have to believe himself to be finally forsaken, and a lost creature ...

This could lead to very pernicious consequences if such things were known about others. It would anticipate the final judgement; it would create hell upon earth; it would tempt those whose doom is already known, to do all the mischief possible, which malice and despair can suggest. Indeed, it would mean mingling devils with men! And fill the world with confusion! How should parents know how to behave toward their children, a husband toward the wife of his bosom ... if it were known that they were no more to counsel, exhort, admonish them, pray with or for them, as if they were devils! ... We are therefore to pay reverence to the divine government, that things of this nature are among the arcana of it. These secrets belong not to us ...

— John Howe, *The Redeemer's Tears*, pp. 55-57 (B.B.)

JUNE

The best and the worst

And we know that all things work together for good to them that love God, to them who are the called according to his purpose (Rom. 8:28).

Sin stimulates the soul into self-reforming. A child of God does not only find out sin, but drives out sin. One foot he sets upon the neck of his sins, and the other foot he turns to God's testimonies (Ps. 119:59). Thus the sins of the godly work for good. God makes the saints' maladies their medicines.

But let no one *abuse* this doctrine. I do not say that sin works for good to an impenitent person. No, it works for his damnation, but it works for good to them that love God. You that are godly, I know you will *not* draw a wrong conclusion from this, either to make light of sin, or to make bold with sin. If you should do so, God will make it cost you dear. Remember David. He ventured presumptuously into sin, and what did he get? He lost his peace, he felt the terrors of the Almighty in his soul, and this in spite of the fact that he had all helps to cheerfulness. He was a king; he had skill in music; yet nothing could administer comfort to him. He complains of his broken bones (Ps. 51:8). And though he did at last come out of that dark cloud, yet some divines are of the opinion that he never recovered his full joy to his dying day. If any of God's people should be tampering with sin, in the belief that God can turn it into good; though the Lord does not damn them, he may well send them to hell in this life. He may put them into such bitter agonies and soul-convulsions, as may fill them with horror and bring them to the brink of despair.

Thus have I shown, that both the best things and the worst things, by the overruling hand of the great God, do work together for the good of the saints.

— Thomas Watson, *A Divine Cordial*, pp. 37-38 (S.G.)

Secret prayer: advantages

But thou, when thou prayest, enter into thy closet, and when thou hast shut thy door, pray to thy Father which is in secret ... (Matt. 6:6).

When you would judge the reality of grace in your hearts, judge yourselves by what you are (when) alone in the most secret duties of religion. Closet prayer, meditation, self-examination, etc.

What men are when alone, that usually they are in the main. The heart which may be awed or swayed when in the company of others, is most likely to discover itself when alone. If ever grace is working at all, it is at such a time; and if none appears then, it is likely that there is none in the heart. As some corruptions may be most apt to show themselves in secret, when men are free from the restraint of fear and shame, and suchlike motives, which many times put a check on and keep them under when in the company of others; so likewise grace may more readily act in secret, where men may feel freer to awaken and excite it than in the presence of others ...

If you would therefore evaluate your spiritual stature, and know what in you is real, do it when alone, and when retired. It is then that hearts are most likely to discover themselves truly; and have the least temptations to deceive you, or impose upon you.

— Edward Veal, *Puritan Sermons*, Vol. 3, p. 56 (P.S.)

A Christian should shut the door of his closet and the door of his lips so close, that none should hear without what he says within.
— Thomas Brooks

The secrets of secret prayer

Thou shalt make thy prayer unto him, and he shall hear thee, and thou shalt pay thy vows. Thou shalt also decree a thing, and it shall be established unto thee: and the light shall shine upon thy ways (Job 22:27-28).

B e sure of an intimate acquaintance with God. Can *we* presume, that are but dust and ashes, to go up to heaven, and boldly enter the presence-chamber, and have no fellowship with the Father, or with the Son? 'Acquaint now thyself with him, and be at peace ... ' The decree of your heart 'shall be established unto thee: and the light shall shine upon thy ways.' First shining acquaintance, and then shining answers. Can you show your face to the Lord your God? Then you may seek him in prayer ...

Does God know your face in prayer? Do you often converse in your closets with him? Believe it, it must be the fruit of intimate acquaintance with God, to meet him in secret with delight. Can you come familiarly, as a child to a father, considering your own vileness, meanness, or unworthiness, in comparison with his divine love? God is our Father, the Father of fathers, and the Father of mercies! How sweetly does the apostle join it! God is 'our Father' because 'the Father of our Lord'; and because his Father, so our Father ... O what generations of mercies, flow from this paternity!

But plead we must to that approach and access of this Father through Christ by the Spirit (Eph. 2:18). We must be gradually acquainted with all three. First with the Spirit, then with Christ, and last with the Father ... he chose us in Christ, and then sends his Spirit to draw us to Christ, and by Christ to himself. Have you this access to God by the Spirit? Bosom communion flows from bosom affection. If your souls are truly in love with God, he will graciously say to your petitions: 'Be it unto you according to your love.'

— Samuel Lee, *Puritan Sermons*, Vol. 2, pp. 176-177 (P.S.)

Communal prayers

These all continued with one accord in prayer and supplication ...
(Acts 1:14).

When you are present at family prayer, give diligent attention, and notice what confessions of sins are made, what petitions are set up, and what praises are returned to God for mercies received.

The devil will do his utmost that you may be absent in prayer, when you are present at prayer; absent in mind when present in body. God is not pleased with the prostrating of the body, when your hearts are not in the work. Do not so dissemble on your knees with God and man. Are you really desiring the mercies you pray for, whether pardon of sin, an interest in Christ, and evidences thereof, when your minds and thoughts are wandering about other things? If that is the case, let conscience remind you of the work you are about. For is this not to sin against God, when you pretend to be serving him? And you are provoking him, when you should be praying to him to be reconciled to you, and turn away his anger from you?

Joint prayer should be made with one mouth and one mind: 'These all continued with one accord in prayer,' which one word is translated, in Romans 15:6, with one mind. 'That ye may with one mind and one mouth glorify God.' But when your thoughts are wandering in family prayer, though there is but '*one* mouth', there are *many minds*. These persons do *not accord* in prayer, when there is *great discord* before God.

— Thomas Doolittle, *Puritan Sermons*, Vol. 2, p. 243 (P.S.)

The model prayer

After this manner therefore pray ye ... (Matt. 6:9).

Our Lord Jesus, in these words, gave to his disciples and to us a directory for prayer. The ten commandments are the rule of our life, the creed is the sum of our faith, and the Lord's prayer is the pattern of our prayer. As God prescribed Moses a pattern of the tabernacle (Exod. 25:9), so Christ has here prescribed us a pattern of prayer. 'After this manner therefore pray ye', etc. The meaning is, let this be the rule and model according to which you frame your prayers ... Not that we are tied to the words of the Lord's prayer. Christ does not say, 'After these words, pray ye'; but 'After this manner': that is, let all your petitions agree and harmonize with the things contained in the Lord's prayer; and well may we make all our prayers consonant and agreeable to this prayer ...

A piece of work has commendation from its creator, and this prayer has commendation from its author; it is the Lord's prayer. As the moral law was written with the finger of God, so this prayer was dropped from the lips of the Son of God ... As Solomon's Song, for its excellence is called the 'Song of Songs', so this may well be called the 'Prayer of Prayers'.

There is a double benefit arising from framing our petitions according to this prayer.

1. Error in prayer is prevented. It is not easy to write wrong after this copy; we cannot easily err when we have our pattern before us.

2. Mercies requested are obtained; for the apostle assures us that God will hear us when we pray 'according to his will' (1 John 5:14). And we certainly pray according to his will when we pray according to the pattern he has sent us.

— Thomas Watson, *The Lord's Prayer* (B.T.)

A withdrawing God

Who is among you that feareth the Lord, that obeyeth the voice of his
servant, that walketh in darkness, and hath no light? Let him trust in the
name of the Lord, and stay upon his God (Isa. 50:10).

T he Christian must trust in a withdrawing God. Let him that walks
in darkness, and sees no light, trust in the name of the Lord, and
stay upon his God.

This requires a holy boldness of faith indeed, to venture into God's
presence, as Esther into Ahasuerus', when no smile is to be seen on his
face, no golden sceptre of the promise perceived by the soul, to embolden
it to come near, then to press in with this noble resolution, 'If I perish, I
perish' (Est. 4:16). More than that, to trust not only in a withdrawing but a
killing God (Job 13:15); not when his love is hid, but when his wrath
breaks forth.

Now for a soul to make its approach to God by a tranquillity of faith,
while God seems to be firing upon it, and shoot his frowns like enven-
omed arrows into it, is hard work, and will try and test the Christian's
mettle. Yet we find such a masculine spirit in that poor woman of Canaan,
that enables her to take up the bullets Christ shot at her, and with a humble
boldness of faith to send them back again in her prayer.

— William Gurnall, *The Christian in Complete Armour,*
Vol. 1, p. 15 (B.T.)

As the wicked are hurt by the best things, so the godly are bettered by
the worst.

— William Jenkyn

Soul food

The Lord is my shepherd; I shall not want. He maketh me to lie down in green pastures: he leadeth me beside the still waters. He restoreth my soul ... (Ps. 23:1-3).

His principal care is of the soul, for he restoreth my soul. But as he did not make me a living soul till he had first made the earth, and the fruits of the earth to serve for my living, so he restores not my soul till he has first led me into green pastures to serve for my sustenance. For what purpose would it be to give a new life, and not a living, to give a being, and not give means to maintain that being? And was it not perhaps from this that Christ took his pattern when he taught us to pray for daily bread before we pray for forgiveness of sins?

But though he provides first for the body, which was made first, yet he provides most for the soul, which was given last. He but feeds my body, but he restores my soul. He ministers to my body by accidental and outward things, but inward and substantial to my soul. And why is it that God provides more for the soul than for the body, if it were not for the fact that the soul is far more worth than the body? ...

But to what is it that God restores my soul? It must be to something that my soul had before, and has not now; and so it is. He restores it to its original purity that was now grown foul and black with sin; for, alas, what good were it to have green pastures and a black soul! He restores it to its natural temper in affections that was grown distempered with the violence of passions; for, alas, what good were it to have still waters and turbulent spirits! He restores it indeed to life that had become, in a manner, quite dead; and who could restore my soul to life but he only that is the good Shepherd, and gave his life for his sheep, which no shepherd ever did but he.

— Sir Richard Baker, *Meditations & Disquisitions,* pp. 309-310 (S.P.)

In pastures green

He maketh me to lie down in green pastures: he leadeth me beside the still waters (Ps. 23:2).

Indeed, God is a shepherd as able as he is good, and as good as he is able. Not only he has green pastures to lead me into, which shows his ability, but he leads me into them, which shows his goodness. He leads me not into pastures that are withered and dry, that would distaste me before I taste them; but he leads me into green pastures, as well to please my eye with the verdure as my stomach with the herbage, and inviting me, as it were, to eat, by setting out the meat in the best colour ... But yet the goodness is not altogether in the greenness. Green after all, is but a colour, and colours are but deceitful things: they might be green leaves, or they might be green flags or rushes; and what good would there be to me in such a greenness? No, my soul, the goodness is in being green pastures, for now they perform as much as they promise ...

I am now I think in a kind of paradise, and seem not to want for anything, unless perhaps a little water with which now and then to wash my mouth, at most to take a sip sometimes ... And now see the great goodness of this shepherd, and what just cause there is to depend upon his providence; for he lets not his sheep want this neither, but he leads them beside still waters—not waters that roar and make a noise enough to frighten a fearful sheep, but waters still and quiet, that though they drink but little, yet they may drink that little without fear ...

And now, O my soul, is it not time to say grace, and to acknowledge with thankfulness this plenty of meat and drink? And can I say a shorter grace than this: 'The Lord is my shepherd; I shall not want.'

— Sir Richard Baker, *Meditations & Disquisitions,* pp. 306-308 (S.P.)

Personal from God

And it shall be with him, and he shall read therein all the days of his life: that he may learn to fear the Lord his God, to keep all the words of this law and these statutes, to do them (Deut. 17:19).

L earn to apply Scripture. Take every word as spoken to yourselves. When the Word thunders against sin, think thus: 'God means my sins.' When it emphasises any duty, 'God intends me in this.' Many put off Scripture from themselves, as if it only concerned those who lived in the time when it was written; but if you intend to profit by the Word, bring it home to yourselves: a medicine will do not good, unless it be applied ...

When King Josiah heard the threatening which was written in the book of God, he applied it to himself: 'He rent his clothes', and humbled his soul before the Lord (2 Kings 22:11).

Compare yourselves with the Word. See how the Scriptures and your hearts agree, how your dial responds to the sun. Are your hearts as it were, a transcript of Scripture? Is the Word copied out in your hearts? The Word calls for humility; are you not only humbled, but humble? The Word calls for regeneration; have you the signature and engraving of the Holy Ghost upon you? Have you a change of heart? Not only a partial and moral change, but a spiritual? Is there such a change wrought in you, as if another soul did live in the same body? 'Such were some of you: but ye are washed, but ye are sanctified,' etc. (1 Cor. 6:11).

The Word calls for love to the saints. Do you love grace where you see it? Do you love grace in a poor man as well as in a rich? ... Bringing the rule of the Word and our hearts together, to see how they agree, would prove very advantageous to us. By this we come to know the true complexion and state of our souls, and see what evidences and certificates we have for heaven.

— Thomas Watson, *Puritan Sermons,* Vol. 2, p. 66 (P.S.)

How can we praise God at all times?

I will bless the Lord at all times: his praise shall continually be in my mouth (Ps. 34:1).

A las! what a vow is this that David makes here, a vow which he is sure beforehand he cannot keep; for is it possible for any man to bless God at all times? Is there not a time of pain and misery, in which Job's wife persuaded him to curse God and die? And can cursing of God stand with blessing of God ? ...

What does blessing God truly mean? Is it only in thought, or only in a good intention? No, my soul; his praise shall continually be in my mouth; for though the heart indeed be the fountain of blessing him, yet out of the abundance of the heart the mouth speaketh. Therefore it shall not be cloistered up in the cells of silence, but it shall have vent, and be brought into the light, that if it be not said that men *seeing* my good *works*, it may at least be said that men *hearing* my good *words*, may glorify our Father which is in heaven ...

When I make this vow to bless God at all times, I make it not presuming upon any ability in myself ... My confidence is that he who hath given me the resolution to will it, will give me also the power to perform it.

— Sir Richard Baker, *Meditations and Disquisitions,* pp. 359-361 (S.P.)

Facts, please

But Zion said, the Lord hath forsaken me, and my Lord hath forgotten me.
Can a woman forget her sucking child, that she should not have compas-
sion on the son of her womb? yea, they may forget, yet will I not forget
thee. Behold, I have graven thee upon the palms of my hands ...
(Isa. 49:14-16).

How often do souls misunderstand God, and that from a fancy of
great discouragements and eclipses, which issue from themselves,
and not from him! What, if some bold and wanton expectations,
irregularly formed and cherished, come to nothing? Suppose some down-
cast Christians (such I have known, and have rather pitied and reproved)
should desire, expect, and pray for some miraculous tokens of strength
and comfort ... or supposing they request from God some ecstatic trans-
ports and experiences, or covet some and then interpret as grace what
could be nothing but a natural gift consistent with a lost condition. Suppose these things were never obtained by them: must it follow then, that
the face of God is hid from them?

O what problems must these men be to God when they obviously take
him for their enemy, or for a discontented and disliked friend, because he
will not transgress the stated methods of dealing with men's souls! If their
natural strength and fervour decay through age or sickness, or other accidental weaknesses; or if God touches them in their darlings here, as inter-
ests, relations, possessions; or casts them upon unwelcome difficulties, all
for their good; O then they think him gone from them in deep dislike and
wrath. And all the time these things are demonstrations and assurances of
God's faithfulness and favour to them, and not any hard thoughts or bad
designs upon them.

Make sure then that God does hide his face from you before you proceed to infer discouragements ... and harbour jealousies or hard thoughts
of God.

— Matthew Sylvester, *Puritan Sermons,* Vol. 4, pp. 104-105 (P.S.)

Behind a frowning providence ...

My son, despise not thou the chastening of the Lord, nor faint when thou art rebuked of him (Heb. 12:5).

No troubles are more afflictive and stinging, than those that are unexpected. Now when we are assured that there is no son whom the heavenly Father does not chasten, we are less surprised and less troubled when we meet with crosses. Indeed there is hardly any kind of affliction that may befall us, but that we have some instance in Scripture of the saints suffering the same thing.

Are we poor and paltry in the world? We should consider that poverty with holiness is a divine complexion; Jesus Christ, the holy and beloved Son of God, hath not where to lay his head. Are we under bodily infirmities? Good Hezekiah was struck with an uncomfortable disease as to the quality of it; and Gaius had a flourishing soul in a languishing body. Are our dear relations taken away? Aaron and David lost some of their sons by terrible strokes. Are our spirits wounded with a sense of God's displeasure? Job and Heman were under strong terrors, yet they were the favourites of heaven.

Briefly: how many, most dear to God, were called to suffer extreme and bloody trials for the defence of the truth? How many deaths did they endure in one torment! How many torments in one death! Yet they were so far from fainting, that the more their pains were exasperated, the more their courage and joy were shining and conspicuous; as the face of the heavens is never more serene and clear, than when the sharpest north wind blows.

— William Bates, *Puritan Sermons,* Vol. 2, p. 597 (P.S.)

Canaanites and Perizzites

... the Canaanite and the Perizzite dwelled then in the land (Gen. 13:7).

C ontentions and animosities among Christians break out on two occasions:

1. Quarrels arise about earthly things. What can heathens think of them, when they see them malign and worry one another, for such things that their own philosophy has taught them to make little account of? Abraham was very apprehensive of the evil consequences that might have attended the strife between his and Lot's herdsmen, probably about their pasturage or watering places. Therefore Abraham would not insist upon such pleas as he might reasonably have alleged on his own side, but stifled the contention ... He dreaded the scandal which would have been given to the heathen by their squabbles. This is suggested: 'The Canaanite and the Perizzite dwelled in the land.'

The contentions and wranglings of the Corinthians, about things that appertain to this life, and their going to law for them, especially the bringing of their suits before heathen tribunals, was to cast reproach on the Christian religion ...

2. If we inquire, 'What spark has kindled this raging fire?' we shall often find that this earnest contending is not for that 'faith which was once delivered unto the saints'; but a dispute 'who shall be greatest?' All that I am able to do at present, for the removal of this scandal, is to beseech individual Christians in the mercies of Christ, to value, love and 'follow after the things which make for peace' (Rom. 14:19). For I fear the Gospel will hardly win ground in the world, until the Spirit of love, reigning, and acting in the hearts of those who profess it, opens the way for it. In the first planting of it ... it became a proverbial speech touching Christians: 'Behold, how they love one another!'

— George Hammond, *Puritan Sermons,* Vol. 4, pp. 426-427 (P.S.)

Three ages of life

Blessed is the man that walketh not in the counsel of the ungodly, nor standeth in the way of sinners, nor sitteth in the seat of the scornful (Ps. 1:1).

I s the prophet alluding here to the three principal ages of our life, which have every one of them their proper vices ... The vice of youth, which is the vigour of life, and delights most in motion and society; he expresses this as walking in the counsel of the ungodly. The vices of the middle age, which is the steadfast age; he expresses this as standing in the way of sinners. The vices of old age, which being weak and feeble, is scarce able to go; he expresses this by sitting in the chair of scorners.

It is as if the prophet had said: 'Blessed is the man that has passed through all the ages of his life, and has kept himself untainted by the vices that are incident to them. He has passed the day of his youth as it were the morning of his life, and is not tainted with the stirring vices of voluptuousness and prodigality. He had passed his middle age as it were the noon of his life, and is not tainted with the more elevated vices of ambition and vain-glory. He has passed his old age as it were the evening of his life, and is not tainted with the sluggish vices of covetousness and avarice ... '

But why would the prophet say, 'Blessed is the man,' as though ... excusing women from the kingdom of heaven? ... Is it not that David knew better the extent of his words than to be superfluous; for ever since the time that Moses said, 'God created man ... male and female created he them,' women have had as good right to the word as men ... And how else could Christ be called *the Son of man*, who we all know was the son of the woman?

— Sir Richard Baker, *Meditations and Disquisitions,*
pp. 15, 19-20 (S.P.)

Prayers: ushers of mercy

Now when Solomon had made an end of praying, the fire came down from heaven ... (2 Chron. 7:1).

Can God be moved with our arguments, or affected with our troubles? He is the unchangeable God ... there 'is no variableness, neither shadow of turning' with him.

The answer is that those holy motions upon the hearts of saints in prayer are the fruits of the unchangeable decrees of his love to them, and the appointed ushers of mercy. God graciously determines to give us a praying, arguing, warm, affectionate frame, as the precursor and forerunner of a decreed mercy. That is the reason that carnal men can enjoy no such mercies, because they pour out no such prayers. The spirit of prayer prognosticates the mercy that follows.

When the Lord by Jeremiah foretold the end of the captivity, he also presignifies the prayers that should open the gates of Babylon (Jer. 29:10,12). Cyrus was prophesied of, to do his work for Jacob, his servant's sake, and Israel his elect; but yet they must ask him concerning those things to come, and they should not seek him in vain ...

The coming of Christ is promised by himself; but yet 'the Spirit and the bride say, Come;' and he 'that heareth' must 'say, come.' And when Christ says he will 'come quickly:' 'Even so, Come, Lord Jesus' (Rev. 22:12,17,20). Divine grace kindles these ardent affections, when the mercies promised are on the wing. Prayer is that intelligible chain, as Dionysus calls it, that draws the souls up to God, and the mercy down to us; or like the cable that draws the ship to land, though the shore itself remains unmoveable.

— Samuel Lee, *Puritan Sermons,* Vol. 2, p. 174 (P.S.)

Fasting and prayer

... that ye may give yourselves to fasting and prayer ... (1 Cor. 7:5).

A fast has two parts; the one, outward, the chastening of the body; the other, inward, the afflicting of the soul; under which are contained all those religious acts which set the heart right toward God ...

To fast strictly for bodily abstinence is an indifferent thing, and is no part of God's worship; but to take it as joined with the inward part, and with a religious end in view, is a profession of extraordinary humiliation, plus giving a stronger and speedier wing to prayer. Reasons for fasting:

♦ Fasting is the opposite of that fullness of bread, which makes both body and soul more disposed to vice, and indisposed to religious duties, through drowsiness of head, heaviness of heart, dullness and deadness of spirit ...

♦ A day of fasting is an assistance to the soul, for the better performing of holy duties, such as meditation, reading, hearing the word, prayer, judging, and reforming a person's self ...

♦ But it is not enough that the body is chastened, if the soul is not afflicted (Isa. 58:5). Otherwise it is but a mere bodily exercise, which profits little ...

♦ Afflicting the soul works repentance; another chief end, and companion of fasting; for godly sorrow causes repentance, never to be repented of (2 Cor. 7:10) ...

♦ When the soul is afflicted, and heavy laden with sin, then a man will readily and earnestly seek after God, even as the sick seek a physician for health ...

My wish is that you observe it on very special occasions, and when an ordinary seeking of God is not likely to prevail.

— Henry Scudder, *The Christian's Daily Walk,* pp. 50-54 (S.P.)

Inward contentment

My soul, wait thou only upon God ... (Ps. 62:5).

Contentment is a sweet inward heart thing. It is work of the Spirit indoors ... 'My soul, wait thou only upon God.' These words may also be translated as: 'My soul, be silent to God. Hold peace, O my soul.' Not only must the tongue hold its peace; the soul must be silent. Many, many sit silently, refraining from discontented expressions, yet inwardly they are bursting with discontent. This shows a complicated disorder and great perversity in their hearts. And notwithstanding their outward silence, God hears the peevish, fretful language of their souls ...

Outwardly there may be great calmness and stillness, yet within amazing confusion, bitterness, disturbance and vexation.

Some people are so weak that they cannot restrain the unrest of their spirits, but in words and behaviour they reveal what woeful disturbances there are within. Their spirits are like the raging sea, casting forth nothing but mire and dirt, and are troublesome not only to themselves but also to all with whom they live. Others, however, are able to restrain such disorders of the heart, as Judas did when he betrayed Christ with a kiss, but even so they boil inwardly and eat away like a canker. So David speaks of some whose words are sweeter than honey ... and yet have war in their hearts. In another place, he says, 'While I kept silence my bones waxed old.'

Contentment is a soul business. First, it is inward; secondly, quiet; thirdly, it is a quiet frame of spirit ... It is a grace that spreads itself through the whole soul.

— Jeremiah Burroughs, *Rare Jewel of Christian Contentment,*
pp. 2-6 (S.G.)

Light and sight

The Lord is my light and my salvation; whom shall I fear ? ... (Ps. 27:1).

But is it enough that God is my light? What if I am blind? What good then will his light do me? This is true; and therefore David does not stop here, but *Deus illuminatio mea*, God is my enlightening too. He is both my light and my sight; my light by which to see, and my sight with which to see; my light to make walls and thresholds visible, and my sight to make me able to avoid them. If it were not for light, I should be always in the dark; if it were not for sight, I should be dark myself. No illumination without both; and never both, but only from God.

There is one, indeed, who hath gotten him a name, called Lucifer (light-bringer), as though it were he that brought us light, when God knows that but for him we should have no darkness. Yet he pretends to both, both to light and to enlightening; but, alas, his light is but an imposture, his enlightening but an illusion; for as he can transform himself into an angel of light, so he can transform the light itself, and make it seem light when it is indeed dark. Therefore his light can never make walls and thresholds to be truly visible, and as little can his enlightening make us able to avoid them. For this was tried with our first parents, who upon his enlightening had their eyes opened indeed, but opened to see good and evil, not to distinguish good from evil, and therefore could not enable them, nor us, to avoid evil ... God is my enlightening; and then we may safely infer, of what, of whom, should I be afraid?

— Sir Richard Baker, *Meditations and Disquisitions,* p. 322 (S.P.)

None lost but ...

... those that thou gavest me I have kept, and none of them is lost, but the son of perdition ... (John 17:12).

T hings are given to Christ in two ways; by the way of reward, or by way of charge.

By way of reward. So all nations are given to him. 'Ask of me, and I shall give thee the heathen for thine inheritance, and the uttermost parts of the earth for thy possession' (Ps. 2:8). He is Lord of all, even of the devils. All flesh are thus given to him, to be ruled by him. This donation is very large and comprises elect and reprobates ...

By way of charge. This refers to the elect, who are redeemed, justified, sanctified, glorified ... None of them that are given to Christ by way of charge can miscarry. 'All that the Father giveth me shall come to me; and him that cometh to me I will in no wise cast out' (John 6:37) ...

It seems however that some may be lost which are given to Christ (like the son of perdition). I answer: The word *given* is here used indefinitely, for those given to Christ by way of reward, and not by way of charge. Hypocrites, because of their external vocation, are said to be given to Christ by way of ministry and service, but not by way of special charge ... (At the last supper) Christ reveals plainly that one of them was not of the number of the elect, and should not receive the privileges of his especial charge. Though he was chosen to the calling of an apostle, yet not to eternal life. Christ knows the number of the heirs of salvation, and who only are given him by way of ministry and service of the church.

— Thomas Manton, *John 17,* pp. 105, 111 (S.G.)

When hope becomes presumption

Many will say to me in that day, Lord, Lord, have we not prophesied in thy name? and in thy name have cast out devils? and in thy name done many wonderful works? And then will I profess unto them, I never knew you: depart from me, ye that work iniquity (Matt. 7:22-23).

I shall distinguish between presumption and hope. The difference between hope and despair is more apparent; but we are too apt to confound presumption and hope, because there is a greater affinity between these than the other. As in morality some virtues come nearer to one extreme than to the other; so here, there is something of the general nature of hope in presumption. Therefore we must be all the more accurate and precise in distinguishing between the grace of hope, and the sin of presumption ...

I must also distinguish between two kinds of presumption ...

1. The first sort of presumption ... is *of ourselves.* We want to stand upon our own feet, insisting not upon what Christ is to us or has done for us, but upon what we are in and to ourselves, and what we have done for Christ. 'Have we not prophesied in thy name?' etc. ... It is not in the promises of free grace, but in the law and their strict observance of it, that these men ground their hope upon. But the true grace of hope is always grounded upon faith in the promises ...

2. The second sort of presumption ... is that by which we presume *upon God and his mercy.* The first presumption makes way for this credulous presumption: 'God is gracious, mercy is promised, Christ has died for sinners, and all will be well; we shall go to heaven, of course, without any more ado.' So they sit down in security all their days, till one day the surprise of their everlasting doom catches them unawares. This is 'a faithless confidence, a fond, credulous presumption'

... This is more fancy than faith or hope.

— Thomas Cole, *Puritan Sermons,* Vol. 2, pp. 509-510 (P.S.)

Does God deal with all alike?

Doth God pervert judgement? or doth the Almighty pervert justice?
(Job 8:3).

How can it square with God's justice, that all men being equally guilty by nature, that he should pass by one and save another? Why does he not deal with all alike? 'Is there unrighteousness with God? God forbid' (Rom. 9:14).

God is not bound to give account of his actions to his creatures. If none may say to a king, 'What doest thou?' (Eccl. 8:4), much less to God. It is sufficient to say that God is Lord paramount; he has sovereign power over his creatures, therefore can do no injustice ...

God has liberty in his own heart, to save one, and not another; and his justice is not at all impeached or blemished. If two men owe you money, you may, without any injustice, remit the debt to one, and exact it of the other. If two criminals are condemned to die, the king may pardon the one and not the other. He is not unjust if he lets one suffer, because he offended the law; nor if he saves the other, because he will make use of his prerogative as a king.

Though some are saved and others perish, yet there is no unrighteousness in God; because, whoever perishes, his destruction is of himself. 'O Israel, thou hast destroyed thyself' (Hos. 13:9). God offers grace, and the sinner refuses it. Is God bound to give grace? If a surgeon comes to heal a man's wound, and he will not be healed, is the surgeon bound to heal him? 'I have called, and ye refused' (Prov. 1:24). 'Israel would none of me' (Ps. 81:11). God is not bound to force his mercies upon men. If they wilfully oppose the offer of grace, their sin is to be regarded as the cause of their perishing, and not God's justice.

— Thomas Watson, *A Body of Divinity,* p. 64 (B.T.)

An oxymoron: sad saints

I will also clothe her priests with salvation: and her saints shall shout aloud for joy (Ps. 132:16).

Christian, what bad news has Christ brought from heaven with him, that makes you walk with your folded arms and pensive countenance? To see a wicked man merry, or a Christian sad, is alike uncomely. 'A feast is made for laughter,' says Solomon. I am sure God intended his people's joy in the feast of the Gospel; mourners were not to sit at God's table (Deut. 26:14).

Truly the saint's heaviness reflects unkindly upon God himself. We do not commend his cheer, if it does not cheer us. What saith the world? 'The Christian's life is but a melancholy walk,' thinks the carnal wretch, 'it is a dry feast they sit at, where so little wine of joy is drunk.' And will you confirm them in this their opinion, Christian? Shall they have your example to produce against Christ and his word, which promises peace and joy to all that will come to this feast? ...

Now they will believe 'tis good news indeed the Gospel brings, when they can read it in your cheerful lives; but when they observe Christians sad with this cup of salvation in their hands, truly they will suspect the wine in it is not so good as the preachers commend it ... O Christians, let the world see you are not losers in your joy, since you have been acquainted with the Gospel; give them not cause to think by your uncomfortable walking, that when they become Christians, they must bid farewell to all joy, and resolve to spend their days in a house of mourning.

— William Gurnall, *A Homiletic Encyclopedia,* p. 757 (H.E.)

A darling sin?

O Jerusalem, wash thine heart from wickedness, that thou mayest be saved.
How long shall thy vain thoughts lodge within thee? (Jer. 4:14).

A beloved sin is like a bias on the bowl; though you throw it ever so straight, yet the bias will draw it off that way, do what you can; so is a beloved sin to the soul. Aim it with the utmost skill, yet there is a secret lodestone in it, which attracts the heart, and makes that prayer to end in hell which began in heaven. Either sin and you must be at a distance, or God and you will. The soul that is in league with sin dares not come to God, dares not look at him, dares not think about him ... An unmortified soul, like the husband of a scolding wife, would rather be anywhere than at home. He makes many a sad bargain abroad, because he has no comfort at home with his wife. Many a heart chooses to be thinking of any thing rather than God ...

Hence, 'let us draw near with a true heart in full assurance of faith, having our hearts sprinkled from an evil conscience' (Heb. 10:22). He that comes to God with a true, upright, honest heart, being sprinkled from an evil conscience, may draw near to God in full assurance of faith: whereas guilt clouds, clogs, and distracts the soul. So that, both the guilt and power of a bosom sin furnish us with too much cause for distractions. Sin, would have all the heart; and God, he will have all or nothing.

As no subject is capable of two contrary qualities, in intense degrees, (heat and cold may be both in the same hand, but not in their intense degrees), so the heart of man cannot entertain Christ and corruption, light and darkness, except the one be loved and served superlatively above the other. 'If I regard iniquity in my heart, the Lord will not hear me' (Ps. 66:18). God first stops his ear above, and then the sinner's mouth below ...

— Richard Steele, *A Remedy for Wandering Thoughts,*
pp. 108-111 (S.P.)

Conquering darling sins?

... the sin which doth so easily beset us ... (Heb. 12:1).

Sit down and think what real good this sin has ever done you. Think what hurt it has done you and others, and what fruit, besides the shame and death, it brings to any. Your dearest sin is but sin, which is the worst thing in the world, and, its masks and diguises being laid aside, more ugly than the devil, more horrid than hell itself. And think, the more you love it the more God hates it, and his rage and jealousy is increased with the increase of your desires. Think how many prayers it has lost you, how many mercies it has poisoned to you, how many smiles it has clouded, besides what unutterable suffering it has inflicted upon Christ, and is preparing for you in hell. Consider, that you may have as much joy, happiness, and true comfort, without it. All converted sinners confess, that Jesus Christ has been better to them than all of their sins. If you may have as good enjoyments, or better, by having Christ with them, and heaven after them, you have a bargain indeed ...

Kneel down and pray with faith in the uprightness of your hearts, for strength from above. All the strength of heaven is engaged by prayer. He that heartily sets himself against his sin by prayer, cannot but dislike it, and when it is truly disliked, its heart is broken.

Augustine complains that when he, in his unconverted state, begged a divorce from his sin, his heart was afraid lest God should hear his prayers. Beware lest your hearts secretly cry spare, when your tongues openly cry, Lord, kill and crucify my corruption. When you really pull on earth, and the Lord will pull from heaven, it will break your sin and soul asunder.

— Richard Steele, *A Remedy for Wandering Thoughts,*
pp. 111-113 (S.P.)

To be continued

... If ye continue in my word, then are ye my disciples indeed (John 8:31).

Every believer should not only take heed that his works are good, and for the present he also does them, but he should carefully study to maintain them, that is, to keep on doing them and continually exercise them.

It is an easier matter to begin to do good than it is to continue to do good; and the reason is, there is not so much of 'the cross' in the beginning of a work as there is in a continual, hearty, conscientious practice of it. So Christians should be persuaded not only to do good but to continue doing so. Man, by nature, is more of a hearer than a doer. Athenian-like, he is continually listening for some new thing; seeing many things, but observing nothing. It is observable, that after Christ had divided his hearers into four parts, he condemned three of them as fruitless hearers. O it is hard to continue believing, continue loving, continue resisting all that oppose; we are subject to be weary of well-doing ...

It is because of this that you find so many 'ifs' in the Scriptures about men's happiness; example, 'if children, then heirs;' and 'if ye continue in faith.' ... Not that their continuing in the way of God is the cause of their works being right; but their works being right causes the continuance therein.

— John Bunyan, *Christian Behaviour,* pp. 92-93 (B.T.)

The upright soul is content in his profession, and changes not his behaviour according to his companions.

— George Swinnock

Servant of all servants

Behold my servant, whom I have chosen; my beloved, in whom my soul is well pleased (Matt. 12:18).

Christ is called a servant: First, in respect of his creation, because being a man, as a creature he was a servant. But that is not all. He was a servant in respect of his condition. Servant implies a base and low condition. Christ took upon himself the form of a servant; he emptied himself; he was the lowest of all servants in condition: for none was ever so abased as our glorious Saviour.

And then, it is a name of office ... There are ordinary servants and extraordinary, as great kings have their servants of state. Christ besides his abasement, he was a servant of state. He was an ambassador sent from the great God; a prophet, a priest, and a king ... an extraordinary servant, to do a piece of service that all the angels of heaven, and all the men on the earth joined together, could not perform. This great masterpiece of service was to bring God and man together again, that were at variance ... It being the greatest work and service that ever was, it required the greatest servant; for no creature in the world could perform it. All the angels of heaven would have sunk under this service ...

And then he was a servant to us; for the Son of Man came to minister, not to be ministered unto (Matt. 20:28). He washed his disciples' feet. He was a servant to us, because he did our work and suffered our punishment. We made him serve by our sins, as the prophet says (Isa. 43:24). He is a servant that bears another man's burden ... He being our surety, being a more excellent person, he did bear our burden, and did our work, therefore he was God's servant, and our servant; and God's servant, because he was our servant.

— Richard Sibbes, *A Description of Christ,* pp. 5-6 (B.T.)

Poise and proportion

Till we all come in the unity of the faith, and of the knowledge of the Son of God, unto a perfect man, unto the measure of the stature of the fulness of Christ (Eph. 4:13).

Some saints are remarkable for having one grace in peculiar prominence. Faith, for instance; or resignation; or courage; or zeal; or benevolence. Yet though this peculiarity may draw most eyes upon them, and win them most praise, if not in all the churches, in their neighbourhood, or even in their nation, these are not the most perfect specimens of Christianity. For it is with men as with trees, amongst which the least symmetrical may be the most noticeable. The more perfect the shape of the tree, the more symmetrical the proportion between its trunk and branches, between its height and width, it strikes the eye the less; and it is only on a near approach and closer scrutiny that we take in its size, and gaze with wonder on its tower form and enormous girth.

The finest specimen of a Christian is he in whom all the graces, like the strings of an angel's harp, are in the most perfect harmony. Therefore, we are to beware of cultivating one grace or attending to any one duty at the expense of others. The head, the heart, and the hand, doctrine, devotion, and work, should each have their due share of our time and attention. We should work on our lives like the ancient sculptor worked on dead marble, when he produced forms where each feature was not only beautiful in itself, but in perfect proportion also to every other ...

It is by growing equally in the knowledge, and the love, and the life of Christ, that we are to reach the true model of a Christian, and, to use Paul's words, grow into 'a perfect man, unto the measure of the stature of the fulness of Christ.'

— William Guthrie, *A Homiletic Encyclopedia*, p. 2546 (H.E.)

189

The brood of Babylon

The Lord reigneth; let the earth rejoice; let the multitude of isles be glad thereof (Ps. 97:1).

The state of affairs is often involved and confused, that we need not wonder if we see men of wisdom greatly perplexed in their spirits, and almost sunk into discouragement. The best of saints, whose hearts are more furnished and fortified with grace, would be of all men most subject to distress, were it not for the fact that they feel peace and comfort flowing into them from the remembrance and sweet consideration of a God above.

What good man could possibly know any enjoyment of himself, or possess his soul in patience, while he observes the eccentric and irregular motions of things below? The restlessness, tumblings and tossings of the world; desirable comforts and delights blasted in a moment; afflictions and troubles breaking in with a sudden surprise; order subverted, laws violated. He would see things indeed turned upside down; wickedness rampant and religion oppressed; the spurious brood of Babylon clothed in scarlet, and prospering in the world, when at the same time the precious sons of Zion ... are esteemed as earthen pitchers, yes, broken pottery, thrown upon dunghills, or cast into prisons ...

These things, I say, would soon break his heart—did he not see him who is invisible, and firmly believe a wheel within a wheel, an unseen hand, which steadily and prudently guides and directs all things ...

If we will repair into the sanctuary, consult the divine oracles, and believe them when they tell us that the eternal God, our God, is the Rector and Governor of the world, it will revive our spirits. It will also reduce our souls into their right frame, and preserve them in a due composure, when the scene of human affairs is most ruffled.

— Samuel Slater, *Puritan Sermons,* Vol. 3, pp. 314-315 (P.S.)

Extempore or set prayers?

But thou, when thou prayest ... (Matt. 6:6).

Some charge extemporary prayers to be a diminution of God's majesty because they cost nothing, and are made without any pains or industry (2 Sam. 24:24). A most false aspersion.

Surely a believer has laboured with his heart and tongue too, before attaining that dexterity of utterance and the ability to express himself. Many hours in the night no doubt he was awake, and was, by himself, practising Scripture phrases and the language of Canaan, whilst those that censure him for his laziness were fast asleep in their beds ...

Set prayers are prescript forms of our own or other's composing. Such are lawful for any, and needful for some.

Lawful for any. Otherwise God would not have appointed the priests a form of blessing the people. Nor would the Saviour have set his prayer which is both a prayer in itself and a pattern of prayer for us. Those that accuse set forms to be pinioning the wings of the dove, will soon affirm that girdles and garters, made to strengthen and adorn, are so many shackles and fetters which hurt and hinder men's free motion.

Needful for some. Namely, for such who as yet have not attained to pray extempore by the Spirit. But as little children that are so ambitious of going alone, that they scorn to take the guidance of a form or bench to direct them, but will adventure by themselves ... often to the cost of a knock and a fall; so many confess their weakness, in denying to confess it. Refusing to be beholden to a set form of prayer, they prefer to say nonsense, rather than nothing, in their extempore expressions. More modesty, and no less piety, it would have been for such men to have prayed longer with set forms that they might pray better without them.

— Thomas Fuller, *A Homiletic Encyclopedia,* pp. 3783-3785 (H.E.)

Should unbelievers pray?

After this manner therefore pray ye ... (Matt. 6:9).

Though an unbeliever sins in praying, yet it is not a sin for him to pray. There is a sin in the manner of his praying; but prayer, as to the act and substance of it, is his duty. He sins, not because he prays, that is required of him, but because he prays amiss, not in that manner that is required of him.

There are abominations in the prayers of a wicked man, but for him to pray is not an abomination; it is the good and acceptable will of God, that which he commands. He commands him to pray, and he sins not in complying with the command, so far as it is obedience; but he prays not as he ought to do, there is his sin. Now he should leave his sin, not his duty. He should pray better in another manner, that is all which can be inferred, not that he should not pray at all ...

A boy is learning to write; he scribbles at first awkwardly, makes, it may be, more blots than letters. It is his fault that he blots, not that he writes, that is his duty. In this case you would have him leave blotting, not leave writing. So here, the act of prayer is a duty, but the manner of performing this act, therein is the fault: this should be corrected, but the act should not be omitted.

— David Clarkson, *A Homiletic Encyclopedia,* p. 3762 (H.E.)

Prayer that is faithless is fruitless.

— Thomas Watson

JULY

True liberality

And there came a certain poor widow, and she threw in two mites ...
(Mark 12:42).

T hose things we delight in, we love to behold; the eye and the heart will go together. And can we think that the Saviour's glory has diminished aught of his gracious respect for our beneficence? Or that his acceptance of our charity was confined to the earth? Even now, as he sits at the right hand of his Father's glory, he sees every hand that is stretched out to the relief of his poor saints here below. And if vanity has power to stir up our liberality, out of conceit to be seen of men, how shall faith encourage our bounty in knowing that we are seen of God, and accepted by God? ...

The nation of Israel, though otherwise faulty enough, in its liberality was commendable. How bounteously open were their hands to the house of God! ... The rich gave much, the poorest gave more. Jesus saw a poor widow woman casting in two mites. It was misery enough that she was a widow. A married woman is under the careful provision of a husband; if she spends, he earns; in that estate, four hands work for her; in her widowhood, but two ... Alas! who could be poorer than that good woman? Wherefore was that *corban* but for the relief of such as her? Who should receive if such gives? Her mites were something to her, nothing to the treasury ...

A mite to her was more than pounds to the rich: pounds were little to them, two mites were all to her. They gave out of their abundance, she out of her necessity. That which they gave left the heap less, yet a heap still; she gives all at once, and leaves herself nothing. She gave not more than any but 'more than they all.' God does not so much regard what is taken out, as what is left. God looked at once into the bottom of her heart and the bottom of her purse, and esteemed her gift according to both.

— Joseph Hall, *Contemplations*, pp. 544-545 (T.N.)

The great distractor

For we wrestle not against flesh and blood, but against principalities, against powers, against the rulers of the darkness of this world, against spiritual wickedness in high places (Eph. 6:12).

One cause of distraction in the worship of God is Satan. And this he does sometimes more remotely by throwing in some cross business before duties, whereby the soul is unhinged ...

Satan is not idle when this and that child is restless and unquiet in the family; whereby perhaps all in the family lose the thought which would most profit them. He can create and promote distraction by every pillar and part of the structure, and every person in the congregation; and he is content that you should read sentences on the walls to hinder and divert your souls from the sentences that drop from the pulpit ... He is in every pew, at every elbow, throwing in his fireballs, and enticing poor souls to commit folly with him; and when God is dealing with the soul about heaven and hell, then comes he ... to break the treaty, and spoil that sacred conference. No road is so full of thieves as the road to heaven.

And though, to give the devil but his due, we can be bad enough in an ordinance without him, yet he waits there, no doubt, to make us worse ... Especially that prayer, or chapter, or sermon, that should do you most good, or most destroy his kingdom will he be most busy in ...

The remedy against Satan's distracting us in God's worship is that of Christ's own prescribing, 'Watch and pray, that ye enter not into temptation' (Matt. 26:41) ... Watch and pray, and pray and watch, and always remember that we have as much need of the strength of Christ for assistance, as the merit of Christ for acceptance, in every duty.

— Richard Steele, *A Remedy for Wandering Thoughts*,
pp. 113-118 (S.P.)

195

The believer's work ethic

For we hear that there are some which walk among you disorderly ...
(2 Thess. 3:11).

When you have begun the day in prayer by yourself, seeking peace with God through Jesus Christ, and craving his gracious presence to be with you, and for you, that day, you must then conscientiously, according to the nature of the day, apply yourself to the business of that day, whether it be in acts of religion, or that of your personal calling ...

If it is a working day, attend to the work of your particular calling with cheerfulness and diligence. For whosoever has no calling by which he may be profitable to society, to family, church and commonwealth; or having a lawful calling does not follow it, that man lives disorderly (2 Thess. 3:10-11). God never made any man just to play or to do nothing. And whatever a man does, he must do it by virtue of his Christian calling, receiving warrant for it, else he cannot do it in faith, without which no man can please God (Heb. 11:6). He has no way to heaven but by walking with God in his personal and particular calling as well as in his general calling (1 Cor. 7:17-24) ...

Let there be truth, plainness, and equity in all your dealings with men (Prov. 10:4).

Consider your neighbour's good as well as your own ...

Be watchful that you do not miss your opportunities of lawful advantage (Prov. 6:6-8) ...

Whereas in every calling there is a mystery, and often each calling has its special sin or sins, which the devil, and custom, have made to seem lawful; ... look diligently at these by the light of God's Word, and by experience, to find out those sins, and then be careful to avoid them.

— Henry Scudder, *The Christian's Daily Walk*, pp. 43-45 (S.P.)

True patriots

Righteousness exalteth a nation: but sin is a reproach to any people (Prov. 14:34).

The sinners of a nation are really the weakness of it ... Wicked men are they that betray nations and kingdoms, expose them to God's wrath, and subject them to his judgements. Did Noah bring the flood upon the old world? Or did the wicked do it by their wickedness? Did Lot bring down fire from heaven upon Sodom? Or did the Sodomites do it by their own lewdness? Did Jeremiah by his preaching ... and those few other godly in Jerusalem by their praying and weeping and mourning, bring on the captivity of that people? Or did not the people themselves, by their idolatry, their profaneness, their swearing, their Sabbath-breaking, their polluting God's ordinances, their shedding innocent blood, etc.?

I do not deny that the sins of the best of saints may sometimes contribute to the bringing down of judgement upon others. Jonah's sin raised a tempest upon the mariners; and David numbering the people brought the plague upon them ... And yet what is this to the numerous instances on the other side?

Which does ordinarily do most mischief: the sins of the truly godly, which are fewer and lesser, and mourned over and repented of; or the sins of the profane, the hypocrites, the impenitent? May we not say, that if the sins of the one have slain their thousands, those of the other have slain their ten thousands? ...

It is in the interest of any people, that where God has a seed of righteous ones, to favour them and make much of them. *They* are their best friends *that* are God's friends.

— John Collins, *Puritan Sermons*, Vol. 4, pp. 145-146 (P.S.)

The government of Christ

... and the government shall be upon his shoulder ... (Isa. 9:6).

Wherever you find true wisdom and judgement, there Christ has set up his government; because where wisdom is, it directs us not only to understand, but to order our ways aright. Where Christ (by his Spirit) as a prophet teaches, he likewise as a king (by his Spirit) subdues the heart to obedience of what is taught. This is that teaching which is promised of God, when not only the brain, but the heart itself, is taught. Men do not only know what they should do, but are taught the very doing of it. They are not only taught that they should love, fear and obey, but they are taught love itself, and fear and obedience itself. Christ sets up his chair in the very heart, and alters the frame of that, and makes his subjects good, together with teaching them to be good. Other princes can make good laws but they cannot write them in their people's hearts (Jer. 32:40) ...

We learn likewise, that men of a poorly governed life have not true judgement: no wicked man can be a wise man. Without Christ's Spirit the soul is in confusion, without beauty and form, as all things were in the chaos before the creation. The whole soul is out of joint till it is set again by him whose office is to restore all things. The baser part of the soul which should be subject, rules all, and subdues that little truth that is in the understanding, holding it captive to base affections. Then Satan by corruption occupies the soul till Christ, stronger then he, comes, and drives him out ... Christ as a new conqueror changes the fundamental laws of the old Adam, and establishes a government of his own.

— Richard Sibbes, *The Bruised Reed and Smoking Flax*,
pp. 82-83 (B.T.)

Health and wealth

... for he maketh his sun to rise on the evil and on the good, and sendeth rain on the just and on the unjust (Matt. 5:45).

No man knows how the heart of God stands toward him by the direction of his hand. His hand of mercy may be toward a man when his heart may be against that man, as you see in the case of Saul and others. And the hand of God may be set against a man when the heart of God is dearly set upon him, as you see in Job and Ephraim.

No man knows either love or hatred by outward mercy or misery; for all things come the same to all, to the righteous and to the unrighteous, to the good and to the bad, to the clean and to the unclean. The sun of prosperity shines as well upon brambles in the wilderness, as upon fruit trees in the orchard; the snow and hail of adversity fall upon the best garden, as well as upon the stinking dunghill or the wild waste. Ahab's and Josiah's ends concur in the very circumstances. Saul and Jonathan, though different in their natures and deportment, yet in their deaths they were not divided. Health, wealth, honours, crosses, sicknesses, losses are cast upon good men and bad men promiscuously.

'The whole Turkish empire,' says Luther, 'is nothing else but a crust cast by heaven's great Housekeeper to his dogs.'

Moses dies in the wilderness as well as those that murmured ... Nabal is rich as well as Abraham; Ahithophel wise as well as Solomon, and Doeg is honoured as well as Saul, as well as Joseph and Pharaoh.

— Thomas Brooks, *A Homiletic Encyclopedia*, p. 3980 (H.E.)

Take your case to God

Be not overcome of evil, but overcome evil with good (Rom. 12:21).

Dear sister, do not faint. The wicked may hold the bitter cup to your head, but God mixes it, and there is no poison in it. They strike, but God moves the rod; Shimei cursed, but it is because the Lord bids him. I tell you, and I have it from him, before whom I stand for God's people, that there is a decree given out, in the great court of the highest heavens, that your present troubles shall be dispersed as the morning cloud ... Let me intreat you, in Christ's name, to keep a good conscience in your proceedings in that matter, and beware of yourself. Yourself is a more dangerous enemy than I, or any without you. Innocence and an upright cause is a good advocate before God, and shall plead for you, and win your cause.

Count much of your Master's approbation and his smiling. He is now as the king that is gone to a far country. God seems to be from home (if I may say so), yet he sees the ill servants, who say, 'Our master deferred his coming', and so strike their fellow-servants. But patience, my beloved; Christ the King is coming home ...

I hope your present process shall be sighted one day by him, who knows your just cause; and the bloody tongues, crafty foxes, double-ingrained hypocrites, shall appear as they are before his majesty, when he shall take the masks off their faces And O, thrice happy shall your soul be then, when God finds you covered with nothing but the white robe of the saint's innocence, and the righteousness of Jesus Christ.

You have been of late in the King's wine cellar, where you were welcomed by the Lord of the inn, upon condition that you walk in love. Put on love and brotherly kindness, and long-suffering; wait as long upon the favour and turned hearts of your enemies as your Christ waited upon you ...

— Samuel Rutherford, *Letters of Samuel Rutherford*, pp. 54-55 (B.T.)

Entrapment

... how then can I do this great wickedness, and sin against God? (Gen. 39:9).

There are no sins to which there is a stronger inclination in our corrupted nature, than acts of sensuality. The temptation of Joseph by his mistress was heightened by the lure of profit and advancement, that he might obtain through her favour the interest of her husband, who was an eminent officer in the Egyptian court. And the denial of such would be extremely provoking, implying both a contempt injurious to her dignity, and a disappointment of her ardent expectations. Hatred and revenge, upon refusal, are equal to the lust of 'an imperious whorish woman' (Ezek. 16:30).

We read the effects of it ... Upon his rejecting her desires she was consumed with rage, and in order to purge herself, she became his accuser, wounded his reputation, deprived him of his liberty, and exposed his life to extreme peril. Joseph chose rather to lie in the dust than to rise by sin ...

Joseph repelled the temptation with this powerful thought: 'How can I sin against God?' ... It is a watchful sentry, that resists temptations without, and suppresses corruptions within ...

This holy fear is not a mere judicial impression, that restrains us from sin because of the dreadful punishment that follows; for such servile affection, though it may stop a temptation, and hinder the eruption of a lust into the gross act, yet it does not renew the nature, and make us holy and heavenly. There may be a respective dislike of sin with a direct affection to it ... Therefore, that we may 'be in the fear of the Lord all the day long', we must regard him in his endearing attributes—his love, his goodness and compassion, his rewarding mercy. This will produce a filial fear of reverence and caution, lest we should offend so gracious a God.

— Willaim Bates, *Puritan Sermons*, Vol. 4, pp. 384-385, 406-407 (P.S.)

Satan's two-pronged attack

And if the righteous scarcely be saved, where shall the ungodly and the sinner appear (1 Pet. 4:18).

The devil has two ways or methods by which he seeks to undermine and overthrow the hope of a Christian ...

1. If your hope is strong and lively, he will slander it with the name of 'presumption.' This that he may shake your confidence, and discourage you from those eminent actings of your hope in which you have so much comfort. He envies your happiness: he would wish to clip the wings of your faith and hope, that he may rob you of the joy of your salvation, and keep you in the doldrums all your days. He would like to take off your helmet, that he may knock you down at one blow ... In such conflicts and fierce assaults, gird-up yourself, stand fast, and hope to the end ...
2. If your hope is small and weak, the devil will call it 'despair'. He would make you believe that a little grace is not grace: he will argue from your weakness in grace to your total want of it. If under such temptation you find your spirit sinking and ready to faint, arouse yourself, and address your soul, as David did: 'Why art thou cast down, O my soul?' Follow these direction:

a. Consider: It is not the degree of grace, but the truth of grace, to which salvation is promised.
b. Put right value and estimate upon the lowest degree of grace, so that grace may not seem contemptible and as nothing in your sight. Grace is of more worth than the whole world, 'a pearl of great price.'
c. Study to distinguish correctly between the weakness of your grace, and the grace itself that is under the weakness. And while you are mourning under one, be sure you rejoice in the other ...

— Thomas Cole, *Puritan Sermons*, Vol. 2, pp. 518-519 (P.S.)

The devil's expertise

... for we are not ignorant of his devices (2 Cor. 2:11).

The world is Satan's bait. He seldom throws out a naked hook. Let murder, fraud, lying or idolatry be presented in their undisguised turpitude, and only few people of good education and correct morals will be taken in by him. But he conceals the hook in a goodly bait, and like a skilful angler, he knows how to use the temptation best suited to our palate ... For one he has a golden bait; for another, pleasure; for a third, worldly fame and honours.

And his line is thrown out everywhere—in our place of business, in our families, in our studies, at our tables, and on our pillows.

— Arthur Jackson, *A Homiletic Encyclopedia*, p. 4680 (H.E.)

(The devil) hath an apple for Eve, a grape for Noah, a change of raiment for Gehazi, a bag for Judas. He can dish out his meat for all palates.

— William Jenkyn

The fencing school of temptation

And lead us not into temptation ... (Matt. 6:13).

L et those that are tempted be wise enough to make good use of their temptations. As we should endeavour to improve our afflictions, so to improve our temptations. We should pick some good out of temptation, as Samson got honey out of the lion. God can make his people get much good by their temptation:

♦ A Christian sees that corruption in his heart which he never saw before. Water in a glass looks pure, but put it on the fire, and the scum boil up; so in temptation a Christian sees the scum of sin boil up ...

♦ A Christian sees more of the wiles of Satan, and is better able to withstand them. Paul had been in the fencing school of temptation, and grew to be an expert in finding out Satan's stratagems. 'We are not ignorant of his devices' (2 Cor. 2:11).

♦ A Christian grows more humble. God would rather let his children fall into the devil's hands than to see them proud. Temptation makes the plumes of pride to fall ... Better is that temptation that humbles than that duty which makes us proud. Thus a Christian may get much good by temptation, which made Luther say that three things make a good divine: prayer, meditation and temptation.

Some have been under the sore temptations and buffetings of Satan, to lust, revenge, self-murder, but God has stood by them, and given them strength to overcome the tempter.

Let them be very thankful to God ... Know that it was free grace that beat back the tempter, and brought us off with trophies of victory.

— Thomas Watson, *The Lord's Prayer*, pp. 216-218 (B.T.)

A glorious intrusion

And it came to pass, that while he executed the priest's office before God ... (Luke 1:8).

When things are at the worst, then God begins a change. The state of the Jewish church was extremely corrupted immediately before the news of the Gospel; yet as bad as it was, not only the priesthood, but the courses of attendance, continued even from David's time till Christ's. It is a desperately depraved condition of a church, where no good orders are left ...

While they were praying to God, Zacharias sees an angel of God: as Gideon's angel went up in the smoke of the sacrifice, so did Zacharias' angel, as it were, come down in the fragrant smoke of his incense. It was ever great news to see an angel of God, but now more, because God had long withdrawn from them all the means of his supernatural revelations. As this wicked people were strangers to their God in their conversation, so was God grown a stranger to them in his apparitions; yet, now that the season of the Gospel approached, he visited them with his angels, before he visited them by his Son. He sends his angel to men in the form of man. The presence of angels is no novelty, but their apparition. They are always with us, but rarely seen that we may awfully respect their messages when they are seen. In the meantime, our faith may see them, though our senses do not ...

When could it be more fit for the angel to appear to Zacharias, than when prayers and incense were offered by him? Where could he more fitly appear than in the temple? In what part of the temple more fitly than at the altar of incense? And whereabouts rather than on the right side of the altar? Those glorious spirits, as they are always with us, so most in our devotions; and as in all places, so most of all in God's house.

— Joseph Hall, *Contemplations*, pp. 404-406 (T.N.)

205

Needed: more than reformation

... Except a man be born again ... (John 3:3).

Reformation may proceed: (a) *From force and fear*. Such a reformation is from impediments, not from inclination. Cutting a bird's wings does not take away its propensity to fly, but its ability. Cutting the claws of a lion or pulling out its teeth does not change its lionish nature. Fear restrained Herod from putting John to death when his will was inclined to the act. Fear may clip the nails of sin, only grace can hinder their growth and take away their life. Fear only stops the streams, not chokes the fountain.

(b) *From a sense of outward interest*. A man may rationally abstain from those sordid pleasures which degrade his esteem and prey upon his reputation. But in the meantime his inward lusts may triumph, while their outward appearances are halted. A splendid life may co-exist with inward vermin, contrary to the pure nature of God, and inconsistent with a man's happiness. Men may cast out one gross devil to make way for seven more and worse ones. The interest which restrains outward acts will not restrain inward lusts.

Well then, an outward reformation without an inward grace can no more rectify nature than abstinence from luxury can cure a disease that a man has contracted through intemperance ... Outward applications of balms and ointments will do little good in a fever, unless the spring of the disease be altered ...

— Stephen Charnock, *A Homiletic Encyclopedia*, p. 4069 (H.E.)

To the death

Thou hast loved righteousness, and hated iniquity ... (Heb. 1:9).

I f friends have weapons in their hands, they will but play with them, but deadly enemies will draw the blood of one another. There is a difference between fencing and fighting for life. Although a man that knows nothing of their meaning might think a fencer is fighting seriously, seeing he seems to make so great a stir ... Yet the issue will show you that it is otherwise, because you see that there is no blood shed, nor men killed.

So it is with a hypocrite in his seeming reformation. He makes the greatest stir against his sin in confessing and prayer, and other means, yet he will not resolvedly cast it away, but secretly uses it as his friend, while he openly abuses it as his enemy ... He will not be brought unfeignedly to renounce it, and give it a bill of divorce, and cast it out as a man does his vomit, with resolution never to take it in again. Oh, how sweetly does he roll it in his thoughts in secret, when he frowns upon it with the severest countenance! How easily is he drawn to it again, when he takes on that he repents of and abhors it!

But it is clean contrary with a man that is converted. Though the remnants of sin will remain in him as long as he lives, yet as to the reign of it, he presently casts it off, and bids defiance to it. He fights against it in good earnest, knowing that either he or it must die.

— Richard Baxter, *A Homiletic Encyclopedia*, p. 1433 (H.E.)

Self-examination

But let a man examine himself ... (1 Cor. 11:28).

L et no soul examine itself by any lower standard than this: *partici-pation of the divine nature, conformity to the divine image.* Examine what alliance your soul has to God; whose is the image and superscription. Religion is a divine accomplishment, an afflux from God, and may, by its affinity to heaven, be distinguished from a brat of hell and darkness ...

There is a vanity which I have observed in many pretenders to nobility and learning. When men seek to demonstrate the one by their coat of arms and the records of their family, and the other by a gown, or a title, or their names inscribed on the register of the university, rather than by the accomplishments and behaviours of gentlemen or scholars, vanity is observed.

A like vanity, I do not doubt, may be observed in many pretenders to religion. Some are searching God's records to find their names written in the Book of Life, when they should be studying to find God's name written upon their hearts, 'Holiness to the Lord' engraved upon their souls. Some are busy examining themselves by the external notes and marks of men, when they should labour to find the marks and prints of God and his nature upon them ... Some glory in the bulk of their duties, and in the multitude of their pompous performances and religious achievements, crying with Jehu, 'Come, see here my zeal for the Lord'; whereas it would be much more excellent if one could see their likeness to the Lord, and the characters of divine beauty and holiness drawn upon their hearts and lives.

— John Shaw, *A Homiletic Encyclopedia*, p. 4466 (H.E.)

Repentance

... except ye repent, ye shall all likewise perish (Luke 13:3).

The more we defer, the more difficult and painful our work will prove to be. Every day will both enlarge our task and diminish our ability to perform it. Sin is never at a stay. If we do not retreat from it, we shall advance in it, and the further on we go, the more we have to come back ...

Vice, as it grows in age, so it improves in stature and strength. From a puny child it soon waxes a lusty stripling, then rises to be a sturdy man, and after awhile becomes a massive giant, whom we shall scarce dare to encounter, whom we shall well nigh find impossible to vanquish ... It grows mighty by stripping us of our best forces, by enfeebling our reason, by perverting our will, by corrupting our temper, by debasing our courage, by seducing all our appetites and passions to a treacherous compliance with itself. Every day our mind grows more blind, our will more rusty, our spirit more faint, our passions more headstrong and untameable. The power and empire of sin encroaches by degrees, and continually gains ground on us, till finally it has subdued and suppressed us.

First we learn to bear it; then we come to like it; by and by we negotiate a friendship with it; then we dote on it; at last we become enslaved to it in a bondage, which we shall hardly be able, or willing, to shake off. Not only are our necks fitted to the yoke, but our hands are manacled and our feet shackled thereby. Our heads and hearts conspire in a base submission to it. When vice has made such an impression on us ... it will demand an extremely toilsome labour to extirpate it.

— Isaac Barrow, *A Homiletic Encyclopedia*, p. 4245 (H.E.)

Can it be done?

I can do all things through Christ which strengtheneth me (Phil. 4:13).

It is often said that it is impossible ... to call on God without distractions. Such is the variety of objects, such the imbecility of our nature, such the weakness of our graces, such the suddenness and swiftness of a thought, that none but angels can do this ...

(We grant that) perfection herein is impossible in this life; perhaps only a prayer or an ordinance may have that intenseness, as to exclude every wandering thought that would step in. However to be perfectly free in every duty from them, is rather to be wished for than hoped for in this life. The angelical perfection is reserved for heaven; the evangelical perfection may be here attained ...

In this sense, there is no divine precept impossible. Although our Lord Jesus said, 'Without me ye can do nothing' (John 15:5), yet the apostle asserts, 'I can do all things through Christ which strengtheneth me' (Phil. 4:13). If all things, then why not this? Though it were impossible in itself, yet is it possible with God's help? We are prone to think that we can perform easy things by our own strength, and that difficult things are too hard for God. Have you ever really tried to find out what God and you can do? Could you not have heard a sermon better if a naked sword had been suspended by a single hair over your bare heads; and prayed more cordially if you had seen every word you uttered written down by the hand of God? The same caution and watchfulness that can keep distraction away two days, can do it for ten, or twenty; and he that can be tempered for a day, might be tempered every day, if he did his best.

— Richard Steele, *A Remedy for Wandering Thoughts*, pp. 46-48 (S.P.)

The battle of short duration

... To him that overcometh ... (Rev. 2:7).

L et this encourage you, O Christian in your conflict with Satan: the skirmish may be sharp, but it cannot be long. Let him tempt you, and his wicked agents trounce you, it is only for a little while, and you shall be rid of both of them. The cloud while it drops rain is passing over you, and then comes fair weather and eternal sunshine of glory.

Can't you watch with Christ a couple of hours? And keep the field for a few days? If you give up, you are finished forever. Persevere, and when the battle is over your enemy shall never rally again. Ask faith to look through the keyhole of the promise, and tell you what it sees there laid up for him that overcomes. Ask it to listen and tell you whether it can hear the shouts of the crowned saints, just as if they were dividing the spoils and receiving rewards for all their services and sufferings. Those sufferings and temptations that come to you are like a little splash of water coming between you and glory.

— William Gurnall, *A Homiletic Encyclopedia*, p. 4795 (H.E.)

If thou hast fallen into sin through violent temptations, seek speedily for repentance for it, recovery out of it, and reformation from it.

— Vavasor Powell

When the Assyrian comes into the land

And this man shall be the peace, when the Assyrian shall come into our land ... (Mic. 5:5).

There is no work which God has made—the sun, moon, stars and all the world—in which so much of the glory of God appears as in a man who lives quietly in the midst of adversity. That was what convinced the king: when he saw that the three children would walk in the midst of the fiery furnace and not be touched, whereas the others who came only to the mouth of the furnace were devoured. So when a Christian can walk in the midst of fiery trials, without his garments being singed, and has comfort and joy in the midst of everything, it will convince men, when they see the power of grace in the midst of afflictions. When they can behave themselves in a gracious and holy manner in such afflictions as to make others roar: O, this is the glory of a Christian.

This is what is said to be the glory of Christ, (for it is thought by interpreters to be meant of Christ) in Micah 5:5. This man shall be the peace when the Assyrian shall come into our land. For one to be in peace when there are no enemies is no great thing, but the text says, when the Assyrian shall come into our land, then this man shall be the peace. That is, when all shall be in a hubbub and uproar, this man shall be peace. That is the trial of grace, when you find Jesus Christ to be peace in your hearts when the Assyrian shall come into the land ...

Suppose you heard the enemy come marching into the city capturing everything and plundering, what would be your peace? Jesus Christ is the peace of the soul when the enemy comes into the city, and into your houses.

— Jeremiah Burroughs, *Rare Jewel of Christian Contentment*,
pp. 50-51 (S.G.)

Monendo et movendo

Make me to go in the path of thy commandments ... (Ps. 119:35).

God leads not only by a naked guidance or directive light beamed into the understanding ... but he leads, also, by the efficacious inclining of the heart, the bowing and bending of the will, the overpowering of the affections, to follow his guidance in the doing of what is good and in the shunning of what is evil. Divines bring the whole of the Spirit's leading under two words, *monendo et movendo*: He first 'counsels and directs' as to what is to be done, and then he 'excites and effectually inclines' to the doing thereof. 'Teach me, O Lord, the way of thy statutes' (Ps. 119:33): here is the informing and directing act of the Spirit. 'Make me to go in the path of thy commandments' (Ps. 119:35): here is the efficacious and powerful act of the Spirit.

His cooperation and corroboration. When one leads another, both the person leading, and the person led, have their proper action and motion, and both unite and concur in it. And so it is in the saints being led by the Spirit, as to what is holy and good. He acts, and they act too; something is done on his part, and something on theirs too: ... They do the thing, but it is by his influx: 'Thou also hast wrought all our works in us' (Isa. 26:12).

The other act of the Spirit—corroboration or strengthening—falls in with this in part. So, his lead resembles the mother or the nurse leading the child. The child being weak, not able to go alone, they take him by the hand, hold him up, join their strength with his weakness; and so they enable him to go. In like manner, the strong and mighty Spirit of God does, as it were, take weak Christians by the hand, and communicates his strength to them ...

— Thomas Jacombe, *Puritan Sermons*, Vol. 3, pp. 590-591 (P.S.)

Epicure and Stoic

Who satisfieth thy mouth with good things; so that thy youth is renewed like the eagle's (Ps. 103:5).

Who is not sensible of good things, and specially when they are good things for the mouth? For all the labour of man is for the mouth; all that the hands work for, and all that the feet toil about, is all for the mouth. So long as we have green pastures and still waters, so long as we have meat and drinks, not only to satisfy hunger, but to please the palate, we don't care much for anything else.

But, O my soul, these are not the good things that are here meant; and even if they were worth caring about if they continued, even then the days will come when I shall say, I have no pleasure in them. The time will come when my mouth will lose its taste, and what good then will these good things of the mouth do me? No, my soul, no fear here of old age; no fear of defect by reason of years, for your youth shall be renewed like the eagle's ...

May we not now begin anew ... and (like David) remember all his benefits ... He begins with forgiveness of sins, because this is the foundation ... His next benefit is the healing of all my infirmities; but, alas, what good will both these benefits do me if he should stay here, and go no further ...

He will now therefore add a concluding flourish ... He crowns you with loving kindness and tender mercies ... He satisfies your mouth with good things, and your youth is renewed like the eagle's; as much as to say, you shall have the happiness of the epicure and the stoic, both at once.

— Sir Richard Baker, *Meditations and Disquisitions*,
pp. 400-402 (S.P.)

In praise of study

Study to shew thyself approved unto God ... (2 Tim. 2:15).

When the Spirit does in an ordinary way help us in remembering or meditating on any text or holy doctrine, he does it according to our capacity and disposition, and therefore there is much of our weakness and error usually mixed with the Spirit's help in the product. As example, when you hold the hand of a child in writing, you write not so well by his hand, as by your own alone, but your skill and his weakness and unskilfulness do both appear in the letters which are made. So it is in the ordinary assistance of the Spirit in our studies, meditations, prayers etc., otherwise all that we do would be perfect, in which we have the Spirit's help. But Scripture and all Christian experience contradict this.

It is not the work of the Spirit to tell you the meaning of Scripture, and give you the knowledge of divinity, without your own study and labour, but to bless that study, and give you knowledge thereby ... Does not experience commonly tell you that men know more who study and have learning than those who do not? Are not ministers and other learned men and godly people that have studied the Scriptures long, the most knowing people in the world? Nothing but mad ignorance or impudence can deny it. What man breathing knew as much the first hour he received the Spirit, as he does after many years of study and diligent labour?

To reject study on the pretence of the sufficiency of the Spirit, is to reject the Scripture itself. As a man rejects his land that refused to till it ... though he praise it never so much; so does he reject the Scripture that refuses to study it.

— Richard Baxter, *A Homiletic Encyclopedia*, pp. 2868-2869 (H.E.)

Meditate on our making, that we may fall in love with our Maker.
— David Dickson

In understanding, be men

But grow in grace, and in the knowledge of our Lord and Saviour Jesus Christ ... (2 Pet. 3:18).

We are to labour after a greater measure of knowledge. And those who are real Christians, have attained to some degree of spiritual understanding. That light which is as the light of the moon, should be increased, so as to equal the light of the sun; and that which is as the light of the sun, should be augmented so as to equal the light of seven days, growing more and more glorious ...

Compare all the knowledge with this knowledge of Christ, and see the vast difference in excellency. And this will stir you to grow in it. The philosophers of old—how restless were their minds, how endless their inquiries! The farther they went, the more they were puzzled; and, after long study, they came to understand that they fully understood nothing. The wise king of Israel, after he had diligently employed his large understanding about human knowledge—cries out, as a man exceedingly vexed and disappointed: 'In much wisdom is much grief: and he that increaseth knowledge increaseth sorrow' (Eccl. 1:18).

But the knowledge of Christ is of another nature. He that rightly understands the Lord Jesus, understands how to have his guilt removed, his heart renewed, his conscience calmed, his soul secured, and that forever. This knowledge is not a *vexation*, but a *satisfaction*, to the spirit ... Here it may truly be said, 'The better Christ is understood, the more the soul that understands him is at rest.'

— Nathanael Vincent, *Puritan Sermons*, Vol. 3, pp. 294-306 (P.S.)

The body and soul of Scripture

... known by his fruit ... (Matt. 12:33).

There is a *caro* and a *spiritus*, a flesh and a spirit, a body and a soul, in all the writings of the Scriptures. It is but the flesh and body of divine truths that is printed upon paper ...

There is however a soul and spirit of divine truths that could never yet be congealed into ink, and could never be blotted upon paper. It is by a secret transference and conveyance, that passes from one soul into another, being able to dwell or lodge only in a spiritual being, in a living thing, because it itself is nothing but life and spirit. Neither can it express itself sufficiently in words and sounds, but will best declare itself in actions; as the old manner of writing among the Egyptians was, not by words, but things. The life of divine truths is better expressed in actions than in words, because actions are more living than words. Words are nothing but dead resemblances and pictures of those truths, which live and breathe in actions. The kingdom of God consists not in word, but in life and power.

Sheep do not come and bring their fodder to their shepherd, and show him how much they eat; but inwardly concocting and digesting it, they make it appear by the fleece which they wear upon their backs, and by the milk which they give. And let not Christians merely talk and dispute of Christ, and so measure our knowledge of him by our words; but let us show our knowledge concocted into our lives and actions. Then it will be manifest that we are Christ's sheep indeed, that we are his disciples, by the fleece of holiness that we wear, and by the fruits that we daily yield in our lives and conversations. 'Herein,' says Christ, 'is my Father glorified, that ye bear much fruit.'

— Ralph Cudworth, *A Homiletic Encyclopedia*, p. 3115 (H.E.)

Credenda and agenda

And it shall be, when he sitteth upon the throne of his kingdom, that he shall write him a copy of this law in a book out of that which is before the priests the Levites (Deut. 17:18).

H ere was a good beginning of a king's reign: the first thing he did after he sat upon the throne, was to copy out the Word of God in a book.

(In the following verse it reads): 'And it shall be with him, and he shall read therein all the days of his life.'

It shall be with him: The book of the law shall be his daily companion ...

And he shall read therein: It is not below the majesty of a prince to peruse the oracles of heaven: in them are comprised sacred axioms: 'I will speak of excellent things' (Prov. 8:6) ... In the Hebrew it is 'princely things'; such as are fit for a God to speak, and a king to read ...

All the days of his life. He must not leave off reading till he leaves off reigning ... (It) is to be read diligently. Ignorance of Scripture is the mother of error, not devotion. 'Ye do err, not knowing the Scriptures' (Matt. 22:29).

Let us enquire at this sacred oracle. Apollos was 'mighty in the Scriptures' (Acts 18:24). Melancthon, when he was young, sucked 'the sincere milk of the word.' Alphonsus, King of Arragon, read over the Bible fourteen times. That Roman lady Cecilia had, by much reading of the Word, made her breast *bibliotheca Christi* (the library of Christ), as Jerome says ...

The Scripture contains in it the *credenda,* the things which we are to believe, and the *agenda*, the things which we are to practise.

— Thomas Watson, *Puritan Sermons*, Vol. 2, pp. 57-58, 63 (P.S.)

The library of the Holy Ghost

All scripture is given by inspiration of God ... (2 Tim. 3:16).

Believe it to be of God; see the name of God in every line ... Whence should the Scriptures come, if not from God? *Sinners* could not be the authors of Scripture. Would they incite such holy lines? Or attack so fiercely those sins which they love? *Saints* could not be the authors of Scripture. How could they be sanctified if they counterfeited God's name, and put 'Thus saith the Lord' to a book of their own devising? *Angels* could not be the authors of Scripture. What angel in heaven would dare impersonate God, and say, 'I am the Lord'? Believe the pedigree of Scripture to be sacred, and to come from the 'Father of lights' (Jam. 1:17). The Scripture's antiquity speaks its divinity ...

The Scripture is the library of the Holy Ghost; it is an encyclopedia of divine knowledge, an exact model and pattern of religion. The Scripture contains in it the *credenda*, the things which we are to believe, and the *agenda*, the things which we are to practise ...

The Scripture is the standard of truth, the judge of controversies; it is the pole-star to direct us to heaven ... The Scripture is the compass by which the rudder of our will is to be steered; it is the field in which Christ, the Pearl of Price, is hid; it is a rock of diamonds; it is a sacred 'eye-salve'; it heals their eyes that look upon it; it is a spiritual optic-glass in which the glory of God is resplendent; it is the panacea of 'universal medicine' for the soul. The leaves of Scripture are, like the 'leaves of the tree [of life] were, for the healing of the nations' (Rev. 22:2). The Scripture is both the breeder and feeder of grace.

— Thomas Watson, *Puritan Sermons*, Vol. 2, pp. 62-64 (P.S.)

Bible contradictions?

Nicodemus answered and said unto him, How can these things be?
(John 3:9).

I t is merely because of our ignorance that the Scriptures seem contradictory ... It is rather a wonder that the Scriptures seem not more self-contradictory, if you consider:

♦ That they are written in another language, and must need lose much in the translation.
♦ That it being the language also of another country, to men that know of the customs, the situation of places, the proverbial speeches and phrases of that country ...
♦ Also, that the Scriptures are of so exceeding antiquity, as no books else in the world are like them ... It is a very foolish audacious thing, that novices in divinity should expect to have all difficulties resolved at once, or else they will censure the Scriptures, and speak evil of the things they know not, instead of censuring themselves ...

How should we deal with contradictions? Common reason tells us that we must first have a general proof that Scripture is God's Word, and argue from there to the verity of the parts, and not begin with a particular proof of each part. It would seem that you would argue like this: This and that text of Scripture is true, therefore they are God's Word. But reason tells you that you should argue like this: This is God's Word, therefore it is true ...

— Richard Baxter, *A Homiletic Encyclopedia*, pp. 584-590 (H.E.)

The sin of addition

Add thou not unto his words, lest he reprove thee, and thou be found a liar (Prov. 30:6).

What is it that we must not add to these words of God?

1. Nothing as God's which is not his; as articles of faith, new points of doctrine, promises, threats, prophecies, revelations, traditions, or miracles, pretending to be of God, but are not so ...

2. Nothing to compete with God's revealed truths or laws, as to authority or importance: for this is to usurp the throne of God, and claim a peerage with absolute supremacy.

3. Nothing that savours of such additional supplements that would seem to imply ignorance to God, or imprudence, or negligence: for this makes us accusers or reprovers of the Holy One, as guilty of defects, miscarriages, and mistakes ...

4. Nothing that builds what God destroys, or ruins what God designs expressly and resolves to build. The wise and righteous governor of the world is most impatient of such contradictions ...

5. Nothing that puts a wrong construction of God's words. False glosses, and corrupt interpretations of the truths of God, are vain and bold additions ...

6. In one word: Nothing that supersedes, or is coordinate with, or derogatory of, God's words, in doctrine, government and worship and is prejudicial, burdensome, or unprofitable to the purity, peace, order, edification, or needful harmony and consolation of souls and churches ...

— Matthew Sylvester, *Puritan Sermons*, Vol. 6, pp. 429-430 (P.S.)

Battling with heresies

Now the Spirit speaketh expressly, that in the latter times some shall depart from the faith, giving heed to seducing spirits, and doctrines of devils (1 Tim. 4:1).

After the persecutor the second enemy that comes forth against the Christian is the *heretic* or *seducer*, who is so much more to be feared than the persecutor because it is worse to part with God's truth than with our own life. It is worse to be corrupted in our minds than to be tortured in our members. In a word, it is worse to have our souls damned by God than our bodies killed by man.

Now, that you may be able to lift up this sword of the Spirit—the weapon to defend you—and have victory against this dangerous enemy, apply yourself in the use of the best means and with utmost care to find out the true sense and meaning of the Spirit in his Word. This sword in another's hand will not defend you. No, it must be in your own, or else you cannot have the benefit of it. The phrase and outward expression are but the shell; the sense and meaning is the pearl ... We are to listen to what the Spirit says in the Word as we hear or read it. And he that has an ear for the Spirit will not have an ear for the seducer.

♦ Take heed that you come not to the Scriptures with an unholy heart.
♦ Make not your own reason the rule by which you measure Scripture truths.
♦ Take heed you come not with a judgement pre-engaged to any party and opinion.
♦ Go to God by prayer ... to unlock the mysteries of his Word.
♦ Compare Scripture with Scripture.
♦ Consult with your faithful guides which God hath set over you in his church.

— William Gurnall, *The Christian in Complete Armour*,
Vol. 2, pp. 251-252 (B.T.)

And the books

The cloak that I left at Troas with Carpus, when thou comest, bring with thee, and the books ... (2 Tim. 4:13).

B ooks are not absolutely dead things, but do contain a progeny of life in them, to be as active as that soul was whose progeny they are; no, they do preserve, as in a vial, the purest efficacy and extraction of that living intellect that bred them.

I know they are as lively, and as vigorously productive as those fabulous dragon's teeth; and being sown up and down, may chance to bring up armed men. And yet, on the other hand, unless caution be used, as good almost kill a man as kill a book. Who kills a man, kills a reasonable creature—God's image, but he who destroys a good book, destroys reason itself, kills the image of God, as it were, in the eye. Many a man lives a burden to the earth: but a good book is the precious life-blood of a master spirit, embalmed and treasured up on purpose to a life beyond life.

— John Milton, *A Homiletic Encyclopedia*, p. 656 (H.E.)

A few books well chosen, and well made use of, will be more profitable to you than a great confused *Alexandrian* library.

— Thomas Fuller

Balanced believers

... lest perhaps such a one should be swallowed up with overmuch sorrow (2 Cor. 2:7).

Because a hardened heart is so great a part of the malady and misery of the unregenerate, and a soft and tender heart is a part of the new nature promised by Christ, many awakened souls think they can never have sorrow enough, and that the danger lies in hard-heartedness, and they never fear excessive sorrow till it has swallowed them up ... This is a great mistake.

Sorrow is excessive when it is fed by a mistaken cause. *All* is too much where *none* is due; and great sorrow is too much when the cause requires but less ...

Superstition always breeds such sorrow, when men themselves perform religious duties which God never made, and then come short in the performance of them. Many darkened souls are assaulted by the erroneous, and told that they are going the wrong way, and they must believe some error as a necessary truth; and so they are thrown into perplexing difficulties, and sometimes repent of the truth which they previously owned. Many fearful Christians are troubled about every meal that they eat, about their clothes, their thoughts and words, thinking or fearing that all is sinful which is lawful, and that unavoidable infirmities are heinous sins. All such as these are troubles and sorrows without cause, and therefore excessive.

— Richard Baxter, *Puritan Sermons*, Vol. 3, pp. 254-255 (P.S.)

AUGUST

Relics of 'the old man'

Behold, I was shapen in iniquity; and in sin did my mother conceive me (Ps. 51:5).

L et us lay to heart original sin, and be deeply humbled for it. It cleaves to us like a disease, it is an active principle in us, stirring us up to evil. Original sin is worse than all actual sin; the fountain is more than the stream. Some think, as long as they are civil, they are well enough; yes, but the nature is poisoned. A river may have fair streams, but vermin at the bottom. You carry a hell around with you, you can do nothing without defiling it; your heart, like muddy ground, defiles the purest water that runs through it. Although you are regenerate, there is much of the old man in the new man.

O, how should original sin humble us! This is one reason why God has left original sin in us, so that it can be a thorn in our side to humble us. As the Bishop of Alexandria reminds us, that after the people had embraced Christianity, they destroyed all their idols but one, so that the sight of that one idol might make them loathe themselves for their former idolatry. In the same way God leaves original sin to pull down the plumes of pride. Under our silver wings of grace are black feet.

Let the sense of this make us daily look up to heaven for help. Beg Christ's blood to wash away the guilt of sin, and his Spirit to mortify the power of it. Beg further degrees of grace ... though grace cannot make sin not to be, yet it makes it not to reign; though grace cannot expel sin, it can repel it.

— Thomas Watson, *A Body of Divinity*, p. 103 (B.T.)

When God came to man to convert him, he found him a dead man.
— John Bunyan

The abuse of mercy

But the mercy of the Lord is from everlasting to everlasting upon them that fear him ... (Ps. 103:17).

Take heed of abusing this mercy of God. Suck not poison out of the sweet flower of God's mercy. Do not think that because God is merciful, you may go on in sin; this is to make mercy become your enemy. None might touch the ark but the priests, who by their office were more holy; none may touch this ark of God's mercy but such as are resolved to be holy.

To sin because mercy abounds is the devil's logic. He that sins because of mercy is like one that wounds his head because he has a plaster. He that sins because of God's mercy shall have judgement without mercy. Mercy abused turns to fury ...

Nothing is sweeter than mercy when it is improved; nothing fiercer when it is abused. Nothing is colder than lead when it is taken out of the mine; nothing more scalding than lead when it is heated. There is nothing blunter than iron; nothing sharper when it is whetted. 'The mercy of the Lord is ... upon them that fear him.' Mercy is not for them that sin and fear not, but for them that fear and sin not. God's mercy is a holy mercy; where it pardons, it heals.

— Thomas Watson, *A Homiletic Encyclopedia*, p. 2349 (H.E.)

Take notice not only of the mercies of God, but of God in the mercies.
— Ralph Venning

Assurance abused

He that loveth not knoweth not God ... (1 John 4:8).

If you have assurance of your justification, do not abuse assurance.

1. It is an abusing assurance when we grow more remiss in duty; as the musician, having money thrown him, leaves off playing. By remissness, or interrupting the exercises of religion, we grieve the Spirit, and that is the way to have an embargo laid upon our spiritual comforts.
2. We abuse assurance when we grow presumptuous and less fearful of sin. What, because a father gives his son an assurance of his love, and tells him he will bequeath his land to him, shall the son therefore be wanton and dissolute? This is the way to lose his father's affection, and make him cut off the inheritance.

It is bad to sin when one wants assurance, but it is worse to sin when one has it. Has the Lord sealed his love with a kiss? Has he left a pledge of heaven in your hands, and do you thus recompense the Lord? Will you sin with manna in your mouth? Does God give you the sweet clusters of assurance to feed on, and will you return him wild grapes? It much pleases Satan, either to see us want assurance, or abuse it; this is to abuse assurance, when the pulse of our souls beats faster in sin, and slower in duty.

— Thomas Watson, *A Homiletic Encyclopedia*, p. 351 (H.E.)

Assurance made David divinely fearless, and divinely careless.
— Thomas Brooks

228

The original of original sin

These six things doth the Lord hate; yea, seven are an abomination unto him: A proud look ... (Prov. 6:16-17).

P ride is a sin that is most hateful to God: He hates all sin, but more especially this sin. There are 'six things doth the Lord hate: yea, seven are an abomination unto him'; and the first and chiefest of those is pride. He hates a proud look, but he hates more a proud heart: 'Every one that is proud in heart is an abomination to the Lord'; not abominable only, but 'an abomination' in the abstract.

Twice it is said in the New Testament—once in the epistle of James (4:6), and the second time in the first epistle of Peter (5:5)—that 'God resisteth the proud ... ' He opposes them, because they oppose him and, if it were in their power, they would depose him too; they would be God to themselves. This is the devilish nature of pride, that whereas other sins are against God's law, this sin is against his sovereignty and his being. Other sins are a turning from God, this is turning on God. Hence it is that God is said to behold 'the proud ... afar off', as if he could not endure the sight of them (Ps. 138:6) ...

There are two ingredients in pride which greatly aggravate it, and make it sinful and abominable beyond measure:

The *antiquity* of it. It was the first enemy that God ever had. This was the sin of the fallen angels, and also of our first parents; this was the original of original sin ...

The *pregnancy* of it. It is a big-bellied sin; most of the sins that are in the world are the offspring and issue of pride.

— Richard Mayo, *Puritan Sermons*, Vol. 3, pp. 382-383 (P.S.)

The faithful God

... but God is faithful, who will not suffer you to be tempted above that ye are able; but will with the temptation also make a way to escape, that ye may be able to bear it (1 Cor. 10:13).

S aints that suffer have other kinds of temptations than other Christians have. The liberty of *others*, while they are in bonds, is a temptation to them. Also the enjoyments of others, while their houses are empty, and their goods taken away ...

Even more, a suffering man has not only these things lying before him as a temptation; but perhaps the wife of his bosom entices him, saying, 'O don't throw your life away; if you continue as you are, what will come of me? You've said that you love me; now prove it by granting me this small request I'm asking you. Don't stand on your integrity.' Next come the children, all pleading poverty, and being reduced to beggars, and all because you failed as a father to provide for them ... Following on their steps come family, relatives and friends. Some criticise, some cry, some argue, some threaten, some promise, some flatter, and some do all of them just to portray you as a fool for throwing your life away, and reducing your wife and children to beggary, and all in the name of religion. These are sore temptations ...

But *God* is faithful. It doesn't say that you are. But God is faithful to his Son, to whom he has given you; to his promise, which he has given you; to his cause to which he has called you; and to your soul, which you have committed to his trust, and which he also has taken charge of, because he is a faithful Creator ...

Not 'tempted above that *ye are able.*' He doesn't say above that you are *well* able. Indeed your strength shall be proportionate to the temptation; but you may have none over, and above, to spare; you shall not have a bigger load than God will give your shoulders to bear.

— John Bunyan, *Advice to Sufferers*, pp. 120-123 (A.B.P.)

A higher focus

... but when I became a man ... (1 Cor. 13:11).

I have perceived that nothing so much hinders the reception of the truth as urging it on men in too demanding a fashion, and condemning too severely their errors ... The older I grew the less emphasis I laid on controversies and curiosities (although my intellect still hates confusion) ... And now it is the fundamental doctrines of the catechism which I value most and daily think of, and these I find most helpful to myself and to others. The creed, the Lord's Prayer and the Ten Commandments provide me now with the most acceptable and plentiful material for all my meditations. They are to me as my daily bread and drink ... and I find in the daily practice and experience of my soul that the knowledge of God and Christ, and the Holy Spirit, and the truth of Scripture, and the life to come, and a holy life, is of more use to me than mere curious speculations ...

And one time I used to meditate on my own heart ... dissecting my own sins or needs, or examining my sincerity; but now, though I am still greatly convinced of the need of heart-acquaintance ... I see a greater need of a higher work, and that I should look oftener on Christ, and God, and heaven, (rather) than on my own heart.

I now see more good and more evil in men that I did before ... I admire less the gifts of utterance and a mere profession of religion than I once did ... I once thought that anyone who could pray eloquently and fluently, and talk well of religion, had to be saints. But experience has revealed to me that low crimes can co-exist with high professions ...

I would hardly look beyond England in my prayers, and did not even consider the world at large ... But now, no part of my prayers are so deeply serious as those for the conversion of the infidel and ungodly world ...

— Richard Baxter, *Reliquiae Baxterianae*, pp. 60-61 (R.&R.)

Walking on water

And he said, Come. And when Peter was come down out of the ship, he walked on the water ... (Matt. 14:29).

It was a bold spirit that could wish it, more bold that could act it. No sooner has our Saviour said, 'Come', than he sets his foot upon the unquiet sea, not fearing either the softness or the roughness of that uncouth passage ... Well did Peter know that he who bade him, could uphold him; and therefore he both pleads to be bidden, and ventures to be upheld. True faith concerns itself with difficulties, and is not dismayed with ordinary impossibilities. True faith concerns itself not with scattering straws, or getting rid of mole-hills, but with the removing of mountains ...

Peter pleads, Jesus bids. Rather will he work miracles, than disappoint the plea of a faithful man ...

True faith rests not in great and good desires, but in acts and executes accordingly. Peter does not wish to go ... but his foot answers his tongue and instantly plunges down into the waters ...

Lo! Peter is walking upon the waves! Two hands uphold him, the hand of Christ's power, and the hand of his own faith. Neither of them could do it alone. The hand of Christ's power laid hold on him; the hand of his own faith laid hold on the power of Christ commanding. Had not Christ's hand been powerful, that faith would have been vain ... While we are here in the world, we walk upon the waters; but the same hands bear us up. If he lets go his hold on us, we drown; if we let go our hold of him, we sink and shriek as Peter did, who, when he saw the wind boisterous was afraid ...

— Joseph Hall, *Contemplations*, pp. 491-492 (T.N.)

Shoes for the journey

And your feet shod with the preparation of the gospel of peace
(Eph. 6:15).

All of you that take the name of Christ, you are urged to put on these shoes of preparation, and to keep them on. In this way you will be ready at all times to follow the call of God's providence, though it should lead you into a suffering condition. Consider these two motives:

First: suffering work may overtake you suddenly, before you are aware of it. Therefore see that you are shod. Sometimes orders come to soldiers for a sudden march; they may not have as much as an hour's warning. They must be gone as soon as the drum beats.

So, as a Christian, you may be called before you are aware, into the field either to suffer for God or from God ... God can soon change the scene in which you live, the public affairs and the conditions. Maybe, at present the authorities smile on the Church of God; but within a while it may frown, and the storm of persecution arise. There was a time when the churches had 'rest throughout all Judea' (Acts 9:31). It was a blessed time. But how long did it last? Alas! not long. Soon 'Herod the king stretched forth his hands to vex certain of the church.' In this persecution James the brother of John lost his life by Herod's cruel sword ...

Second: if your feet are not shod with a preparation to suffer for Christ here on earth, your head cannot be crowned in heaven ... Now mark the following words: 'If so be that we suffer with him, that we may be also glorified together' (Rom. 8:17).

— William Gurnall, *The Christian in Complete Armour*,
Vol. 1, pp. 573-575 (B.T.)

This is the day ...

If thou turn away thy foot from the sabbath, from doing thy pleasure on my holy day; and call the sabbath a delight, the holy of the Lord, honourable; and shalt honour him, not doing thine own ways, nor finding thine own pleasure, nor speaking thine own words: Then shalt thou delight thyself in the Lord; and I will cause thee to ride upon the high places of the earth ... (Isa. 58:13-14).

I f we would sanctify the sabbath acceptably, we must call the Sabbath 'a delight' ... We must reckon the Sabbath *inter delicias*, as it is said of Jerusalem: she 'remembered ... all her pleasant things' (Lam. 1:7).

But we must also remember to take in, with the day, all the ordinances, religious services and duties of the day. They must not only be done spiritually, holy and universally, but they must be done with delight and satisfaction. We must prefer them to our chiefest joy; yes, the very approach of the Sabbath should be our delight. So have all the saints and servants of God in all ages of the church done; they have been to them the very joy and life of their souls. 'I was glad when they said unto me, Let us go into the house of the Lord ... ' (Ps. 122:1).

I was never more affected with joy and gladness in all my life, than when I used to hear the people encouraging one another to assemble themselves for the public worship of God, in the house of God, on God's day. O! it did my heart good to hear with what alacrity and rejoicing they did provoke one another: 'Come, let us go to the house of the Lord.' ...

From the creation of the world to this day, God never suffered his church to be without a Sabbath. As soon as ever there was a church, though it was but in its infancy, and confined within the narrow limits of a single family, and few souls therein, God did immediately institute a Sabbath for it ...

— Thomas Case, *Puritan Sermons*, Vol. 2, pp. 30-32 (P.S.)

Miracles

And God wrought special miracles ... (Acts 19:11).

W e call those 'miracles' which happen outside the track of nature, and contrary to the usual stream and current of it, which men wonder at because they seldom see them and hear of them. They are things rarely brought forth in the world. But the truth is, there is more power expressed in the ordinary station and motion of natural causes, than in those extraordinary exertions of power.

Is there not more power signalized in that whirling motion of the sun every hour for so many ages, than in the suspending of its motion one day, as in the days of Joshua? That fire should continually ravage and consume, and greedily swallow up everything that is offered to it, seems to be the effect of as admirable a power as the stopping of its appetite a few moments as in the case of the Three Children ...

Is not the chemical producing so pleasant and delicious a fruit as the grape from a dry earth, insipid rain, and sour vine, as admirable a token of divine power as our Saviour's turning of water into wine? Is not the cure of diseases by the application of a simple trivial weed ... as wonderful as the cure of it by a powerful word? ...

Miracles indeed affect more, because they testify to the immediate operation of God without the concurrence of second causes; not that there is more of the power of God shining in them than in the other.

— Stephen Charnock, *A Homiletic Encyclopedia*, p. 3560 (H.E.)

Are we credible?

In meekness instructing those that oppose themselves ... (2 Tim. 2:25).

They who design and endeavour to win others ... must religiously avoid that which is the greatest obstruction of all, the profligate and atrocious lives of some that call themselves Christians. If men were prompted and employed by the devil himself, they could not be more effective in making the Gospel to be abhorred, than by living as some Christians do. How can it be expected, that the poor, ignorant heathen should have any reverence for the great and sacred name of God, when they hear those who pretend that they have a deep veneration for him, reproach and blaspheme him? ...

Will they believe those that tell him, 'the Son of God was manifested, that he might destroy the works of the devil' (1 John 3:8), and that they act under him as the Captain of their salvation, while they employ all their time, parts, and power to establish and defend Satan's kingdom?

Can you persuade men that you believe there is a hell and eternal flames prepared for the ungodly and the impenitent ... when they observe those that say they believe this, to run posting, sporting, and laughing into it? They will never apprehend, that the heaven which the Gospel promises to the faithful and holy, is any other than a poetical Elysium ... Can any man convince them, that the saints are such excellent creatures, when they see those who call themselves so, live like brutes or devils?

— George Hammond, *Puritan Sermons*, Vol. 4, pp. 431-432 (P.S.)

Communion with God

If any man will come after me, let him deny himself ... (Matt. 16:24).

Communion with God is attained, and then maintained, if we practise self-denial. He that abides in himself, and lives in and to himself, lives at a distance from God. God and self are as two opposite terms: we must forsake the one, if we would approach the other. When man first fell from God, he fell in with himself; and therefore must forsake himself, if he would return to God and have communion with him. There is a twofold self-denial:

One is *internal*. When we can deny ourselves confidence in ourselves, all self-ends, self-applause, self-sufficiency, and even annihilate ourselves: this is highly needful for our communion with God. Self is that Dagon that must fall before God's ark; that idol that must be cast out of the temple of man's soul, that God may enter in, and dwell there.

Then there is a self-denial that is *external*. God sometimes calls his people to this, in order to have communion with himself. This may mean forsaking father, mother, house, land, liberty, etc.; and all this in order to receive the 'hundredfold' in this life, as our Saviour promised (Matt. 19:29); which they shall receive in this communion with God ...

Communion with God is the life of religion. It is but a dead thing without it ... What the body is without the soul, and matter without form, that is religion, where men find no influence from heaven upon their hearts, and have no communion with God.

— Matthew Barker, *Puritan Sermons*, Vol. 4, pp. 48, 51 (P.S.)

Curiosity

And though I have the gift of prophecy, and understand all mysteries, and all knowledge ... (1 Cor. 13:2).

H e that would comprehend all things, apprehends nothing. As he that comes to a corn heap, the more he opens his hand to take, the less he grasps, the less he holds. Where the Scripture has no tongue, we should have no ear ...

Why do we study that which is impossible to learn? Whatever kind of fruit it was that our first parents sold their birthright for in Paradise, I am sure there was no juice enough in it to quench that hot thirst of forbidden knowledge which they imparted to their posterity. But that which only distempered Adam's taste is now become inherent in all mankind; that the more they know, the more they desire; and admitting them to one secret, only encourages them to seek for another. We all take after Eve, and setting our shoulders to the very portals of God's privy chamber, in we must go, and be made acquainted with the divine counsel ...

Men may soon be too bold with hidden mysteries. He that modestly looks upon the sun, sees a glorious torch, and receives a comfortable light; but he that fixes his eyes too earnestly upon it, is struck blind; and because he will see more than he should, comes in the end to see nothing at all.

— Thomas Adams, *A Homiletic Encyclopedia*, pp. 1509-1512 (H.E.)

Remember that the greatest misery to an honest heart is this, a misdrawing of rules out of the Word of God.

— Walter Cradock

A thorn in the flesh?

And lest I should be exalted above measure through the abundance of the revelations, there was given to me a thorn in the flesh, the messenger of Satan to buffet me, lest I should be exalted above measure (2 Cor. 12:7).

The one great design of God in all his dispensations to his people, is to prevent and cure the pride of their hearts. This, you see, was the thing that God designed by letting Satan loose to afflict the apostle; by so doing he gave him a thorn in his flesh. This was his design in giving the children of Israel such a dance in the wilderness. They might well have gone from Egypt to Canaan in less than forty weeks; yet he made them to wander for the space of forty years: and why was it? The Spirit of God tells us, that it was 'to humble' them (Deut. 8:2).

I might show you how God designed this in his *creating* of man. At first he made him of the dust of the earth; and this might well keep him humble, just a sense of his origin. God designed this in his way of *redeeming* man by his Son Jesus Christ. By so doing, we are given to understand, that we could no more have redeemed ourselves, than we could have created ourselves. We are as much subject to a Redeemer for salvation and eternal life, as to a Creator for our natural life.

Yes, God designs this in his way and method of *saving* man; which is by his grace, and 'not by the works of righteousness which we have done' (Titus 3:5). We must condemn ourselves, before he will justify us; and renounce our own righteousness, if ever we will be made righteous. And why is this, so that pride should not be exalted, and that no flesh might ever glory, or exalt itself, in his sight? (Rom. 3:20; 1 Cor. 1:29).

— Richard Mayo, *Puritan Sermons*, Vol. 3, pp. 380-381 (P.S.)

Never stop growing

But speaking the truth in love, may grow up into him in all things, which is the head, even Christ (Eph. 4:15).

The growth of grace will hinder the growth of corruption. The more health grows, the more the distempers of the body abate. So it is in spirituals; the more humility grows, the more the swelling of pride is decreased. The more purity of heart grows, the more the fire of lust is abated. The growth of flowers in the garden does not hinder the growing of weeds; but the growing of this flower of grace hinders the sprouting of corruption ...

The more we grow in grace, the more will God love us. Is it not that we pray for? The more growth, the more will God love us. The gardener loves his thriving plants; the thriving Christian is God's Hephzibah, or chief delight ... Christ accepts the truth of grace, but commends the growth of grace. 'I have not found so great faith, no, not in Israel.' Would you be as the beloved disciple that lay in Christ's bosom? Would you have much love from Christ? Labour for much growth, let faith flourish with good works, and let love increase into zeal ...

The more we grow in grace, the more we shall flourish in glory. Though every vessel of glory shall be full, yet some vessels hold more.

— Thomas Watson, *A Homiletic Encyclopedia*, pp. 2560-2562 (H.E.)

All grace grows as love to the Word of God grows.

— Philip Henry

Don't invite suffering

But when they persecute you in this city, flee ye into another ...
(Matt. 10:23).

I f they persecute you in one city, flee ye to another. 'If they will not let me preach here, I will take up my Bible and be gone. Perhaps this is because I must preach in another place.' A minister can quickly pack up, and carry his religion with him, and offer what he knows of God, to another people (Acts 13:44-47).

Nor should a minister strive, I think, with the magistrate for place, or time. But let him listen to hear what God shall say by such opposition. Perhaps the magistrate must drive you out of this place, because the soul that is to be converted is in another place ...

Every Christian is bound by God's Word to hold to, or stand by his profession, his profession of faith, and to join to that profession, a holy, godly life ... And more particularly, by all this, that we should hide our faith from no man, but should rather reveal it by a life that will do so. For our profession ... is the badge, and the Lord's livery, by which we are distinguished from other men ... This is what Peter intends when he says ... 'And be ready always to give an answer to every man that asketh you a reason of the hope that is in you with meekness and fear' (1 Pet. 3:15). Here then is a call ... to walk in our Christian profession, and to adorn it with all good works; and if any or many will meddle with me, and ask me a reason of the hope that I have, to give it him with meekness and fear, whatever follows from it. This is the very thing Peter should have done himself, when he denied his Master thrice.

— John Bunyan, *Advice to Sufferers*, pp. 65-67 (A.B.P.)

Fondling a snake

But thou, O man of God, flee these things ... (1 Tim. 6:11).

I once walked into a garden with a lady to gather some flowers. There was one large bush whose branches were bending under the weight of the most beautiful roses. We both gazed upon it with admiration. There was one flower on it which seemed to outshine all the rest in beauty. This lady pressed forward into the thick bush, and reached far over to pluck it. As she did this, a black snake, which was hid in the bush, wrapped itself round her arm. She was alarmed beyond all description; she ran from the garden, screaming and almost in convulsions. During all that day she suffered very much with fear; her whole body trembled, and it was a long time before she could be calmed. That lady is still alive. Such is her hatred now of the whole serpent race that she has never since been able to look at a snake, even a dead one. No one could ever persuade her to venture again into a cluster of bushes, even to pluck a beautiful rose.

Now this is the way the sinner acts who truly repents of his sins. He thinks of sin as the serpent that once coiled itself around him. He hates it. He dreads it. He flees from it. He fears the place where it inhabits. He does not willingly go into the haunts. He will no more play with sin than this lady would afterwards have fondled snakes.

— Joseph Meade, *A Homiletic Encyclopedia*, p. 4602 (H.E.)

A sin of infirmity may admit apology; a sin of ignorance may find an excuse; but a sin of defiance can find no defence.

— Sir Richard Baker

When other Christians fall

Watch and pray, that ye enter not into temptation: the spirit indeed is willing, but the flesh is weak (Matt. 26:41).

There are two things that are very apt to be an occasion of offence to the weak:

♦ When the cross attends religion.
♦ When others that profess religion suffer for evil doing.

To the first, I would say this: though the cross, indeed is grievous to the flesh, yet we should with grace bear up under it, and not be offended at it. To the second, though we should and ought to be offended with such misdeeds; yet not with religion, because of such misdeeds.

Some, indeed, when they see these things, take offence against religion itself. Yes, perhaps are glad of the occasion, and so fall out with Jesus Christ, saying to him, because of the evils that attended his ways, as the ten tribes said to Rehoboam, the son of Solomon the king: 'What portion have we in David? Neither have we inheritance in the son of Jesse: to your tents, O Israel: now see to thine own house, David' (1 Kings 12:16). So they leave the Lord, and cleave no more to him, to his people, or to his ways. But this is bad.

Shun therefore the evil ways of Christians, but cleave to the way that is Christian. Cast away that bad spirit you see in any; but hold fast to your Head and Lord. Where can you go? The Lord Jesus has the words of eternal life (John 6). Where will you go? There is no salvation in any other (Acts 4:12). Take heed therefore of picking a quarrel with Jesus Christ, and with his ways, because of the evil doings of some of his followers. Judas sold him; Peter denied him; and many of his disciples went back and walked no more with him; but neither himself nor his ways were the worse for that.

— John Bunyan, *Advice to Sufferers*, pp. 47-49 (A.B.P.)

Numero uno

The law of thy mouth is better unto me than thousands of gold and silver (Ps. 119:72).

C an he be proficient in any art, who slights and deprecates it? Prize this book of God above all other books ...
'Take away the word, and you deprive us of the sun,' said Luther ... King Edward VI on the day of his coronation, had presented before him three swords, signifying that he was the monarch of three kingdoms. The king said that there was one sword missing. Being asked what that was, he answered, 'The Holy Bible, which is the sword of the Spirit, and is to be preferred before these ensigns of royalty.' Robert, king of Sicily, did so love God's Word, that, speaking to his friend Petrarcha, he said, 'I protest, the Scriptures are dearer to me than my kingdom; and if I must be deprived of one of them I had rather lose my diadem than the Scriptures.'

Prizing relates to judgement, *love* to the affections. 'Consider how I love thy precepts' (Ps. 119:159) ... Augustine tells us that before his conversion he took no pleasure in the Scriptures, but afterwards they were his 'chaste delights'. David tasted the word 'sweeter ... than honey and the honeycomb' (Ps. 19:10). Thomas À Kempis used to say he found no contentment but to be 'in a corner, with the book of God in his hand.'

What infinite pleasure should we take in reading the Book of Life! There is enough in the Word to breed holy felicity and delight; it is a specimen and demonstration of God's love to us. The Bible is God's love-token, his love-letter.

— Thomas Watson, *Puritan Sermons*, Vol. 2, pp. 63-64 (P.S.)

Eternal

... for the things which are seen are temporal; but the things which are not seen are eternal (2 Cor. 4:18).

Eternal! What a sound does this word 'eternal' make in my ears! What strings does it cause within my heart! What casting about of thought! What word is next to be added to it? ...

My trembling heart is still solicitous as to what other word this word 'eternal' might be prefixed. This regarding myself, or those that hear me this day, when they and I, who, through the long-sufferance of God are yet in this present and temporal world, but shall be in that eternal world? Shall it be *eternal damnation* in that eternal world? How? After so many pleadings of Christ, strivings of the Spirit, tenders of mercy, wooings of grace, calls of ministers, warnings of conscience, admonitions of friends, waitings of patience? All of which offered us a fair probability of escaping eternal damnation. O dreadful words! Can more terror be contained, can more misery be comprehended, in any two words, than in 'eternal damnation'?

But we in time are praying, hearing, repenting, believing, conflicting with devils, mortifying sin, weaning our hearts from this world, that, when we shall go out of time, we might find 'life' or 'salvation' added to 'eternal'. *Eternal salvation!* These are words as comfortable as the others were terrible, as sweet as they were bitter.

What, then? This word 'eternal' is the horror of devils, the amazement of damned souls, which causes desperation in all that hellish crew; ... for they most certainly know that they are damned to all eternity. Eternal! It is the joy of angels, the delight of saints, that while they are made happy in the beatific vision, they are filled with perfect love and joy, they sit and sing, 'All this will be eternal.'

— Thomas Doolittle, *Puritan Sermons*, Vol. 4, pp. 1-2 (P.S.)

Ordinances

... and keep the ordinances, as I delivered them to you (1 Cor. 11:2).

I t is not enough to make use of ordinances, but we must see if we can find God in them. There are many that hover about the palace, and yet do not speak with the prince: so possibly we may hover about ordinances, and not meet with God there. To go away with the husk and shell of an ordinance, and neglect the kernel, to please ourselves because we have been in the courts of God, though we have not met with the living God, is very sad.

A traveller and merchant differ thus: a traveller goes from place to place only that he may see; but a merchant goes from port to port, that he may take in his freight, and grow rich by trade. So a formal person goes from ordinance to ordinance, and is satisfied with the works; a godly man looks to take in his freight, that he may go away from God with God; that he may meet God here, and there, in this duty and in that, and go away from God with God.

A man that makes a visit only by constraint, and not by friendship, it is all the same to him whether the person be at home or not; but another is glad to find his friend there. It is the same with us, if from a principle of love we come to the ordinances with the desire of finding the living God.

— Thomas Manton, *A Homiletic Encyclopedia*, p. 3427 (H.E.)

A man may go to hell with baptismal water upon his face.

— John Trapp

Means of grace

... ordinances of divine service ... (Heb. 9:1).

Please do not misunderstand me: religious exercises are necessary and should be practised, but still a man must not stay there. Prayer says, 'There is no salvation in men.' The sacraments and fasting say, 'There is no salvation in us.' All these are subservient helps, not absolute causes of salvation. A man will use his bucket, but he expects water *from the well.* The means are the buckets, but all our comfort, and all our life and grace, is only in Christ.

Use your religious exercises, as Noah's dove did her wings, to carry you to the ark of the Lord Jesus Christ, for only there is rest. If she had never used her wings, she would have fallen into the water; and if she had not returned to the ark, she would have found no rest. So, if you will not use these religious duties, but neglect them, you are sure to perish. And if they don't convey you to Christ, you may well 'lie down in sorrow.' Or as the case of a poor man, who has to cross great water for a treasure on the other side, though he cannot fetch the boat, he calls for it, and uses it to carry him over to the treasure.

Christ is in heaven, and you on earth. He does not come to you, and you can't get to him. Now call for a boat; though there is no grace, no good, no salvation in a dull duty, yet use it to carry you over to the treasure, the Lord Jesus Christ. When you come to church to listen, say, 'Come to me, Lord, by this sermon.' When you come to pray, say, 'Come to me, Lord, by this prayer.'

— Isaac Ambrose, *A Homiletic Encyclopedia*, pp. 3432, 3449 (H.E.)

The art of musing

I will meditate in thy precepts ... (Ps. 119:15).

Labour to remember what you read. Satan would steal the word out of your mind (Matt. 13:4, 19); not that he intends to make use of it himself, but lest we should make use of it. The memory should be like the chest in the ark, where the law was put ... Such as have a disease they call *lienteria*, the meat comes up as fast as they eat it, and stays not in the stomach, and they are not nourished by it. If the word stays not in the memory, it cannot profit. Some can better remember an item of news than a line of Scripture; their memories are like these ponds, where the frogs live, but the fish die ...

Meditate upon what you read ... In meditation there must be a fixing of the thoughts upon the object: the Virgin Mary 'pondered' those things, etc. Meditation is the concoction of Scripture: reading brings a truth into our head, meditation brings it into our heart: reading and meditation must, like Castor and Pollux, appear together. Meditation without reading is erroneous; reading without meditation is barren. The bee sucks the flower, then works it in the hive, and so turns it to honey: by reading we suck the flower of the word, by meditation we work it in the hive of our mind, and so it turns to profit. Meditation is the bellows of the affections: 'While I was musing the fire burned' (Ps. 39:3). The reason we come away so cold from reading the word is because we do not warm ourselves at the fire of meditation.

— Thomas Watson, *Puritan Sermons*, Vol. 2, pp. 61-62 (P.S.)

The only cause why you forget so fast as you hear ... is because you went from sermon to dinner, and never thought any more of the matter ...

— Henry Smith

Jubilee in the soul

Make me to hear ... (Ps. 51:8).

L et us strive to secure the evidence that our sins are forgiven. A man may have his sins forgiven and not know it; he may have a pardon in the court of heaven when he does not have it in the court of conscience. David's sin was forgiven as soon as he repented. God sent Nathan a prophet to tell him so (Ps. 51:3). But David did not feel the comfort of it immediately, as is apparent by the penitential psalm he composed afterwards. 'Make me to hear joy.' ... It is one thing to be pardoned and another to feel it.

Why does God sometimes conceal the evidence of pardon? Though he pardons, he may withhold the sense of it for a time:

1. Because he would lay us lower in contrition. He would have us see what an evil and bitter thing it is to offend him. Therefore we must lie longer in the salty tears of repentance before we have the sense of pardon ...
2. Though God has forgiven sin, he may deny the manifestation of it for a time, in order to make us prize pardon and make it sweeter to us when it comes. The difficulty of obtaining a mercy enhances its value ... The longer mercy is in the birth the more welcome will the deliverance be.

Let us not be content, however, without the evidence and sense of pardon. He who is pardoned and knows it not, is like one who has an estate bequeathed to him, but knows it not. Our comfort consists in the knowledge of forgiveness ... There is a jubilee in the soul when we are able to read our pardon. To the witness of conscience God adds the witness of his spirit; and in the mouth of these two witnesses our joy is confirmed.

— Thomas Watson, *The Lord's Prayer*, pp. 171-172 (B.T.)

The royal stamp

... and holiness, without which no man shall see the Lord (Heb. 12:14).

Y ou may as well see without light, and be supported without earth, or live without food, as to be saved without holiness, or be happy without the one thing necessary (Heb. 12:14). And when this has been determined by God, and established as his standing law, and he has told it so often and plainly, for any man then to say, 'I will yet hope for better, I hope to be saved on easier terms, without all this ado', is no better for that man than to set his face against the God of heaven. Instead of believing God, he believes the contradiction of his own ungodly heart; and hopes to be saved whether God wills it or not. He gives the lie to his Creator, under the pretence of trust and hope. This is indeed to hope for impossibilities. To be saved without holiness is to see without eyes, and to live without life ...

Who is so foolish as to hope for this? Few of you are so unreasonable as to hope for a crop at harvest, without ploughing or sowing: or for a house without building; or for strength without eating and drinking ... And yet this would be a far wiser kind of hope, than to hope to be saved without one thing necessary for salvation.

— Richard Baxter, *A Homiletic Encyclopedia*, p. 2820 (H.E.)

God loves purity so well he would rather see a hole than a spot in his child's garments.

— William Gurnall

The river of pleasures

... glorious in holiness ... (Exod. 15:11).

Y ou have an art above God himself, if you can locate any true pleasure in unholiness. It is the lowest of blasphemies for you to claim that the way of holiness is an enemy to true pleasure. By doing so you are claiming that God himself lacks true pleasure, if such be the case that holiness does not supply it. 'Thou shalt make them drink of the river of thy pleasures.' God has his pleasures, and God gives his saints drink of his pleasures ...

Pray not only against the power of sin, but for the power of holiness also. A wicked heart may pray against his sins, not out of any inward enmity to them, or love to holiness, but because they are troublesome guests to his conscience. His zeal is false that seems hot against sin, but is cold to holiness.

A city is rebellious that keeps their rightful prince out, though it receives not his enemy in. Nay, the devil needs not fear, for at last he shall make that soul his garrison again, out of which for a while he seems shut out, but so long as it stands empty, and is not filled with solid grace he will come back in. What indeed should hinder Satan's re-entry into that house which has none in it to keep him out.

— William Gurnall, *A Homiletic Encyclopedia*, pp. 2826-2833 (H.E.)

Here is the Christian's way and his end ... his way is holiness, his end is happiness.

— John Whitlock

Discord of the saints

And when there had been much disputing ... (Acts 15:7).

The servants of God consider the matter of religion more seriously than others do; and therefore their differences are more observable to the world. They cannot make light of the smallest truth of God ... whereas the ungodly differ not about religion, because they have hardly no religion to differ about. Is this a unity and peace to be desired? I would rather have the discord of the saints, than such a concord of the wicked.

They (the saints) are so careful about their duty that they are afraid of misusing it in the least particular; and this (with their imperfect light) is the reason of their disputings about these matters. But you that are careless concerning your duty, can easily agree about the ways of sin, or anything that comes along. The saints honour the worship of God so much, that they would not have anything out of order; but you consider it so unimportant that you will be of the same religion as the king, let it be what it will be ...

The controversies of lawyers, historians, chronologers, geographers, physicians, and such like, never trouble the brains of the ignorant; but for all that, I would rather be in controversy with the learned, than without such controversy with you. If you scatter a handful of gold or diamonds in the street, perhaps men will scramble for them, and quarrel about them, while swine will trample on them and quietly despise them, because they do not know their worth. Will you therefore think that swine are happier than men? The living are vexed with strifes and controversies, about almost every matter in the world, while dead carcasses in the grave lie still in peace, and are not troubled with any of these differences. Will you say therefore that the dead corpse is happier than the living?

— Richard Baxter, *A Homiletic Encyclopedia*, p. 1374 (H.E.)

The crown

Henceforth there is laid up for me a crown of righteousness ...
(2 Tim. 4:8).

Seeing we are freely justified, and brought to glory by free grace, through the redemption that is in Jesus Christ ... may not the doctrine of reward for good works be not only needless, but an impairing and a lessening of the completeness of that glory?

That we are justified in the sight of the Divine Majesty, from the whole lump of our sins, both past and present, and to come, by free grace, through that one offering of the body of Jesus Christ, once for all, I bless God. I believe it. That we shall be brought to glory by the same grace, I believe that also .. Yet, not withstanding all this, there is a reward for the righteous, a reward for their works of faith and love, whether in a doing or a suffering way, and that principally to be enjoyed not here, but hereafter. 'Great is your reward in heaven ... '

Paul was as great a maintainer of the doctrine of God's free grace, and of justification from sin ... as any that ever lived in Christ's service, from the world's beginning till now ... Paul expected himself, and encouraged others also to expect such a reward, for working and suffering for Christ, which he calls 'a far more exceeding and eternal weight of glory' (2 Cor. 4:17) ...

Now, could I tell what those rewards are that Christ has prepared and will one day bestow upon us ... I should say more than I dare say or ought to say. Yet, let me say this, they are such rewards that would make us leap to think about, and that we would remember them with exceeding joy. Never think that it is contrary to the Christian faith, to rejoice and be glad for that which we understand not.

— John Bunyan, *Paul's Departure and Crown*, pp. 46-47 (R.P.)

They can taste our humility

Him that is weak in the faith receive ye, but not to doubtful disputations
(Rom. 14:1).

Christian charity and reception will sooner win weak ones to the truth than rigid arguments ... Opposition breeds opposition. A man will never believe that a person loves his soul who cheats on his salary, reviles his actions, torments his body. Passion begets passion, but only love kindles love ...

Now passions do nothing well. One emperor used to say over and over to himself the alphabet, in order to get dominion over his anger. Ahasuerus fanned himself in the garden (Est. 7:7); and a character in Plutarch would not smite his servant, because he was angry. Passionated persecution makes only hypocrites become proselytes; and in their hearts lodges such a revenge as will be satisfied, one time or another, on those who made them act contrary to their consciences. Religion is a matter of free choice, or it is not religion; therefore it gets in by persuasion, not persecution ...

Sincere love and converse breed a good opinion of persons who differ from us. They can taste humility, meekness and kindness, better than the more speculative principles of religion. These get into men's affections, and drill into their judgements, causing them to change their minds. Two heads, like two globes, touch but in one point, the whole bodies being at a distance; but two hearts touch *in plano*, and fall in with each other in all points. Love opens the heart and ear to cooler considerations and second thoughts. The Spirit of God directed Elijah, not in the strong wind which rents rocks and mountains, nor in the earthquake, or fire, but in the silent whisper or tranquil voice.

— Thomas Woodcock, *Puritan Sermons*, Vol. 4, pp. 377-378 (P.S.)

Empty names

... leaving us an example, that ye should follow his steps (1 Pet. 2:21).

C hrist frequently speaks to you to follow him, and observes whether and how you do it. His Word is plain, that you should learn his doctrine, and live after his example ... To this effect Christ speaks to you:

'Look unto me, and be ye saved, all ye ends of the earth.' Look unto me, and become like me, all you that profess yourselves to be my members. What you see in me, should not for any reason turn away your faces or your hearts from me. 'Blessed is he whosoever shall not be offended in me.' The Father is well-pleased in me, and so should you, if you value his favour, and consider your own interest. I never took so much as one step in the ways of misery and destruction; be sure to avoid them. I always trod in those paths which to you will prove pleasantness and peace; though, to satisfy for your deviations and going astray, I was willing myself to be 'a man of sorrows, and acquainted with grief' (Isa. 53:3). Consider your Lord and Master, you that call yourselves my disciples. Many look upon you that will not look unto my word, and will judge me by your practices. Do not damage me, by misrepresenting me; as if I allowed those evils which you allow yourselves. Why should I be 'wounded in the house of my friends' (Zech. 13:6). Why should you crucify me afresh, and put me to an open shame? ...

All you upon whom my name is called, don't be content yourselves with an empty name! Be my disciples indeed. Live as I did in the world: to honour God, and to do good to man. Let that be your business; for I have left you an example, that you should follow my steps.

— Nathanael Vincent, *Puritan Sermons*, Vol. 4, p. 448 (P.S.)

Now is the time

Remember now thy Creator in the days of thy youth ... (Eccl. 12:1).

Omnipotence can suffer no difficulty, and that which is immense can admit no limits. Unto the divine power all things are as perfectly easy, as they are certainly possible: and the heavenly grace is fruitful equally of all things consistent with its spotless purity. God-Creator strained no harder to make this great world, than to make the smallest atom of it. And the God-Redeemer saves Mary Magdalenes, as well as Virgin Marys ...

But, in respect of things themselves, and of their appearances unto us, all effects are not of equal facility, nor all events to be alike hoped for. Much easier is the bending of a green twig, than of an old oak; more hopeful the cure of a green wound, than of an old putrefied sore. There is more to be done to convert a man of Belial, than a child of Belial; and to convert an old man, than any other man And we may justly expect better success when we call unto God the boys and girls playing in the streets, than when we call old men and women that can scarcely walk in them ...

This I am desired to show ... the promoting of early piety ... The time wherein all of you are commanded to convert, is the present. 'Remember' has its 'now' expressly added; forbidding both your delay until the afternoon of your life-day, and your delay unto any other day, hour, or minute of your forenoon. It requires that God's tribute be paid, as the king's tax is, upon sight; and that not the least distance of time be admitted between your discerning, and your doing.

— Daniel Burgess, *Puritan Sermons*, Vol. 4, pp. 550-553 (P.S.)

SEPTEMBER

Little by little

Train up a child in the way he should go: and when he is old, he will not depart from it (Prov. 22:6).

In all your instructions, be careful to avoid all tedious verbosity. Nothing more disgusts a child's spirit than long and tedious discourses. Make up for the shortness of your discourse with frequency; a little now, and a little then, not all at once; drop by drop, as you pour liquor into a narrow-mouthed bottle. Just as you do when you first begin to feed their bodies with a spoon, so must you do when you first begin to feed their souls with instruction. Long speeches burden their small memories too much; and men's imprudence may unhappily make them to loathe spiritual manna. As physicians, therefore, in their dietetic prescriptions to children, say, 'little and often'; so must we. Young plants may quickly be over-glutted with rich manuring, and rotted with too much watering. Weak eyes, newly opened from sleep, at first can hardly bear the glare of a candle. 'Line upon line', therefore, and 'precept upon precept; ... here a little, and there a little' (Isa. 28:10). You must drive the little ones towards heaven, as Jacob did his toward Canaan, very gently (Gen. 33:13). Fair and soft goes far ...

To holy, hearty, serious, affectionate, frequent admonition, add an exemplary behaviour. Inferiors are apt to be led by example rather than rule, and more prone to imitate practices than to learn principles. They are more mindful of what we do, than of what we say; and they will be very prone to suspect that we are not in good earnest, when they see that we command them one thing, and do another ourselves. When we teach them well, and do wrong ourselves, we only pull down with one hand what we build with the other.

— Thomas Lye, *Puritan Sermons*, Vol. 2, pp. 120, 125 (P.S.)

Weeds need no cultivation

And ye shall teach them your children ... (Deut. 11:19).

The church began at first in a family, and was preserved by the godly care of parents in instructing their children and household in the truths of God, whereby the knowledge of God was transmitted from generation to generation. Though now the church is not confined to such straight limits, yet every private family is as a little nursery to the church. If the nursery be not carefully planted, the orchard will soon decay.

Oh, would you be willing, Christians, that your children when you are laid in the dust, should be turned into the degenerate plants of a strange vine, and be a generation that do not know God? Atheism needs not to be planted, you do enough to make your children such, just by not planting religion in their minds. The very neglect of the gardener to sow and dress his garden, gives advantage enough to the weeds to come up. This is the difference between religion and atheism, religion does not grow without planting, but will die even where it is planted without watering. Atheism, irreligion, and profaneness are weeds that will grow without setting, but they will not die without plucking up ...

Therefore, you that are parents, and do not teach your children, deal the more unrighteously with God, because you neglect the best season in their whole life for planting in them the knowledge of God, and plucking up the contrary weeds of atheism and irreligion. Young weeds come up with most ease, sinful ignorance in youth becomes wilful ignorance, yes, impudence in age. If you will not instruct them when young, they will scorn their ministers when old.

— William Gurnall, *A Homiletic Encyclopedia*, p. 804 (H.E.)

That little spark ...

... and their conscience being weak is defiled (1 Cor. 8:7).

C onscience, as an expression of the law or will and mind of God, is not now to be implicitly depended on. It is not infallible. What was true of its office in Eden, has been deranged and shattered by the fall. It now lies, as I have seen a sundial in the neglected garden of an old desolate ruin, thrown from its pedestal, prostrate on the ground, and covered by tall rank weeds ... Conscience has often lent its sanction to the grossest errors, and prompted the greatest crimes. Did not Saul of Tarsus, for instance, drag men and women to prison; compel them to blaspheme; and stain his hands in saintly blood, while conscience approved the deed— he believed that he was doing God service ...

Read the *Book of Martyrs*, read the sufferings of our own forefathers; and under the cowl of a shaven monk, or the trappings of a haughty churchman, you shall see conscience persecuting the saints of God, and dragging even tender women and children to the bloody scaffold or the burning stake. With eyes swimming in tears, or flashing fire, we close the painful record, to apply to conscience the words addressed to Liberty by the French heroine. When passing its statue, she rose in the cart that bore her to the guillotine, and throwing up her arms, exclaimed, 'O Liberty, what crimes have been done in thy name!' And what crimes in thine, O conscience!

So far as doctrines and duties are concerned, not conscience, but the revealed Word of God, is our one only sure and safe directory.

— William Guthrie, *A Homiletic Encyclopedia*, p. 1303 (H.E.)

When conscience can be a hindrance

... their conscience also bearing witness ... (Rom. 2:15).

The discovery of forgiveness in God is great, holy, and mysterious ... The difficulty of making this discovery is partly due to the hindrances that lie in the way of it ... One of these hindrances is the constant voice of *conscience* which is against the discovery of forgiveness ...

Conscience naturally knows nothing of forgiveness; yes, it is against its very work and office, to hear anything of it. If a man of courage and honesty is entrusted to keep a garrison against an enemy, let one come and tell him that peace is made between those whom he serves and their enemies, so that he may leave his guard, and open the gates, and cease to watch; how wary will he be, lest under this pretence, he is betrayed! No, says he, I will keep my post until I have express orders from my superiors.

Conscience is entrusted with the power of God in the soul of a sinner, with command to keep all in subjection, with reference to the judgement to come. Conscience will not betray its trust, in believing every report of peace. No! It says, and speaks in the name of God: Guilt and punishment are inseparable. If the soul sin, God will judge. What tell you me of forgiveness? I know what my commission is, and that I will abide by ...

Conscience has two works in reference to sin; one to condemn the acts of sin, another to judge the person of the sinner ... When forgiveness comes, it severs these offices, and takes one of them out of the hand of conscience. It will condemn the sin; but it does not condemn the sinner. The sinner shall be freed from its sentence ... But this cannot be done but by the blood of Christ ...

— John Owen, *The Forgiveness of Sins,* pp. 76-79 (B.B.)

A sin not always recognised

... he that believeth not God hath made him a liar ... (1 John 5:10).

Concerning the greatness of the sin of unbelief, there are two things greatly to be regarded:

1. As great as this sin is, and as surely damning as it is, yet it never disturbs the conscience of a natural ungodly man. He may be disturbed in his mind for sin, he may be disturbed in his conscience for his own lying, but he is never disturbed in his conscience for calling God a liar. He may be disturbed in his conscience for disobeying God's law, but he never thinks it a sin to disbelieve God's promise ...

2. As great as this sin is, and as much as there is of it in the godly, yet it is a sin that very rarely disturbs even godly men's consciences. This is sad, that Christians are seldom troubled about their unbelief. Our Lord speaks concerning it (John 16:9), that he will send the Comforter to convince the world of sin, because, says he, 'they believe not on me.' Moses may convince men of sin, or murder, of adultery, of swearing falsely ... but only the Spirit of God can convince believers of the sin of unbelief ... Of the very promises that they have formerly believed, and have given glory to God by believing, they take back again and glory by unbelieving.

The most spiritual attainment of a Christian in the world, the most spiritual, evangelical mourning and repentance that can be done by a Christian, is mourning over his unbelief; that the Word of the Lord is not more precious to him; that he cannot trust God's Word naked without props; that he doubts it so often, when darkness comes on; and that he lets go his hold of this great rock, the faithfulness of God.

— Robert Traill, *The Works of Robert Traill,* Vol. 3, pp. 102-103 (J.O.)

Are there grades of sin?

... he that delivered me unto thee hath the greater sin (John 19:11).

Some sins in themselves, and by reason of several aggravations, are more heinous in the sight of God than others ... The stoic philosophers held all sins were equal; but this Scripture clearly holds forth that there is a gradual difference in sin; some are greater than others; some are 'mighty sins', and 'crying sins'. Every sin has a voice to speak, but some sins cry. As some diseases are worse than others, and some poisons more venomous, so some sins are more heinous. 'Ye have done worse than your fathers', your sins have exceeded theirs (Jer. 16:12) ...

That some sins are greater than others appears because:

1. There was a difference in the offerings under the law; the sin offering was greater than the trespass offering.
2. Some sins are not capable of pardon as others are, therefore, they must be more heinous, as the blasphemy against the Holy Ghost (Matt. 12:31).
3. Some sins have a greater degree of punishment than others. 'Ye shall receive the greater damnation ' (Matt. 23:14) ...

God would not punish one more than another if his sin was not greater.
— Thomas Watson, *The Ten Commandments,* p. 139 (B.T.)

A sin that reaches beyond the grave

He that backbiteth not with his tongue, nor doeth evil to his neighbour, nor taketh up a reproach against his neighbour (Ps. 15:3).

Among the many sins which God is contending with ... and especially with the professors of religion, I have no doubt that one of them is the gross misgovernment of our tongues. The abuses of the tongue are many, one of which is the malignity of it. And whereas in David's time a malignant and virulent tongue was the badge of an atheist: 'Behold, they belch out with their mouths: swords are in their lips: for who, say they, doth hear?' (Ps. 59:7), now, alas! this blotch is become the blotch of God's children, and of high professors of religion ...

I shall reveal to you how pregnant a sin this is ... It causes a great injury to the person whom you censure and reproach ... you rob him of the best treasure which he has in the world. 'A good name is rather to be chosen than great riches' (Prov. 22:1). Consequently, you are more criminal than he that dies by the hands of justice for taking away another man's goods: you robbed him of that which you are not able to give him back; you robbed him of the most lasting good which he has, and that which alone will abide after death. Your cruelty extends beyond the grave, and leads to this—to make his name rot above ground, while his body rots in it.

And injury is the greater, because it cannot be prevented: there is no fence against this vice; it is the arrow that flies by night, which no man can observe or avoid, and it is an injury which can hardly be repaired. Breaches in men's estates may be made up, liberty lost may be recovered, a conscience wounded may be healed; but a reputation can hardly ever be restored.

— Matthew Poole, *Puritan Sermons,* Vol. 2, pp. 443, 449, 452-453

(P.S.)

Soul and body

For what is a man profited, if he shall gain the whole world, and lose his own soul? ... (Matt. 16:26).

This soul is your own, and you have not, nor ever will have, another, and therefore it is important that you keep it safe. The text calls our souls *ours*—'his own soul'. Christ does not call the world, or anything in it, ours; but he calls our souls ours. And certainly they are ours as nothing else is; for we must forego all other things, and be parted from them; but without our souls we never were, nor ever can be ...

This will enhance our opinion of the soul, that *our bodies follow the condition of our souls.* As our souls are, so shall our bodies be, when raised up, to all eternity. And therefore St. Stephen, when he was dying, commends only his soul to our Saviour (Acts 7:59); and our Saviour himself in his last breath commends his 'spirit', or soul, to his Father (Luke 23:46); neither making any mention of their bodies. They knew that their bodies by consequence would be happy; that they would be cared for by God, and raised up in God's time, to be blessed with their souls to all eternity.

If our souls are found unbelieving and impenitent, without God's image and favour, all the rich attire and sumptuous fare will not keep our bodies, no more than they did Dives' body, from being tormented in those flames ... On the other hand, if our souls are sanctified and accepted, notwithstanding any present poverty, disease, or misery they shall hereafter 'sit down with Abraham, and Isaac, and Jacob, in the kingdom of heaven' (Matt. 8:11).

The welfare of the body even in this life depends upon the soul ... I shall say nothing to vilify the body ... which we overprize and value. It is enough to say, with Bernard: 'Trim thy body, pamper it, bestow all thy care and pains upon it; it is but flesh still.'

— Peter Vinke, *Puritan Sermons,* Vol. 3, pp. 584, 577 (P.S.)

Thoughts: words of the mind

Repent therefore of this thy wickedness, and pray God, if perhaps the thought of thine heart may be forgiven thee (Acts 8:22).

'The Lord,' whose knowledge is infallible, 'knoweth the thoughts of man, that they are vanity' (Ps. 94:11); yes, and of the wisest men too, according to the apostle's interpretation (1 Cor. 3:20). And who were they that 'became vain in their imaginations,' but the wisest men that the carnal world produced? ...

As good thoughts and purposes are acts in God's account, so are bad ones. Abraham's intention to offer Isaac is accounted as an actual sacrifice: that the stroke was not delivered, was not from any reluctance of Abraham's will, but the gracious indulgence of God ... Thoughts are the words of the mind, and are as real in God's account as if they were expressed with the tongue ...

We are accountable to God and punishable for thoughts. If thoughts need a pardon, as they certainly do, then it follows that if mercy does not pardon them, justice will condemn them. And it is absolutely stated that 'a man of wicked devices', or 'thoughts', God will condemn (Prov. 12:2) ...

If our thoughts be not judged, God would not be a righteous Judge. He would not judge according to the merit of the cause, if only outward actions were scanned, without regard to their intents ... Those very thoughts will accuse you before God's tribunal, which accuse you here before your conscience, his deputy ... Our good thoughts will be our accusers for not observing them, and our bad thoughts will be indictments against us for complying with them ... The tongue is only an instrument to express what the heart did think.

— Stephen Charnock, *Puritan Sermons,* Vol. 2, pp. 396-397 (P.S.)

Angel's tongue; devil's heart

Ye hypocrites ... (Luke 12:56).

Hypocrites are like pictures on canvas, they show fairest at farthest. A hypocrite's profession is in folio, but his sincerity in *decimo-sexto*, nothing in the world to speak of. A hypocrite is like the Sicilian Etna, flaming at the mouth when it has snow at the foot: their mouths talk hotly, but their feet walk coldly. The nightingale has a sweet voice, but a lean carcass; a voice, and nothing else but a voice: and so have all the hypocrites ...

Hypocrites labour to seem saints, not to be so, but the holy labour to be saints, more than to seem saints. The kite may fly aloft, but her eye and mind is to the earth. She seems to be a gallant bird at her pitch, till she falls down upon a carrion. Oh how the pretentious zealot makes a show to honour Christ with his lofty profession, as if he were altogether a man of heaven: tarry but a little, throw the bait of glory in his way, and he will stoop to a carrion, and be taken with the pride of his own commendation ...

If you have an angel's tongue and a devil's heart, you are no better than a post in the crossway, that rots itself to direct others; or a torch that, having pleasured others with the light, goes out itself in smoke and stench.

— Thomas Adams, *A Homiletic Encyclopedia,*
pp. 2999, 3011, 3018 (H.E.)

Feigned equity is double iniquity.

— George Downame

267

Hypocrisy exposed

... Beware ye of the leaven of the Pharisees, which is hypocrisy (Luke 12:1).

Hypocrites are certain to miscarry at last; so true is that proverb, 'Frost and fraud have dirty ends.'

The Christian, like a star in the heavens, wades through the cloud that for a time hides his comfort; but the hypocrite, like a meteor in the air, blazes for a while, and then drops into some ditch where he is quenched. 'The light of the righteous rejoiceth: but the lamp of the wicked shall be put out.'

Hypocrites are like tops that go no longer than they are whipped; but the sincere soul is ever ready. It does not want a will, but only skill and strength to act ...

God taught man to make coats to cover his naked body, but the devil taught him to weave deceit to cover his naked soul. Yet the more subtle you are in concealing your sin, the more flagrantly you play the fool. There are none so shamed as the liar when found out, and you are sure to be ...

The Jews covered Christ's face, and then buffeted him. So does the hypocrite. He first says in his heart, God sees not, and then makes bold to sin against him. He ought to say with Augustine, 'I may hide thee from myself, but not myself from thee.'

— William Gurnall, *A Homiletic Encyclopedia,*
pp. 3012, 3020-3021 (H.E.)

A chameleon from hell

And no marvel; for Satan himself is transformed into an angel of light (2 Cor. 11:14).

It is observable that a forester goes usually in green, suitable to the leaves of the trees and the grass of the forest. By this means the most observant in all the herd never so much as distrusts him till the arrow pierces his side.

And thus the devil shapes himself to the fashions of all men. If he meets with a proud man, or a prodigal man, then he makes himself a flatterer; if a covetous man, then he comes with a reward in his hand. He has an apple for Eve, a grape for Noah, a change of raiment for Gehazi, a bag for Judas.

He can dish out his meat for all palates. He has a last to fit every shoe. He has something to please all conditions, to suit with all dispositions whatsoever.

— William Jenkyn, *A Homiletic Encyclopedia,* p. 1670 (H.E.)

Saul has slain his thousands, and David his ten thousands: but Satan his millions.

— Thomas Adams

269

Vain thoughts

For as he thinketh in his heart, so is he ... (Prov. 23:7).

The best Christian's heart is like Solomon's ships, which brought home not only gold and silver, but also apes and peacocks. It has not only spiritual and heavenly, but also vain and foolish thoughts. But these latter are there as a disease or poison in the body, the object of his grief and abhorrence, not of his love and complacency.

Though we cannot keep vain thoughts from knocking at the door of our hearts, nor from entering in sometimes, yet we may cease bidding them welcome, or giving them entertainment. 'How long shall thy vain thoughts lodge within thee?' It is bad to let them lie or lodge with us. It is better to receive the greatest thieves into our houses than vain thoughts into our hearts.

John Huss, seeking to reclaim a very profane wretch, was told by him, that his giving way to wicked, wanton thoughts was the original of all those hideous births of impiety which he was guilty of in his life. Huss answered him, that though he could not keep evil thoughts from courting him, yet he might keep them from marrying him.

— George Swinnock, *A Homiletic Encyclopedia,* p. 1843 (H.E.)

A lustful thought is from the same defiled puddle, as actual filthiness: and the thought is but the passage to the action: it is but the same sin in its minority, tending to maturity.

— Richard Baxter

Seasoned with grace

... for the imagination of man's heart is evil from his youth ... (Gen. 8:21).

There is nothing so unaccountable as the multiplicity of thoughts in the minds of men. They fall from them like the leaves off trees when they are shaken with the wind in autumn. To have all these thoughts, all the several fragments of the heart, all the conceptions that are framed and agitated in the mind, to be evil, and that continually, what a hell of horror and confusion must it be! A deliverance from this loathsome, hateful state is more to be valued than the whole world. Without it neither life, nor peace, nor immortality, nor glory, can ever be attained ...

The minds and hearts of men are continually minting and coining new thoughts and imaginations; the cogitative faculty is always at work. As the streams of a mighty river running into the ocean, so are the thoughts of a natural man, and through self they run into hell ... The mighty streams of the evil thoughts of men will admit of no bounds or dams to put a stop to them. There are but two ways of relief from them, the one respecting their moral evil, the other their natural abundance. The first is by throwing salt into the spring, as Elisha cured the waters of Jericho—that is, to get the heart and mind seasoned with grace; for the tree must be made good before the fruit will be so.

The other is to turn their streams into new channels, setting new aims and goals to them, fixing them on new objects; so shall we abound in spiritual thoughts; for abound in thoughts we shall, whether we will or no.

— John Owen, *A Homiletic Encyclopedia,* p. 1849 (H.E.)

Flee to the throne

Let us therefore come boldly unto the throne of grace, that we may obtain mercy, and find grace to help in time of need (Heb. 4:16).

W hat shall we get by coming to God? The greatest blessings: *mercy* and *grace*. These blessings contain all things needful to make a sinner happy ...

This throne of grace is to be distinguished from all other thrones of God referred to in the Word. *The throne of his essential glory* is unapproachable by all creatures. *The throne of justice* is dreadful to all sinners. We should pray against coming before this throne ... There is also *the throne of the Judge at the last day*. But this throne is not yet set up, though it will surely be; we know not how soon, so we should prepare for our appearing before it.

But this throne of grace is the gracious manifestation of God in Christ, reconciling the world to himself ...

But who shall be welcomed? Surely all that come shall be welcome ... For as the Son refused none that were given to him by the Father in their eternal counsel, but took every one of them as his charge to redeem them; so all they, and only they, being drawn by the Father, and made willing to come to Christ, are made welcome by him (John 6:37).

But there are some that are specially welcomed to Christ, and do well at this throne of grace. As those who come when they can do nothing else; they come to the throne of grace as their last hope ... Believing is called *fleeing*: We 'have fled for refuge to lay hold upon the hope set before us' (Heb. 6:18). Now, who flees? Only he that can stand no longer ... It is the greatest sin of all, to count all lost, as long as this throne stands, and the Lord calls men to come to it.

— Robert Traill, *The Works of Robert Traill,* Vol. 1, pp. 33, 40-41 (J.O.)

Careful for nothing

Cast thy burden upon the Lord, and he shall sustain thee ... (Ps. 55:22).

Nothing will bring ill success upon us sooner than unbelieving and distrustful fears about the future. For when any person shall, in spite of the experience he has had, or might have had, of God's power, love, care, and truth, become so distrustful, as not to be contented with his own work, but proceeds to make God's work his burden as well, only caring about success ... such a man is foolish and presumptuous. Such a person provokes God so much that God, out of his wise justice, ceases caring for such a one, leaving him to his own care ...

Commit your ways unto the Lord, and trust in him. Cast all your care on the Lord; be careful in nothing (Ps. 55:22).

O! how happy are we Christians, if we did but know, or knowing would enjoy our happiness! We are cared for in everything that we need, and that can be good for us. We may live without taking thought, or care for anything. Our work is only to study and endeavour to please God, walking before him in sincerity, and with a perfect heart; then we may cleave to him, and rest on him both our bodies and souls without fear or distraction (1 Cor. 7:35). God is all-sufficient, and all in all to such. He is known by his name Jehovah to such (Exod. 6:3), even to being the accomplisher of his promises to them. If we shall wisely and diligently care to do our work, we, serving so good and so able a Master, need not take thought about our wages. If we would only obey and please so good, rich, and bountiful a Father; then we need not be careful for our maintenance here, in our youth or old age; nor yet our eternal inheritance, when we shall come to full age.

— Henry Scudder, *The Christian's Daily Walk*, pp. 190-192 (S.P.)

The danger of delay

The harvest is past, the summer is ended, and we are not saved (Jer. 8:20).

Do you not find by experience that the longer you delay, the farther you wander from God and holiness, and the more unfit you are for, and the more unwilling to, the work of conversion? Is it not time therefore to turn with speed, when continuance in sin insensibly hardens your heart, and gradually indisposes it to the work of repentance? As the ground, so is your heart, the longer it lies fallow, not ploughed up, the harder it will be. Will you go one step farther from God, when you must come back every step, and that by 'Weeping-cross' all the way, or be damned forever? ...

A stain which has been long in clothes is not easily washed out; a house that has long run to ruin will require the more cost and labour for its reparation; diseases that have been long in the body are cured, if at all, with much difficulty. The devil which had possessed the man from his infancy was hardly cast out, and not without much rending and raging (Mark 9:21-26). Satan thinks his evidence as good as eleven points at law, now that he has got possession. The longer he continues commander-in-chief in the royal fort of your heart, the more he fortifies it against God, and strengthens himself against the Almighty.

All the while you delay, God is more provoked, the wicked one more encouraged, your heart more hardened, your debts more increased, your souls more endangered, and all the difficulties of conversion daily more and more multiplied upon you, having a day more to repent of, and a day less to repent in.

— George Swinnock, *A Homiletic Encyclopedia,* p. 1446 (H.E.)

Almost

Then Agrippa said unto Paul, Almost thou persuadest me to be a Christian (Acts 26:28).

What will become of those that have grown weary before they have got half way to heaven?

Why, man, it is he that holds out to the end that must be saved. It is he that overcomes that shall inherit all things—not every one that begins. Agrippa gave a fair step all of a sudden, he steps almost into the bosom of Christ in less than half an hour. 'Thou', said he to Paul, hast 'almost persuaded me to be a Christian.' Ah! But it was but almost; and so he might as well have been never a whit. He stepped fair indeed, but yet he stepped short. He was hot while he was at it, but he was quickly out of wind.

All this but almost! I tell you, this but almost, it lost his soul. Sometimes I imagine these poor wretches that get but almost to heaven, how fearful their almost, and their but almost, will torment them in hell. They shall carry it in the bitterness of their souls, saying 'I was *almost* a Christian. I *almost* got into the kingdom. *Almost* from under the curse of God. *Almost,* and that was all. *Almost,* but not altogether. O that I should be *almost* at heaven, and should not go quite through!'

Friend, it is a sad thing to sit down before we are in heaven, and to grow weary before we come to the place of rest. If this should be your case, I am sure it is because you did not so run as to obtain.

— John Bunyan, *The Heavenly Footman,* pp. 38-39 (R.P.)

Hidden in light

... I flee unto thee to hide me (Ps. 143:9).

But why should I think that God will assist me flying, when he would not assist me fighting? How can I hope he will be my sanctuary, when he would not be my fortress? O my soul, who can tell whether God has not left me in distress on purpose, to try what help I would seek? Who can tell whether he has not therefore been my fortress, in order that he might be my sanctuary? Did he ever fail to deliver any that put their trust in him, and shall I think he will begin with me? Did he ever refuse to protect any that fled to him for help, and shall I fear to fare worse than anybody ever did? ...

I fly to him, not as the world used to do, for preferment in the world; but I fly to him only that he may hide me; and he will do little for me if he will not do so much as hide me. To hide me is no more to him than to receive me, seeing he dwells in light inaccessible, whither my enemies, that are children of darkness, can never come to find me. I fly not to be hidden in thickets and bushes, that may be felled with axes and burnt with fire; but I fly to the bush, burning and not consuming, where I know myself safe against fire and sword ...

But why should David fly to God to hide him, seeing hiding is best done by darkness, and God is all light? O my soul, God hides with light, as he is hidden with light, and takes not away visibility but by addition of lustre; his *tegere* (covering) is *protegere* (protecting), a hiding that makes not obscure, but more conspicuous. David, for all his other glories, would never have shined so much to posterity, if he had not fled to God, and been hidden by him.

— Sir Richard Baker, *Meditations and Disquisitions,* pp. 291-292 (S.P.)

A divided heart

But let him ask in faith, nothing wavering. For he that wavereth is like a wave of the sea driven with the wind and tossed (Jam. 1:6).

The forlorn picture of a roving heart, carried up and down as the wind of any temptation pleases: the cause, a double mind ... The word signifies one that has two souls; one that speaks with a double heart (Ps. 12:2). Like that profane wretch that boasted he had two souls in one body: one for God, the other for anything that came. This man is the unstable man in God's service, off and on with God, unfixed to his business, knows not what he would have, prays and unprays, wants faith for the ballast of his soul, and so is carried at the pleasure of every wave ... 'Let not this man think that he shall obtain anything of the Lord': Though God may answer such requests out of his superabundant mercy, yet such a man can look for nothing. Though a distracted prayer may receive something, yet it cannot expect anything from God. When a man's supplication is a provocation, there is little hope. He that puts treason into his petition has little reason to hope for a good answer ...

The remedy for a divided heart is to get sincerity and seriousness. And, indeed, the soul that is sincere is serious. The real beggar entreats in good earnest; he cries, he weeps, he heeds not the playing of the children, nor the barking of the dogs; his wants pinch him, his stomach craves, nothing but food will please him ... So it is the same with the upright and serious heart; he is really and deeply pressed down with sin, and needy of grace and comfort ... and therefore let the devil or the world disturb what they can, or suggest what they will, he plies his business, he must have pardon and grace.

— Richard Steele, *A Remedy for Wandering Thoughts,* pp. 131-137
(S.P.)

The dark night of desertion

Then I said, I am cast out of thy sight; yet I will look again toward thy holy temple (Jon. 2:4).

God being a Father, if he hides his face from his child, it is in love. Desertion is sad in itself, a short hell (Job 6:9). Yet when the light is withdrawn, dew falls. We may see a rainbow in the cloud, the love of a Father in all this.

Firstly, God hereby quickens grace. Perhaps grace lay dormant (Canticles 5:2). It was as fire in the members; and God withdraws comfort, to invigorate and exercise grace. Faith is a grace that sometimes shines brightest in the dark night of desertion (Jon. 2:4).

Secondly, when God hides his face from his child, he is still a Father, and his heart is towards his child. Joseph spoke roughly to his brethren, and made them believe he would take them for spies; still his heart was full of love, and he was fain to go aside and weep. So God's heart yearns for his children, even when he seems to look strange. 'In a little wrath I hid my face from thee ... but with everlasting kindness will I have mercy on thee.' Though God may have the look of an enemy, he still has the heart of a Father.

— Thomas Watson, *A Homiletic Encyclopedia,* p. 1656 (H.E.)

He who has engaged to be our God forever cannot depart forever.
— Timothy Cruso

Obedience is paramount

Take heed, and hearken, O Israel; this day thou art become the people of the Lord thy God. Thou shalt therefore obey the voice of the Lord thy God, and do his commandments ... (Deut. 27:9-10).

I t is not enough to hear God's voice, but we must obey. Obedience is a part of the honour we owe to God. 'If then I be a father, where is mine honour?' (Mal. 1:6). Obedience carries in it the lifeblood of religion.

'Obey the voice of the Lord thy God, and do his commandments.' Obedience without knowledge is blind, and knowledge without obedience is lame. Rachel was fair to look upon, but, being barren, said, 'Give me children, or I die.' So, if knowledge does not bring forth the child of obedience, it will die.

'To obey is better than sacrifice' (1 Sam. 15:22). Saul thought it was enough for him to offer sacrifices, though he disobeyed God's command; but 'to obey is better than sacrifice.' God disclaims sacrifice, if obedience be wanting.

— Thomas Watson, *The Ten Commandments,* p. 1 (B.T.)

This is the true obedience, whether to God or man, when we look not so much to the letter of the law, as to the mind of the law-maker.
— John Trapp

Temptation

Watch and pray, that ye enter not into temptation ... (Matt. 26:41).

Satan tempts God's children, not because they have sin in them, but because they have grace in them. Had they no grace, the devil would not disturb them. Where he has possession all is at peace (Luke 1:21). His temptations are to rob the saints of their grace.

A thief will not break into an empty house, but to the house where he thinks there is treasure. Similarly the devil wishes to possess the people of God, because he thinks they have a rich treasure of grace in their hearts, and he wants to rob them of that.

What makes people throw stones at a tree is the fact that there is an abundance of fruit hanging from its branches. In the same way the devil throws his temptations at you, because he sees that you have much fruit of grace growing upon you. Although to be tempted is a trouble, yet to consider why you are being tempted is a comfort ...

Godly temptation causes the increase of grace. 'One tempted Christian,' said Luther, 'is worth a thousand.' He grows more in grace. As the bellows increases the flame, so the bellows of temptation increases the flame of grace.

This is no small blessing that Christ succours the tempted. A mother succours a child most when he is sick; she sits by his bedside and brings him cordials. In the same way, when a soul is most assaulted, it shall be most assisted.

— Thomas Watson, *A Homiletic Encyclopedia,*
pp. 4773, 4785, 4793 (H.E.)

Reading makes a full man, prayer a holy man, temptation an experienced man.

— John Trapp

Fruitful virginity

And in the sixth month the angel Gabriel was sent from God unto a city of Galilee, named Nazareth, to a virgin espoused to a man whose name was Joseph ... (Luke 1:26-27).

The messenger is an angel: a man was too mean to carry the news of the conception of God ... God appointed his angel to be the first preacher, and has since called his preachers angels. The message is well suited: an angel comes to a virgin, Gabriel to Mary ...

In this whole work, God would have nothing ordinary: it was fit that she should be a married virgin, which should be a virgin mother. He that meant to take man's nature without man's corruption, would be the son of the man without man's seed, and would be the seed of the woman without man. And amongst all women, a pure virgin; but, amongst virgins, one espoused, that there might be at once a witness and a guardian of her fruitful virginity. If the same God had not been the author of virginity and marriage, he would never have countenanced virginity by marriage.

Whither does this glorious angel come to find the mother of him that was God, but to obscure Galilee—a place which even the Jews themselves despised, as forsaken of their privileges? 'Out of Galilee ariseth no prophet.' Behold, an angel comes to that Galilee out of which no prophet comes, and the God of prophets arises! He that fills all places makes no difference of places: it is the person which gives honour and privilege to the place, not the place to the person. The presence of God makes heaven, heaven does not make the honour glorious. No blind corner of Nazareth can hide the blessed Virgin from the angel. The favours of God will find out his children, wheresoever they are withdrawn.

— Joseph Hall, *Contemplations,* pp. 408-409 (T.N.)

The art of probing

Search me, O God, and know my heart ... (Ps. 139:23).

I f you truly realise what you say you believe, would you not be convinced that the most pleasant, gainful sin is worse than madness? And would you not spit on the mere mentioning of it?

2. What would you think of the most serious, holy life, if you truly realised the things you say you believe? Would you ever again criticize it as too legalistic, or too concerned with trivialities, and think your time better spent in playing than in praying; in drinking, and sports, and filthy lusts, than in the holy service of God?

3. If you truly realised what you say you believe, would you ever again be offended with the ministers of Christ for their candid reproofs, devastating exhortations, and strict precepts and discipline ... ? You would appreciate why they were so imploring for your conversion, and that serious preaching is far better than indulging in trivialities.

4. I dare to ask the worst one of you that hears me: Dare you now be drunk, or gluttonous, or worldly? Dare you be voluptuous, proud, or fornicators any more? Dare you go home and make a joke of piety, and neglect your souls as you have done? ...

5. And, O, how such a sight would magnify the Redeemer, his grace, promises, word, and ordinance in your estimation? It would quicken your desires and make you fly to Christ for life, as a drowning man to the one who rescues him. How sweetly you would then relish the name, the word, the ways of Christ, which now seem so dry and commonplace!

— Richard Baxter, *Practical Works,* pp. 585f (S.D.G.)

Giving and receiving reproof

... he that refuseth reproof erreth (Prov. 10:17).

Reprove seriously. Reproof is an edged tool, and must not be jested with. Cold reproofs are like the noise of cannons a great way off, not frightening us in the least. He that reproves sin merrily, as one that takes pride to show off his wit and to make the company laugh, will destroy the sinner instead of the sin ...

Reprove compassionately. Soft words and hard arguments go well together. Passion will heat the sinner's blood, but compassion will heal his conscience. Our reprimanding may be sharp, but our spirits must be meek ... The reprover should have a lion's heart, or he will not be faithful, and a lady's soft hand, or he is not likely to be successful ...

Let us as wise men be patient in receiving admonition ... There are two things that cause men to rage against reproof:

a. Guilt of the sin objected. Guilt makes men angry when they are searched; and, like horses that are galled, to kick if they are touched. The easiest medicines and mildest waters are troublesome to sore eyes. There is scarcely a more probable sign that the crime objected to was true, than wrath and bitterness against the person that charged us with it.
b. Love for sin makes men impatient under reproof. When a person's sin is to him as 'the apple of his eye,' no wonder he is offended at any that touches it.

But grace will teach a Christian contentedly to take those potions that are wholesome, though they are not toothsome.

— George Swinnock, *A Homiletic Encyclopedia,*
pp. 4306, 4314, 4323 (H.E.)

The lost art of reproving

Thou shalt not hate thy brother in thine heart: thou shalt in any wise rebuke thy neighbour, and not suffer sin upon him (Lev. 19:17).

There is a special obligation upon friends to be helpful to one another in this matter. The laws of friendship require us to discover what things endanger us. You would count him unworthy to be called a friend, who, knowing a thief or an arsonist to be lurking in your neighbourhood with a design to kill, or rob, or burn your house, and he concealed it from you, and did not acquaint you with it on his own accord.

There is no such thief, murderer or arsonist as sin. It is a greater danger to us and to those values that are more precious than goods, houses, or life. And what really makes it dangerous is that it can kindle the Lord's anger against us.

Silence or concealment in this case is treachery. He is the most faithful friend, and worthy of most esteem and affection, that deals most plainly with us in reference to exposing our sin. He that is reserved in this case is but a false friend, a mere pretender to love, whereas, indeed, he hates his brother in his heart (Lev. 19:17).

— David Clarkson, *A Homiletic Encyclopedia*, p. 4277 (H.E.)

It is well done of Paul to reprove Peter to his face, and it was well done of Peter to praise Paul in his absence.

— Thomas Adams

Perseverance in grace

... Holy Father, keep through thine own name those whom thou hast given me, that they may be one, as we are (John 17:11).

The perseverance of the saints, or their conservation in a state of grace, is sure and certain ...

However, seeming grace may be lost ' ... But from him that hath not shall be taken away even that which he hath' (Matt. 25:29). Blazing comets and meteors are soon spent, and may fall from heaven like lightning, while stars keep their orb and station ...

Initial or preparative grace may fail: ' ... those who were once enlightened, and have tasted of the heavenly gift, and were made partakers of the Holy Ghost, And have tasted the good word of God, and the powers of the world to come', may fall away; such as illumination, external reformation, temporary faith, some good beginnings. Some die in pangs of the new birth and are stillborn. Plenty of blossoms do not always foretell a store of fruit.

True grace may suffer a shrewd decay, but not an utter loss. In temptations it may be sorely shaken; the heel may be bruised, as Christ's was, but 'his seed remaineth in him' (1 John 3:9) ...

Grace indeed, if left to us, would be soon lost; we showed that in innocency. But it is our advantage that our security lieth in God's promises, not our own strength, that we are not our own keepers. God would not trust this jewel but in safe hands. Perseverance is God's gift, not man's act.

— Thomas Manton, *An Exposition on John 17,* pp. 186-188 (S.G.P.)

Still within God's reach

And delivered just Lot, vexed with filthy conversation of the wicked (2 Pet. 2:7).

We must mourn the sins of our bitterest enemies, as well as of our most beloved relatives ... I suppose there is no godly man but bitterly mourns for the impieties of his dear yoke-fellow or child; but to mourn because a cruel enemy either dishonours God or damns his own soul, I doubt if there are very many that conscientiously do that. Nothing is more common than to rail at our enemies for their impieties, and to expose them to reproach and public hatred; but I fear there is nothing more unusual than to mourn their self-destroying sins, before God in secret ... The holy attitude of Christ, and Paul, moved by his Spirit reveals them wailing and shedding tears for these that desired to shed their blood ... It is a thousand times more sea of my tears, than that their persons should be swept away by the stream of my powers.

In presenting before God the wickedness of great sinners, admire his infinite *power*, that can not only stop the worst of men in, but turn them from, their continued rebellion against God. In spite of our mourning, we are not to despair for the conversion of the worst. They are as much within the converting reach, as the destructive reach, of God's hand. Say to God: 'I censure his way, but I dare not determine his end. Thou hast made white paper from black and filthy dunghill rags: what cannot the infinite power of God accomplish for the conversion of the greatest sinner? ... O, how glorious would pardoning grace and converting power appear in causing such a change?'

— William Jenkyn, *Puritan Sermons,* Vol. 3, pp. 112-113 (P.S.)

The reward of the saints

... I am thy shield, and thy exceeding great reward (Gen. 15:1).

Nothing besides God can be the saints' reward. Nothing on *earth* can be their reward. The glamour of the world dazzles men's eyes; but, like the apples of Sodom, it does not so much delight as delude. The world is gilded emptiness (Prov. 23:5). The world is made circular, the heart in the figure of a triangle; a circle cannot fill a triangle. The world is enough to busy us, but not to fill us ...

Heaven itself is not the saints' reward: 'Whom have I in heaven but thee?' (Ps. 73:25). 'There are angels and archangels,' says Musculus; yes, but those are for a saint's comfort, and not properly for his reward. Communion with seraphims is excellent, and yet it can no more make a saint's reward than the light of the stars can make a day ...

The great blessing of the covenant is, 'I am thy God.' The Lord told Abraham that kings should come out of his loins, and he would give the land of Canaan to him and his seed (Gen. 17:6); but all this did not amount to blessedness. 'I will be their God' (Gen. 17:8). God will not only see that the saints are rewarded, but he himself will be their reward. A king may reward his subjects with gratuities, but he bestows himself upon his queen.

— Thomas Watson, *Puritan Sermons,* Vol. 3, pp. 67-68 (P.S.)

O Christian! Get above.

— Richard Baxter

OCTOBER

Taste and see

O taste and see that the Lord is good ... (Ps. 34:8).

Seeing the angels are so beneficial and so good to us ... O taste and see how good the Lord is. It is by the goodness we find in the angels, we may take a taste of the goodness that is in God. If it be a great goodness in the angels to encamp about us, how great is his goodness that gives the angels that charge? For the angels would not do it if God did not command them; alas, they could not do it if God did not enable them. O, then, taste, and see how good the Lord is; not how good the angels are, though they be good, and exceeding good in their rank as ministers; yet what is this to the goodness of God, who is the fountain of goodness to the angels themselves?

O, then, taste and see how good the Lord is; for taste him we may, but we can but taste him while we live here. We shall not have a full comprehension of him till we come to see as we are seen, when we shall need no more encamping of angels round about us ...

But how can we taste him that is not bodily? How can we see him that is not visible? Not him, indeed, but his goodness; and not his goodness in itself, but in its effects; and not in its effects as they shall be, but as they are, which, God knows, is but a small part of what they shall be.

O, then, taste and see how good the Lord is. If you would but taste him, you would never take pleasure in other things. If you would but see him, you would never delight in another object. O my soul, if you could but taste the sweetness, if you could but see the goodness that is in God, it would make you fall into a greater ecstasy than that of Peter at the sight of Christ's glory in the Mount.

— Sir Richard Baker, *Meditations and Disquisitions*, pp. 368-369 (S.P.)

The throne of grace

Let us therefore come boldly unto the throne of grace, that we may obtain mercy, and find grace to help in time of need (Heb. 4:16).

What is to be inferred from the term 'throne of grace'?
1. To be sure, this is inferred, that converted men are not in every way, or in every sense, free from the being of sin. For, were they, they need not go to a throne of grace for help. When it says there is grace in God, it infers that there is sin in the godly; and when it says grace reigns, as upon a throne, it implies that sin would like to ascend the throne, reign, and have the dominion over the children of God ... And the only way to prevent it is to apply ourselves, as told by the text, to the throne of grace for help against it.

2. The text implies, that at certain times the most godly man in the world may be hard put to it by the sin that dwells in him, yes, so hard put to it, that there can be no way to save himself from a fall, but by imploring heaven and the throne of grace for help. This is called the needy time, the time when the wayfaring man that knocked at David's door shall knock at ours (2 Sam. 12); or when we are pushed into the sieve into which Satan pushed Peter (Luke 22:31); or when those fists are about our ears that were about Paul's ... But now here we are presented with a throne of grace, to which, as David says, we must 'continually resort'; and that is the way to obtain relief, and to find help in time of need (Ps. 71:3).

3. As Christians are sometimes in imminent danger of falling, so sometimes ... they are fallen, they are down, and down dreadfully, and can by no means lift themselves up ... Now, as they which are falling are kept from it by coming to this throne of grace, so those that are fallen must rise by the sceptre of love extended to them from the same throne. Men may fall by sin, but cannot rise up themselves without the help of grace.

— John Bunyan, *Prayer*, pp. 72-74 (B.T.)

Cry for grace

Repent ye therefore, and be converted, that your sins may be blotted out ... (Acts 3:19).

The internal cause of salvation is free grace alone. 'Not by works of righteousness which we have done, but according to his mercy he saved us' and 'by the ... renewing of the Holy Ghost' (Titus 3:5). 'Of his own will begat he us' (Jam. 1:18). We are chosen and called unto sanctification, not for it (Eph. 1:4).

God finds nothing in man to turn his heart, but enough to turn his stomach; he finds enough to provoke his loathing, but nothing to excite his love ... hear and blush, you children of the Most High. O unthankful men blush, that free grace is no more in your mouths, in your thoughts; no more adored, admired and commended by such as you! One would think you should be doing nothing but praising and admiring God wherever you are. How can you forget such grace? ...

The subject of conversion is the elect sinner, and that in all his parts and powers, members and mind. Whom God predestinates, them only he calls (Rom. 8:30). None are drawn to Christ by their calling, nor come to him by believing, but his sheep, whom the Father has given him (John 6:37, 44). Effectual calling runs parallel with eternal election (2 Pet. 1:10).

You begin at the wrong end if you first dispute about your election. Prove your conversion, and then never doubt your election. If you cannot yet prove it, then start on a present and thorough turning. Whatever God's purposes be, which are secret, I am sure his promises are plain. How desperately do rebels argue! 'If I am elected I shall be saved, do what I will. If not, I shall be damned, do what I can'. Perverse sinner, will you begin where you should end? Is not the Word before you? What says it? 'Repent ... and be converted, that your sins may be blotted out' (Acts 3:19). What can be plainer? Instead of disputing about your election, just repent and believe. Cry to God for converting grace.

— Joseph Alleine, *An Alarm to the Unconverted*, pp. 9-10, 12 (B.T.)

Natural affections?

... for as ye have yielded your members servants to uncleanness and to iniquity unto iniquity; even so now yield your members servants to righteousness unto holiness (Rom. 6:19).

Christianity abolishes not affection, but rectifies it. It dries not up the streams of sorrow, joy, hatred, etc., but only turns them into the right channel; it removes not away their being, but their ill-being.

Religion slays not, but sanctifies affections; it does not *unman* a man, but only *undevil* him. Grace is like the percolation or draining of salt water through the earth; it only takes away the brackishness and unsavouriness of our affections and faculties. It kills not Isaac, but the ram: it does not break, but only tune, the strings of nature. It destroys not, but advances, nature.

When you are godly, you have more innocent humanity than ever: you may exercise human affections and actions as much as you desire, but do not damn yourselves. You may eat, though not be gluttons; drink, through not be drunk; buy and sell, but do not make a sale of a good conscience. Grace gives leave to every thing except damning your souls.

— William Jenkyn, *Puritan Sermons*, Vol. 3, p. 125 (P.S.)

He that says he will be good tomorrow, says he will be wicked today.
— James Janeway

Christian vagabonds

Take heed therefore how ye hear ... (Luke 8:18).

Reading the Scriptures and good books is not sufficient for those that have a capacity to hear. The preaching of the Word is the great ordinance appointed by God, for the instruction, edification, and conversion of those that are to be saved ... As in other cases, so it is for the most part here: you are commonly more affected with what you hear men speak, than with what men write. Ministers may write or print their sermons, but not their emotions ... You are most likely to be warmed by the Word when you hear it coming out of a hot heart ...

But, above all, be sure to be regular in your hearing. Take heed *how* you hear; and take heed *what* you hear; and from both these will follow, that you must take heed *whom* you hear too. Hear those that are most knowing, and best able to instruct you; those that are most sound, and least likely to mislead you. Do not choose to put your souls under the care of blind guides ... Settle yourselves under the guidance of some faithful pastor, upon whose ministry you may ordinarily attend. This running to and fro, which is usual among us, is quite different from what Daniel speaks of, and, I am sure, it is not the way to increase knowledge (Dan. 12:4) ... They that run from one minister to another, may soon run from one opinion to another, and from one error to another.

I dare safely say, you will get more sound knowledge of the things of God by constant attendance upon the ministry of *one* of less abilities, than by rambling up and down to hear *many,* though of greater gifts ... It is no wonder if men that run to and fro, be 'tossed to and fro.' They that are so light of hearing may easily be 'carried about with every wind of doctrine' (Eph. 4:14); the Word of Christ seldom dwells in such vagabond hearers.
— Edward Veal, *Puritan Sermons*, Vol. 2, p. 16 (P.S.)

To get and not to give

And the publican, standing afar off, would not lift up so much as his eyes unto heaven, but smote upon his breast, saying, God be merciful to me a sinner (Luke 18:13).

Specially welcomed to the throne of grace are they that come ... to get, and not to give. Watch your spirits in this matter. When you come to the throne of grace, come to receive out of Christ's fullness, and come not to bring grace with you to add to Christ's store. He loves to give, and glories in giving; but he scorns to receive grace from you; and in truth you have none to give but what he gives you. Bring your wants to him to supply, but bring not your fullness to brag about. Spread your sins before his throne with shame and sorrow, and plead for a gracious pardon; but watch that you don't bring your sorrow, tears and repentance, no, nor your faith itself, as a plea for that pardon.

How abominable it is to Christian ears, and how much more to Christ's to hear a man plead thus for pardon: 'Here is my repentance; where is thy pardon? Here is my faith; where is thy justification?' I know men hate to say so, but watch carefully, lest any thought bordering on it enters into your heart.

Faith is the tongue that begs for pardon. Faith is the hand that receives it; it is the eye that sees it; but it is not the price to buy it. Faith uses the Gospel-plea for pardon; but, neither in habit nor act, is the plea itself. That can only be Christ's blood ...

The publican was a far better man than he (the Pharisee), as Christ testified. He came to the throne of grace, like a man that would carry something away. It is a rule of this court, 'He hath filled the hungry with good things; and the rich he hath sent empty away' (Luke 1:53).

— Robert Traill, *The Works of Robert Traill*, Vol. 1, pp. 31-32 (B.T.)

Doctrine and experience

... ye have obeyed from the heart that form of doctrine which was delivered you (Rom. 6:17).

O f all dangers in profession, let professors take heed of this; namely, of a customary, traditional or doctrinal acceptance of such truths as ought to have an effect on them, but in fact they have no experience of their reality or efficacy. This is plainly to have a form of godliness, and to deny the power thereof ...

You will say, then, what shall a man do who has no experience in himself of what is affirmed in the Word? He cannot find the death of Christ crucifying sin in him, and he cannot find the Holy Ghost sanctifying his nature, nor can he find joy in believing. What shall he then do? Shall he not believe or profess those things to be so, because he has no blessed experience of them?

I answer that our Saviour has given full direction in this case: 'If any man will do his will, he shall know of the doctrine, whether it be of God, or whether I speak of myself' (John 7:17). Continue in the things revealed in the doctrine of the Gospel, and you shall have a satisfactory experience that they are true, and that they are of God. Cease not to act in faith regarding them, and you shall enjoy their effects; for 'then shall we know, if we follow on to know the Lord' (Hos. 6:3) ...

There is a great correspondence between the heart of a believer and the truth he believes. As the Word is in the Gospel, so is grace in the heart; yes, they are the same thing variously expressed. 'Ye have obeyed from the heart that form of doctrine which was delivered you.' The meaning is that the doctrine of the Gospel begets the form, figure, image or the likeness of itself, in the hearts of them that believe; so that they are cast into the mould of it. As is the one, so is the other. As is regeneration, so is a regenerate heart. As is the doctrine of faith, so is a believer.

— John Owen, *The Forgiveness of Sin*, pp. 154-156 (B.B.)

Specious pretences

... for he found no place of repentance (Heb. 12:17).

H e that resolves to be virtuous, but not till some time later, resolves against being virtuous in the meantime. And as virtue at such a distance is easily resolved on, so it is as easy a matter always to keep it at a distance. 'The next week,' says the sinner, 'I will begin to be sober and temperate, serious and devout.' But the true sense of what he says is this, 'I am fully bent to spend this present week in riot and excess, in sensuality and profaneness, or whatever vice it is that I indulge myself in.' And if we do this often, and it becomes our common practice to put off our repentance from time to time, this is a shrewd sign that we never intended to repent at all ...

It is with wicked men in this case, as it is with a bankrupt. When his creditors are loud and clamorous, speaking big and threatening high, he answers them with many good words and fair promises. He arranges for them to come another day, entreats their patience but a little longer, and then he will satisfy them all, when all the time the man never intends to pay them one farthing ... In the same way men endeavour to pacify and calm their consciences, by telling them they will listen to them another time. All this is only to delude and cheat their consciences with good words and specious pretences, making them believe they will certainly do what yet they cannot endure to think of, and what they would fully desire to excuse themselves from.

— Edmund Calamy, *A Homiletic Encyclopedia*, p. 4248 (H.E.)

If God's today be too soon for thy repentance, thy tomorrow may be too late for his acceptance.

— William Secker

A single sin

For whosoever shall keep the whole law, and yet offend in one point, he is guilty of all (Jam. 2:10).

He that yields to one sin casts contempt upon the authority that made the whole law, and upon this account breaks it all. For he that said, Do not commit adultery, said also, Do not kill. Now if you commit no adultery, yet if you kill, you are a trangressor of the law. Not that you are guilty of all distributively, but collectively ... For the law is one combination; one commandment cannot be wronged, or broken without all being involved. The whole body suffers by a wound given to one part. 'God spake all these words'; they are ten words, but one law ...

Consider what you do before you gratify Satan in any one action; for by one sin you strengthen the whole body of sin. Give to one sin, and that will send more beggars to your door, and they will come with a stronger plea than the former ... Your best way is to keep the door shut to all, lest, while you intend to entertain only one, all the others will crowd in with it ...

By allowing one sin, we disarm and deprive ourselves of having a conscientious argument to defend ourselves against any other sin. He that can go against his conscience in one, cannot plead conscience against any other; for if the authority of God awes him from one, it will from all. 'How can I do this, and sin against God?' said Joseph. I have no doubt but that his answer would have been the same if his mistress had bid him to lie for her, as now when she enticed him to lie with her. The ninth commandment would have bound him as well as the seventh. This is why the apostle exhorts us not to give place to the devil. This implies that by yielding to one, we lose our ground, and what we lose he gains ... Once the little drill enters, the workman can then drive in a great nail.

— William Gurnall, *A Homiletic Encyclopedia*, pp. 4504-4505, 4508

(H.E.)

Justifying faith

Above all, taking the shield of faith, wherewith ye shall be able to quench all the fiery darts of the wicked (Eph. 6:16).

W hat faith is it that is here commended? ... Now, look upon the several kinds of faith, and among them must be the faith ... which enables the creature to quench Satan's fiery darts, yes all his fiery darts. *Historical faith* cannot do this, and therefore is not it. This is so far from quenching Satan's fiery darts, that the devil himself, that shoots them, has this faith. 'The devils also believe' (Jam. 2:19). *Temporary faith* cannot do it. This is so far from quenching Satan's fiery darts, that it itself is quenched by them ... *Miraculous faith*, this falls as short as the former. Judas' miraculous faith—as far as we can read—enabled him to cast devils out of others, but left himself possessed of the devil of covetousness, hypocrisy, and treason ...

There is only one kind of faith that remains ... and that is *justifying faith*. This indeed is a grace that makes him, whoever has it, the devil's match ...

What is this justifying faith as to its nature? ... It is not a naked assent to the truths of the Gospel ... Judas knew the Scriptures, and without a doubt did assent to the truth of them ... but he never had so much as one dram of justifying faith in his soul ... Yes, Judas' master, the devil himself—one far enough, I suppose, from justifying faith—yet he assents to the truth of the Word ... When he tempted Christ he did not dispute against the Scripture, but *from* the Scripture ... Assent to the truth of the Word is but an act of the understanding, which reprobates and devils may exercise; but justifying faith is a compounded habit, and has its seat both in the understanding and the will; and therefore it is called a believing with the heart (Rom. 10:10), yes, a believing with all the heart (Acts 8:37).

— William Gurnall, *The Christian in Complete Armour*,
Vol. 2, pp. 2-3 (B.T.)

Presumptions

Yet hath he not root in himself, but dureth for a while ... (Matt. 13:21).

Many ... presume that their faith is a lively and saving faith, because, as they think, they have repented, and are become new creatures. And all because they had such an enlightening that they could not naturally attain; the Word has affected them, and somewhat altered them from what they were ... They find that they do not commit many of those sins which they used to be committing; and that they do many good duties towards God and man, which they used not to do.

But what of all this? These men, as far as they go, yet going no further, are far from salvation. The common gifts of God's Spirit, given unto men in the ministry of the Gospel, may elevate a man higher, and carry him further towards heaven, than nature, art, or mere human industry can do; and yet if the saving grace of the same Spirit is not added, he will fall far short of heaven ...

True conversion and repentance consist of a true and thorough change of the whole man, whereby not only some actions are changed, but first and chiefly the whole frame and disposition of the heart is changed. He is now set aright toward God, from evil to good, as well as from darkness to light (Eph. 4:22-24). And whereas man is naturally earthly-minded, and makes himself his utmost love; he will either mind earthly things, or if he minds heavenly things, it is in an earthly manner, as did Jehu (2 Kings 10). If this man has truly repented, and been indeed converted, he becomes heavenly-minded (Col. 3:1-2) and makes God and his glory his chief and highest end.

— Henry Scudder, *The Christian's Daily Walk*, pp. 216-218 (S.P.)

The presumption of forgiveness

These things hast thou done, and I kept silence; thou thoughtest that I was altogether such an one as thyself: but I will reprove thee ... (Ps. 50:21).

An atheistic presumption that God is not so just and holy, or not just and holy ... as he is represented, is the ground on which multitudes persuade themselves of forgiveness. Men think that some declarations of God are intended only to make them mad: that he takes little notice of their sins, and those he does notice, he will easily pass by ... Come, 'let us eat and drink; for tomorrow we die.'

Their inward thought is, 'The Lord will not do good, neither will he do evil', which, says the psalmist, is men's 'thinking that God is such a one as themselves.' They have no deep nor serious thoughts of his greatness, holiness, purity, severity, but think he is like themselves, so far as not to be moved much with what they do. What thoughts they have of sin, the same they think God has. If, with them, a slight exclamation is enough to atone for sin so that their consciences are no more troubled, they think the same is enough with God, so that it will not be punished.

The generality of men make light of sin; and he that has slight thoughts of sin, had never great thoughts of God. Indeed, men's undervaluing of sin arises from their contempt of God ...

This is the state of most men; they know little of God, and are little troubled about anything that relates to him. God is not reverenced, sin is but a trifle, forgiveness a matter of nought. Whosoever will, may have it for the asking! But shall this atheistic wickedness of the heart of man be accounted a discovery of forgiveness? Does not this make God an idol? He who is not acquainted with God's holiness and purity, who knows not sin's desert and sinfulness, knows nothing of forgiveness.

— John Owen, *The Forgiveness of Sin*, pp. 83-84 (B.B.)

Weak faith not to be disparaged

And the apostles said unto the Lord, Increase our faith (Luke 17:5).

A child of God may have the kingdom of grace in his heart, and yet not know it. The cup was in Benjamin's sack, though he did not know it was there; so you may have faith in your heart, the cup may be in your sack, though you don't know it. Old Jacob wept for his son Joseph, when Joseph was alive; you may weep for want of grace, when grace may be alive in your heart. The seed may be in the ground, when we don't see it spring up; so the seed of God may be sown in your heart, though you don't perceive it springing up. Don't think that grace is lost because it is hid ...

There is a great distance between the weakness of grace and the want of grace. A man may have life, though he is sick and weak. Weak grace is not to be despised, but cherished. Christ will not break the bruised reed. Do not argue from the weakness of grace to the nullity of grace.

1. Weak grace will give us a title to Christ as well as strong grace. A weak hand of faith will receive the alms of Christ's merits.
2. Weak faith is capable of growth. The seed springs up by degrees, first the blade, then the ear, and then the full corn in the ear. The faith that is strongest was once in its infancy. Grace is like the waters of the sanctuary, which rose higher and higher. Don't be discouraged at your weak faith; though it is but blossoming, it will by degrees come to more maturity.
3. The weakest grace shall persevere as well as the strongest. A child was as safe in the ark as Noah.

— Thomas Watson, *The Lord's Prayer*, p. 52 (B.T.)

301

Blessings in all seasons

Thus saith the Lord, the God of Israel; Like these good figs, so will I acknowledge them that are carried away of Judah, whom I have sent out of this place into the land of the Chaldeans for their good (Jer. 24:5).

C hristian reader, let me beg of you, that you will not be offended, either with God or men, if the cross is laid heavy upon you. Not with God; for he does nothing without a cause: nor with men; for they are the hand of God; and they are the servants of God to you for good. Accept therefore what comes to you from God by them, thankfully.

If the messenger that brings it is glad that it is in his power to do you hurt, and to afflict you; if he jumps for joy at your calamity; be sorry for him, pity him, and pray to your Father for him. He is ignorant and does not understand the judgement of your God; yes, he shows by his behaviour, that, though he as God's instrument serves you by afflicting you: yet he means nothing less than to destroy you. This indicates to you that he himself is working out his own damnation by doing you good. Lay to your heart his woeful state, and render him that which is good for evil; love for his hatred; and by so doing you will prove that you are actuated by a spirit of holiness, and are like your Heavenly Father. And if it is that your pity and prayers can do him no good, yet they must land somewhere; or return again as ships come laden from India, full of blessings into your own bosom ...

Is there nothing of God, of his wisdom, power and goodness, to be seen in thunder and lightning, in hailstones, in storms, in darkness, in tempests? Why then is it said, he has his way in the whirlwind and storm (Nah. 1:3)? ... There is that of God to be seen in such a day as cannot be seen in another ...

It is said that in some countries trees will grow, but will bear no fruit, because there is no winter there. The Lord will bless all seasons to his people ...

— John Bunyan, *Advice to Sufferers*, pp. 7-9 (A.B.P.)

Assurance

... Lord, I believe; help thou mine unbelief (Mark 9:24).

I t is a mistake to think that everyone who is in Christ knows that he is in him; for many are truly gracious, and have a good title to eternal life, who do not know so much, until afterwards: 'These things have I written unto you that believe ... that ye may know that ye have eternal life' (1 John 5:13). This implies that they may know they are believers, and implies they did not know it before.

It is a mistake to think that every one who attains a strong relationship with Christ has an equal certainty about it. One may say that he is persuaded that nothing present, or to come, can separate him from the love of God (Rom. 8:18). Another comes but this far, 'Lord, I believe; help thou mine unbelief' (Mark 9:24).

It is a mistake to think that every one who attains a strong relationship with Christ will always do so; for he who may say of the Lord today, he is his refuge (Ps. 91:2), and his portion (Ps. 11:5-7), will say at another time, that he is cut off (Ps. 31:22), and will ask if the truth of God's promise doth fail for evermore (Ps. 77:7-9).

It is also a mistake to think that every one who attains a good knowledge of their gracious state can formally answer all objections made to the contrary; but yet they may hold fast to the conclusion, and say, 'I know whom I have believed' (2 Tim. 1:12).

— William Guthrie, *The Christian's Great Interest*, p. 21 (B.T.)

Faith is our seal; assurance is God's seal.

— Christopher Nesse

Christ on any terms

Him hath God exalted with his right hand to be a Prince and a Saviour ...
(Acts 5:31).

All of Christ is accepted by the sincere convert. He loves not only the wages but the work of Christ, not only the benefits but the burden of Christ. He is willing not only to tread out the corn, but to draw under the yoke. He takes up the commands of Christ, yes, the cross of Christ.

The unsound convert takes Christ by halves. He is all for the salvation of Christ, but he is not for sanctification. He is for the privileges, but does not appropriate the person of Christ. He divides the offices and benefits of Christ. This is an error in the foundation. Whoever loves life, let him beware here. It is an undoing mistake, of which you have been often warned, and yet none is more common. Jesus is a sweet name, but men do not love the Lord Jesus in sincerity. They will not have him as God offers, 'to be a Prince and Saviour' (Acts 5:31). They divide what God has joined, the King and the Priest. They will not accept the salvation of Christ as he intends it; they divide it here. Every man's vote is for salvation from suffering, but they do not desire to be saved from sinning. They would have their lives saved, but still would have their lusts. Indeed, many divide here again; they would be content to have some of their sins destroyed, but they cannot leave the lap of Delilah, or divorce the beloved Herodias. They cannot be cruel to the right eye or right hand. O be infinitely careful here; your soul depends upon it.

The sound convert takes a whole Christ, and takes him for all intents and purposes, without exceptions, without limitations, without reserve. He is willing to have Christ upon any terms; he is willing to have the dominion of Christ as well as deliverance by Christ. He says with Paul, 'Lord, what wilt thou have me to do?' Anything, Lord. He sends the blank for Christ to set down his own conditions.

— Joseph Alleine, *An Alarm to the Unconverted*, pp. 45-46 (B.T.)

By appointment

That no man should be moved by these afflictions: for yourselves know that we are appointed thereunto (1 Thess. 3:3).

He that suffers for righteousness' sake ... suffers by the order and design of God ...

It is not what enemies will, but what God wills, and what God appoints, that shall be done ...

This then should be well considered by God's church, in the cloudy and dark day. 'All his saints are in thy hand' (Deut. 33:3). It is not the way of God to let the enemies of God's church do what they will ...

♦ God has appointed *who* shall suffer. Suffering comes not by chance ... but by the will and appointment of God. We are apt to forget God when affliction comes, and to think it strange that those that fear God should suffer (1 Pet. 4:12).

♦ God has appointed *when* they shall suffer for his truth in the world ... The people of God, are not in the hands of their enemies, but in the hand of God.

♦ God has appointed *where* this, that, or the other good man shall suffer. Moses and Elias, when they appeared on the holy mount, told Jesus of the suffering which he should accomplish at Jerusalem. Jerusalem was the place assigned for Christ to suffer at ...

♦ God has appointed *what kind of sufferings* this or that saint shall undergo at this place, and at such a time. God said he would show Paul beforehand how great things he should suffer for his sake (Acts 9:16) ...

Our sufferings as to the nature of them, are all written down in God's book; and though the writing seems as unknown characters to us, yet God understands them very well.

— John Bunyan, *Advice to Sufferers*, pp. 87-89 (A.B.P.)

Unprofitable servants

So likewise ye, when ye shall have done all those things which are commanded you, say, We are unprofitable servants: we have done that which was our duty to do (Luke 17:10).

There is not one instance of any one, not even the most holy man that ever breathed on God's earth, that was so holy and perfect as to be freed from having sin in him ... Noah once betrays his internal and external nakedness. Abraham the father of the faithful, is ambiguous more than once. Moses, that conversed with God mouth to mouth, the great secretary of heaven, is guilty of unbelief, and speaks 'unadvisedly with his lips' (Ps. 106:33). What shall I speak of David, Hezekiah, Josiah, those stars of highest magnitude? As for Paul, even after he had been transported up into the third heavens, groans, 'O wretched man that I am! Who shall deliver me?' (Rom. 7:24) ...

It is utterly impossible in this life to keep the commandments of God perfectly, because the best of saints in this life are but imperfectly sanctified ...

Objection: Does God command the creature that which is impossible?

Solution: We reply, as Augustine did: What is simply and absolutely impossible in itself God does not impose upon the creature; but what apostate man himself has made impossible to himself, voluntarily, and by his own default, that the great Lawgiver may and does justly impose ...

Objection: But did not Christ come in the flesh for this end, that we might be able fully to keep the law in our persons, that the righteousness of the law might be fulfilled in us?

Solution: Mark: the Scripture says: 'in us,' not 'by us.' Christ came, 'that the righteousness of the law might be fulfilled' for us, and in us (Rom. 8:4).

Thomas Lye, *Puritan Sermons*, Vol. 6, pp. 229-232 (P.S.)

The right approach to election

Wherefore the rather, brethren, give diligence to make your calling and election sure ... (2 Pet. 1:10).

Some are much troubled because they proceed by a false method and order in judging their estates. They begin with election, which is the highest step of the ladder; whereas they should begin from a work of grace wrought within their hearts, from God's calling by his Spirit, and their answer to his call, and then raise themselves upward to know their election by their answer to God's calling.

'Give diligence,' says Peter, 'to make your calling and election sure.' Your election by your calling. God descends to us from election to calling, and so to sanctification. We must ascend to him beginning where he ends. Otherwise it is a great folly as in removing a pile of wood, to begin at the lowest first, and so, besides the needless trouble, to be in danger to have the rest to fall upon our heads.

— Richard Sibbes, *A Homiletic Encyclopedia*, p. 1798 (H.E.)

You begin at the wrong end if you first dispute about your election. Prove your conversion, and then never doubt your election.
— Joseph Alleine

No merit or credit

But grow in grace ... (2 Pet. 3:18).

The good works of believers are imperfect; and therefore they cannot merit by them. How can a man merit any reward of the lawgiver by doing that which does not fulfil the law, which requires not only good works, but perfectly good ones? He does not deserve his wages that does not do his whole work, and do it as he should. Or how can a man deserve a reward by those works that merit punishment? Can he deserve blessing and curse at the same time, and by the same works? ... 'There is not a just man upon earth, that doeth good, and sinneth not', says Solomon (Eccl. 7:20) ...

If we look at the good works of the saints in particular, we shall find some defect in every one of them. The best proceed but from an imperfect principle—the new nature; which, in believers, during their present state, is but in its growth, and not come to its full maturity. It shall be made perfect; so therefore it is not yet perfect. God promises that believers shall grow in grace ... They are commanded to grow: 'Grow in grace' (2 Pet. 3:18) ... But if grace reaches its full perfection, there would be no more need of growing in it, and no more obligation to do so. Besides, there is no saint, but, as he has some grace in him, so he has some remainders of corruption too. Sin dwells in him, as well as it did in Paul (Rom. 7:17) ...

As sin dwells in the same soul, the same mind, the same will and the same affections with grace, so it mingles itself with the actions of grace: there being something of mud in the fountain, it dirties the stream ...

— Edward Veal, *Puritan Sermons*, Vol. 6, pp. 195-197 (P.S.)

More grace

... Verily I say unto you, If ye have faith, and doubt not ... (Matt. 21:21).

One common and great cause of doubting and uncertainty is the weakness and small measure of our grace. A little grace is next to none: small things are hardly discerned. He that will see a small needle, a hair, a mote, or an atom, must have clear light and good eyes; but houses, and towns, and mountains are easily discerned. Most Christians content themselves with a small measure of grace, and do not follow on to spiritual strength and manhood. They believe so weakly, and love God so little, that they can scarce find whether they believe and love at all ...

The chief remedy for such would be to continue with their duty, till their graces be increased. Ply your work; wait upon God in the use of his prescribed means, and he will undoubtedly bless you with increase and strength. O! that Christians would spend their time in getting grace which they now spend in anxious doubtings, even doubting whether they have any; it would be better if they spent their time in praying, and asking Christ for more grace, instead of bestowing complaints of their supposed grace-lessness!

I beseech you, Christian, take this advice as from God; and then, when you believe strongly, and love fervently, you cannot doubt whether you believe and love or not ... A great measure of grace is seldom doubted of.
— Richard Baxter, *A Homiletic Encyclopedia*, p. (H.E.)

Growth in grace does not always consist in doing other works of a different kind, but in doing the same works over and over again but better ...
— William Bridge

Saving faith

Who are kept by the power of God through faith unto salvation ...
(1 Pet. 1:5).

S aving faith is to cast myself and my own soul upon Christ for salvation. Whatever your faith may be, it is not come to saving faith till you do this. You may carry all your knowledge and all your faith to hell with you. Any faith that is not saving, but remains separate from it, will prove a damning faith to you. It will greatly aggravate your condemnation, that you who knew such things, assented to such truths and Gospel doctrines, should never put forth an act of saving faith for your own souls in particular, according to the import of those doctrines ... Let me tell you, the church, nor all the churches in the world, all the angels in heaven, and all the saints upon earth, cannot believe for you. You must every one believe for himself ...

How many knowing historical believers are there in hell, who have prophesied in his name, prayed in his name, have written, disputed, argued strongly for the faith, have done everything that belongs to a common faith, but could never be brought to put forth one act of saving faith upon Christ for the salvation of their own souls!

'Come unto me, all ye that labour and are heavy laden,' etc. (Matt. 11:28). Is this done, till you personally come to Christ for the pardon of your sins, and for the justification of your persons by name? John, Thomas, Mary, whatever your names are, he or she, I am sent this day to give you a particular call to come to Christ; and I do warn every one of you, and exhort everyone, to go to Christ by a personal act of your own faith for eternal life. He has purchased it for all who come unto him: if you neglect it and will not go, your blood be upon your own heads ...

— Thomas Cole, *Puritan Sermons*, Vol. 4, p. 338 (P.S.)

Naked faith

Now faith is ... the evidence of things not seen (Heb. 11:1).

Some believe the better for having seen Christ's sepulchre; and when they have seen the Red Sea, they doubt not the miracle. Now contrarily, I bless myself, and am thankful, that I don't live in the days of miracles, and that I never saw Christ nor his disciples. I would not wish to have been one of those Israelites that passed through the Red Sea, nor one of Christ's patients on whom he wrought his wonders. If such had been the case then my faith would have been forced upon me; and I would have missed that greater blessing pronounced to all that believe and see not.

'Tis an easy belief to credit what our eye and sense have examined: I believe he was dead and buried, and rose again; and I desire to see him in his glory, rather than contemplate him in his cenotaph or sepulchre.

— Sir Thomas Browne, *A Homiletic Encyclopedia*, p. 2020 (H.E.)

Will you put God to this, that either he must work constant miracles in every age, and before every man, or else he must not be believed?
— Richard Baxter

The mystery of grace

But by the grace of God I am what I am ... (1 Cor. 15:10).

*Q*uestion: Why is it that *we* repent, believe, obey; for if all grace is from Christ, and if Christ does work all our works, why is it not said, that *Christ* repents, believes, obeys?

Answer: No. You know the persons that are responsible. If I owe a man a thousand pounds, and have not a penny to pay it; and another man comes and lends me the money, and then goes along with me to the creditor. The bond is taken up, and discharge is made; but he is not said to have paid the money, but I am said to have paid it. I am the one responsible.

Similarly, you are responsible, although you have received all your strength from Christ to do it. You are the one said to repent, believe, obey. The devil is not said to commit adultery, and commit murder, yet it is by his instigation it is done. The sun works with the tree, when the tree brings forth fruit; and yet it is not said that the sun brings forth fruit. Why? Because the sun works as an universal cause, and the tree as a particular cause.

So no, though Jesus Christ does work in all our workings, yet he is not said to repent, or believe, or obey. He works as an universal cause, and you work as a particular cause. Behold here the mirror of grace: all is of Christ, and yet all is ours. All is ours in denomination, and all is Christ's in operation. All is ours in regard of encouragement, and all is Christ's in regard of glory. Here is grace! Here is the mystery of grace! But still all, whatsoever grace a man has, he has it from Jesus Christ.

— William Bridge, *A Homiletic Encyclopedia*, p. 1015 (H.E.)

What if ... ?

... give diligence to make your calling and election sure ... (2 Pet. 1:10).

There are those who never doubt God's power. They believe he can forgive them; but they fear, yes strongly conclude, that he will not pardon them, and that because they are reprobates. They are reprobates, they say, because they see no signs of election, but rather much to the contrary.

This is my answer to them. When your consciences are first wounded with a sense of God's wrath for sin, it is very likely that before you believed and repented you could not discern any signs of God's favour, only of his anger. Because at that time you were not actually in a state of grace, nor in his favour. And often after a Christian does believe, though there are always plenty of proofs of his election, yet he cannot always see it. If you are in either of these states, even supposing the worst, yet you have no reason to conclude that you are reprobates.

It is true that God before the foundation of the world, fully determined with himself, whom to choose to salvation by grace, and which he ordained; and also whom to pass by, and leave in their sins, for which he determined in his just wrath to condemn them. But who these are, is a secret, which even the elect themselves cannot know, until they are effectually called. And even when called, not until by some experience and proof of their faith and holiness will they understand the witness of the Spirit, which testifies to their spirits, that they are the children of God. This makes their calling and election, which was always sure in God, sure to themselves (2 Pet. 1:5, 10) ...

After you have done this, you may look into yourselves, and there you shall read your election written in golden and great letters.

— Henry Scudder, *The Christian's Daily Walk*, pp. 235-236 (S.P.)

On his terms

... As I live, saith the Lord God, I have no pleasure in the death of the wicked; but that the wicked turn from his way and live ... (Ezek. 33:11).

I learn conversion to be both God's work, and ours, and our children's too ...

It is *God's work*; and he promises it: 'I will put my law in their inward parts, and write it in their hearts; and will be their God, and they shall be my people' (Jer. 31:33).

It is *ours*; and he commands it. 'I have no pleasure in the death of the wicked; but that the wicked turn from his way and live.' ...

It is *his*, we say, as to its rise; he gives to will and to do. It is *ours* as to the act itself; we do it, and move, by him moved ... All I add is this: Act up to the light and power you have received, not daring to dream that conversion is not the duty of children, because it is the work of God ...

We are indeed certified from the divine oracles that God has his special people, his 'peculiar chosen ones' (Exod. 19:5). We ascribe to him, and no other, the grace that 'makes us to differ' (1 Cor. 4:7). But it also certifies, that God is not wanting regarding the happiness of any souls: unblemished goodness governs his absolute sovereignty. His decrees are as firm as though no man had the liberty of will: yet we all have a choice as truly as if there were no fore-determining decree. God suffers men to make a free choice, and gives to all men that which they finally choose. He gives not to his elect either grace or glory without their knowledge and against their consent: and he does not utterly desert or destroy others, till they harden their hearts, and choose darkness rather than life.

— Daniel Burgess, *Puritan Sermons*, Vol. 4, p. 573 (P.S.)

Core Christians

Let us hold fast the profession of our faith without wavering ...
(Heb. 10:23).

He lies to God and to the world, who makes a profession of faith, when he has none; he pretends to God and the world, who says that he has it, and does not profess it ... The glory of our Lord Jesus Christ is promoted by our professing him ... The good of others calls for this. The truth of faith is profitable to us; the profession of faith is profitable to others.

Some reckon, that their physical presence at the ordinances, and physical attendance in church services, is enough to get them the name of professors. It may do so, but this is still short of a profession of faith. Sometimes there is required and expressed assent to points of truth or doctrine that a particular church espouses; and if men pass that test, this is thought to be profession by a great many. In the meantime, the thing in my text is still omitted, and that is, the profession of a man's faith. It is not only profession to the truth of a point of doctrine he assents to, but his assent in it, that is necessary. It is mainly for the honour of Jesus Christ, that men should knit themselves visibly under his standard and banner ...

You know there are two great plagues that have distressed the church of Christ and it will never be quite free from them; a multitude of hypocrites on a fair day, and a multitude of apostates on a foul day. When it is summer weather, hypocrites increase to a multitude; when a storm comes, they are blown away as chaff by the wind. What is the way to prevent the abounding of these dreadful scandals? If we were more strict in demanding the reality of peoples' faith, then, truly they would adhere to the Lord, far more closely in a day of trial.

— Robert Traill, *The Works of Robert Traill*, Vol. 3, pp. 13, 19-20
(B.T.)

A daily faith?

And Jesus said unto them, I am the bread of life: he that cometh to me shall never hunger; and he that believeth on me shall never thirst (John 6:35).

Maintain your faith in frequent exercise, and be as conscientious regarding your daily faith as you are of your daily prayer. For we are apt to rest in a previous call to Christ, and in the original work of faith; instead of coming continually to Christ, and that as earnestly and studiously as if we have never come before.

'He that *is coming* unto me,' says Christ (John 6:35). The word in the original is a participle of the present tense. Through the neglect of this daily coming the soul is often in the dark, and seems to have lost the promise by which it was formerly drawn to Christ ... For instance: 'By faith, Abraham, when he was called,' not only unto Canaan, but unto Christ, 'obeyed'; for he looked more to the promised seed than to the promised land; else, what had his faith been? But now, in the process of time, namely, about ten years later, he begins to call the promise into question, and to make the steward of his house his heir (Gen. 15:2); till God renewed the promise, to revive thereby the actions of his sleeping faith. 'Look now toward heaven,' says God, 'and tell the stars, if thou be able to number them: and he said unto him, So shall thy seed be.' Upon this, Abraham, 'believed in the Lord; and he counted it to him for righteousness.'

Why? Did he not believe before? Yes; the apostle dates his faith from his coming out of Ur of the Chaldees (Heb. 11:8); and yet here we meet with a second date, that is, as to an eminent reviving act of his faith, as if he had omitted to believe (as indeed he did), and now began again; which was only an interruption, not an incision.

— William Hook, *Puritan Sermons*, Vol. 2, p. 684 (P.S.)

'Tis mercy all

Also unto thee, O Lord, belongeth mercy: for thou renderest to every man according to his work (Ps. 62:12).

There is scarcely any sin more natural to us than pride, and no pride worse than spiritual pride. It was the condemnation of the devil. And spiritual pride shows itself most of all in those high and over-weening thoughts that we are apt to have of our own worth and excellency. Though when we have done evil we are filled with guilt, yet, when we think that we have done well, we are tickled with conceit: one while we are conscious that we have offended God, another while we are ready to believe that we have obliged him. We can scarcely be engaged in religious work, pray with any life or warmth, listen with attention and affection, but we are at the same time ready to take our Lord's word out of his mouth, and greet ourselves with a 'Well done, good and faithful servant' (Matt. 25:23) ...

But good works are rewarded solely out of God's mercy and grace; and therefore not out of man's merit. What could be more opposite than mercy and merit? 'Not by works of righteousness which we have done, but according to his mercy he saved us' (Titus 3:5). When man's work really deserves a reward, it still cannot be said that the best works of God's children are ever rewarded with eternal blessedness ... Were God not infi-nite in mercy, the best saint upon earth would fall short of a reward in heaven ...

Men never need mercy more than when they come before God's tribu-nal; and even there, when they look for the reward of their good works, they must expect it from the mercy of the Judge.

— Edward Veal, *Puritan Sermons*, Vol. 6, pp. 183, 191 (P.S.)

Error, schism, heresy

... Hereby know we the spirit of truth, and the spirit of error (1 John 4:6).

There is a difference between error, schism, and heresy. Error is when one holds a wrong opinion alone; schism, when many consent in their opinion; heresy runs further, and contends to root out the truth. Error offends, but separates not; schism offends and separates; heresy offends, separates, and rageth ...

Error is weak, schism strong, heresy obstinate. Error goes out, and often comes in again; schism comes not in, but makes a new church; heresy makes not a new church, but no church. Error untiles the house, schism pulls down the walls, but heresy overturns the foundations. Error is as a child, schism a wild stripling, heresy an old dotard. Error will hear reason, schism will wrangle against it, heresy will defy it. Error is a member blistered, schism is a member festered, heresy a member cut off.

He that returns quickly from error, is not a schismatic; he that returns from schism, is not a heretic. Error is reproved and pitied, schism is reproved and punished, heresy is reproved and excommunicated. Schism is in the same faith, heresy makes another faith. Though they may be thus distinguished, yet without God's preventing grace, one will run into another ...

— Thomas Adams, *A Homiletic Encyclopedia*, p. 1823 (H.E.)

Not to be capable of errors is the inseparable attribute of God himself ... which cannot be said of any creature.

— John Preston

A divine tonic

... we know that all things work together for good to them that love God, to them who are the called according to his purpose (Rom. 8:28).

There are two things, which I have always looked upon as difficult. The one is to make the wicked sad; the other is to make the godly joyful. Dejection in the godly arises from a double spring; either because their inward comforts are darkened, or their outward comforts are disturbed ... I would prescribe them to take, now and then, a little of this cordial: 'All things work together for good to them that love God.' To know that nothing hurts the godly is a matter of comfort; but to be assured that *all* things which fall out shall cooperate for their good, that their crosses shall be turned into blessings, that showers of affliction water the withering root of their grace and make it flourish more; this may fill their hearts with joy till they run over ...

As axioms and aphorisms are evident to reason, so the truths of religion are evident to faith. 'We know', says the apostle. Though a Christian has not a perfect knowledge of the mysteries of the Gospel, yet he has a certain knowledge. 'We see through a glass, darkly' (1 Cor. 13:12), therefore, we have not perfection of knowledge; but we behold with 'open face' (2 Cor. 3:18), therefore we have certainty ... A Christian may know infallibly that there is an evil in sin, and a beauty in holiness. He may know that he is in the state of grace. 'We know that we have passed from death unto life' (1 John 3:14).

He may know that he shall go to heaven ... The Lord does not leave his people at uncertainties in matters of salvation. The apostles say, We know. We have arrived at a holy confidence. We have both the Spirit of God, and our own experience, setting a seal to it ...

— Thomas Watson, *A Divine Cordial*, pp. 6, 8-9 (S.G.)

NOVEMBER

The law and the gospel

... the law was our schoolmaster to bring us unto Christ ... (Gal. 3:24).

What is the difference between the moral law and the Gospel? The law requires that we worship God as our Creator; the Gospel, that we worship him in and through Christ. God in Christ is propitious; out of him we may see God's power, justice, and holiness: in him we see his mercy displayed.

The moral law requires obedience, but gives no strength (as Pharaoh required brick, but gave no straw), but the Gospel gives strength; it bestows faith on the elect; it sweetens the law; it makes us serve God with delight.

Of what use then is the moral law to us? It is a glass to show us our sins, that, seeing our pollution and misery, we may be forced to flee to Christ to satisfy for former guilt, and to save from future wrath.

But is the moral law still in force to believers? Is it not abolished to them? In some sense it is abolished to believers, in respect of justification. They are not justified by their obedience to the moral law. Believers are to make great use of the moral law, but they must trust only in Christ's righteousness for justification. Noah's dove made use of her wings to fly, but trusted only the ark for safety. If the moral law could justify, what need was there of Christ's dying?

— Thomas Watson, *The Ten Commandments*, pp. 33-34 (B.T.)

The law, though it has no power to condemn us, has power to command us.

— Thomas Adams

Either ... or

... choose you this day whom ye will serve ... (Josh 24:15).

In eternity there will be no mixture. In the other world it is all pure love, or all pure wrath; all sweet, or all bitter; without all pain, or without all ease; without all misery, or without all happiness: not partly at ease, and partly in pain; partly happy, and partly miserable; but all the one or the other.

This life is a middle place betwixt heaven and hell; and here we partake of some good and some evil. There is no judgement on this side of hell upon the worst of men but that there is some mercy mixed with it. It is mercy that they are still on this side of hell: and there is no condition on this side of heaven but that there is some evil mixed with it; for, till we get to heaven, we shall have sin in us. In heaven all are good, in hell all are bad; on earth some are good, but more are bad. In hell misery, without mixture of mercy or of hope: they have no mercy—and that is bad; and they can hope for none—and that is worse.

While they are in time, they are pitied; God pities them, and Christ pities them, and good men pity them; their friends and relations pity them; they pray for them, and weep over them: but when time is past, all pity will be past, and they remain in misery without pity to all eternity ...

Then, for the Lord's sake, and for your souls' sake, I beseech you upon my knees, if you have any dread of God, any fear of hell, any desire of heaven, any care whither you must go, take no rest night or day in time, till you have secured your everlasting happy state, that you might have everlasting rest night and day in eternity. Make sure that you might pass into that eternity where it is always day, and no night; and not into that where it shall be always night, and never day.

— Thomas Doolittle, *Puritan Sermons*, Vol. 4, pp. 35-36 (P.S.)

Judicial hardening

And if it bear fruit, well: and if not, then after that thou shalt cut it down
(Luke 13:9).

There is a difference between that hardness of heart that is incident to all men, and that which comes upon some as a special judgement of God. And although all kinds of hardness of heart may in some sense be called a judgement, yet to be hardened with this second kind, is a judgement peculiar only to them that perish, a hardness that is sent as a punishment for the abuse of light received, for a reward of apostasy.

This is a hardness that comes after some great light received, because of some great sin committed against that light, and the grace that gave it. Such hardness as Pharaoh had, after the Lord had done wondrous works before him ... A hardness that is caused by unbelief, and a departing from the living God ...

But how will this man die?

God and Christ, and pity, have left him: sin against light, against mercy, and the longsuffering of God, is come up against him. His hope and confidence is now dying by him, and his conscience totters and shakes continually within him.

Death is at work, cutting him down, hewing both bark and heart, both body and soul asunder. The man groans, but death hears him not ...

And now, could the soul be annihilated, or brought to nothing, how happy it would count itself! But it seems that may not be. Wherefore it is put in a wonderful predicament: stay in the body it may not, go out of the body it dares not.

— John Bunyan, *The Barren Fig-Tree*, pp. 68-76 (R.P.)

Public enemy

For I acknowledge my transgressions: and my sin is ever before me
(Ps. 51:3).

Meditate upon the aggravations of your sins, as they are the grand enemies of the God of your life, and of the life of your soul: in a word, they are the public enemies of all mankind ...

O, the work that sin has done in the world! This is the enemy that has brought in death; that has robbed and enslaved man, that has turned the world upside down, and sown the dissensions between man and the creatures, between man and man, yea, between man and himself, setting the physical part against the rational, the will against the judgement, lust against conscience; yea, worst of all, between God and man, making the sinner both hateful to God and the hater of God.

This is the traitor that thirsted for the blood of the Son of God, that sold him, that mocked him, that scourged him, that spat in his face, that mangled his body ... condemned him, nailed him, crucified him ...

This is the bloody executioner that has killed the prophets, burned the martyrs, murdered all the apostles, all the patriarchs, all the kings and potentates; that has destroyed cities, swallowed empires, and devoured whole nations. Whatever weapon it was done by, it was sin that caused the execution.

Do you still think it is only a small thing? If Adam and all his children could be dug out of their graves, and their bodies piled up to heaven, and an inquest was made as to what matchless murderer was guilty of all this, it would be all found in sin.

— Joseph Alleine, *A Sure Guide to Heaven*, pp. 102-103 (B.T.)

Abortive convictions

W hat makes convictions prove abortive? Wherein is the defect? 1. They are not deep enough: a sinner never saw himself lost without Christ; the seed that wants depth of earth withers. These convictions are like blossoms blown off before they come to maturity.
2. These convictions are involuntary; the sinner does what he can to stifle these convictions; he drowns them in wine and mirth; he labours to get rid of them: as the deer when it is shot, runs and shakes out the arrow, so does he that arrow of conviction. Or as the prisoner who files off his fetters, and breaks loose; so a man breaks loose from his convictions. His corruptions are stronger than his convictions.
3. Men have some kind of humiliation, and have shed tears for their sins, therefore now they hope the kingdom of grace is come into their hearts. But this is no infallible sign of grace; Saul wept, Ahab humbled himself.
— Thomas Watson, *A Homiletic Encyclopedia*, p. 1488 (H.E.)

God made you 'little lower than the angels'; 'sin has made you little better than the devils.'
— Ralph Venning

Secret atheism

The fool hath said in his heart, There is no God. They are corrupt, they have done abominable works, there is none that doeth good (Ps. 14:1).

The first cause of distraction in God's service is secret atheism. There is an atheism of the head, an atheism of the heart, and an atheism of the life. In the first, 'The fool hath said in his heart, there is no God' (Ps. 14:1). Mark, it is not, he has thought in his heart, but says it by rote to himself, rather as what he would have, than what he does believe ... It is notorious madness to conclude, from the variety and diversity of opinions about religion and government, that there is no God, seeing you are supported by him, while you dispute and argue about him.

Atheism of the heart is that whereby the fool says 'also in his heart, There is no God'; that is, either secretly questions or heartily wishes there were none at all. And it is worth observing both of these, that they are such as are obnoxious to the divine Majesty ...

Atheism of the life is to 'profess that they know God; but in works they deny him' (Titus 1:16). Now these latter originate from the first, and the last is most visible in our distractions; for if you did truly believe God present in an ordinance, as he that sits next to you, dare you trifle so egregiously as you do? The minister looks at you, and you dare not talk; if you saw him that looks at you from heaven, you would dare not wander ...

The remedy of this evil is, humbly to read the Scriptures, which is the most clear, certain, and convincing way to work faith herein. Prayer and the Bible have convinced more than any other arguments ...

— Richard Steele, *A Remedy for Wandering Thoughts*, pp. 60-63 (S.P.)

Judgement day

And as it is appointed unto men once to die, but after this the judgement (Heb. 9:27).

*T*he day of judgement is remote, *thy* day of judgement is at hand. As you go out in particular, so will you be found in the general. Your passing-bell and the archangel's trumpet have both one sound to you. In the same condition that your soul leaves your body, shall your body be found of your soul. You cannot pass from your deathbed a sinner, and appear at the great assizes a saint. Both in your private sessions, and the universal assizes, you will be sure of the same Judge, the same jury, the same witnesses, the same verdict.

How certain you are to die, you know; how soon to die, you don't know. Measure not your life with the longest; that would be flattery. You cannot name one living man, not the sickest, which you are sure will die before you. Daily we follow the dead to their graves, and in those graves we bury the remembrance of our own death with them. Here drops an old man, and there a child; here an aged matron, there a young virgin: with mourning eyes we attend their funerals, yet before we lay the flowers out of our hands, the thought of death has vanished from our hearts ... When we lose a neighbour, a friend, a brother, we weep and howl, and lament, as if, with Rachel, we could never be comforted; but once the body is interred, and the funeral ceremony ended, if we do not stay to inquire for some legacies, we run back with all possible haste to our former sins and turpitudes ...

Alas! that the farthest end of all our thoughts should be the thought of our ends!

— Thomas Adams, *A Homiletic Encyclopedia*, p. 3063 (H.E.)

Limiting God

... and limited the Holy One of Israel (Ps. 78:41).

Many are ignorant of the different ways and degrees of God's working with his people, and this darkens their knowledge considerably and diminishes their interest in him. This ignorance consists mainly of three things:

1. They are ignorant of the different degrees and ways of the law, by which God ordinarily deals with men, and of the different ways in which the Lord brings people initially to Christ. They fail to realize that the jailer is not kept an hour in bondage (Acts 16); Saul is kept in suspense three days (Acts 9); Zaccheus not one moment (Luke 19).

2. They are ignorant of, or at least they do not consider, how different are the degrees of sanctification in the saints, how in some men holiness is honourably apparent, whilst in others one only sees some very sad blemishes. Some are blameless, and free of gross outbreakings of sin, an adornment to their profession, as Job and Zacharias ... Others were subject to very gross and sad evils, as Solomon, Asa, etc.

3. They are ignorant of the different communications of God's face and the expressions of his presence. Some walk in the light of God's countenance, and are in close fellowship with him, as David was; others are all their days kept in bondage, through fear of death (Heb. 2:15). Surely ignorance of the different ways by which God works and deals with his people darkens their knowledge and interest in him. They are the ones who limit the Lord to one way of working, but he will not be confined to such ...

— William Guthrie, *The Christian's Great Interest*, pp. 13-14 (B.T.)

Nothing and something

He stretcheth out the north over the empty place, and hangeth the earth upon nothing (Job 26:7).

This creation of things from nothing speaks of an infinite power. The distance between nothing and being has always been counted so great, that nothing but an Infinite Power can make such distances meet together, that is for nothing to become being, or for being to return to nothing. To have a thing arise from nothing, was so difficult a truth to these that were ignorant of the Scriptures, that they did not know how to comprehend it. They therefore laid it down as a fixed rule, that of nothing, nothing is made. This is true, of course, of a created power, but not true of an uncreated and Almighty Power. A greater distance cannot be imagined than that which is between nothing and something; between that which has no being, and that which has; and a greater power cannot be imagined than that which brings something out of nothing.

We don't know how to conceive a nothing, and afterwards a being from that nothing; but we must remain overwhelmed with admiration for the cause that gives it being, and acknowledge it to be without any limits or boundaries of greatness and power. The further anything is from being, the more immense must be that power which brings it into being. It is not conceivable that the power of all the angels in one can give being to the smallest blade of grass. To imagine, therefore, so small a thing as a bee, a fly, a grain of corn, or an atom of dust, can be made out of nothing, would stupefy any creature who considered it. But how much more is it to behold the heavens, with all the troops of stars; the earth, with all its embroidery; and the sea, with all her inhabitants of fish; and man, the noblest creature of all, and all to have risen out of the womb of mere emptiness.

— Stephen Charnock, *The Existence and Attributes of God*,
Vol. 2, p. 38 (B.B.)

Frowns and favours

... He hath done all things well ... (Mark 7:37).

A s no man is so loaded with benefits, that he is in all respects happy; so there is none so oppressed with afflictions, that he is in every way miserable. And this mixture was made by the wise Judge of heaven and earth, to keep us balanced, and not too prone to run into extremes. And because we would be too much exalted with continual prosperity, and too much dejected if we should feel nothing but affliction, the Lord never suffers us to abound with worldly happiness, but that we have something to humble us. Neither does he plunge us in so much misery, but that we have some cause of present comfort or future hope. And like a wise father, he does not pamper us too much, which would make us wantons, nor beat us all the time, which would make us desperate. He judiciously mingles the one with the other, not letting us have our wills in all things, lest we should neglect him; nor yet always crossing us in them, lest we should hate and rebel against him. Not always indulging us, lest we should grow proud and insolent, and not always correcting us, lest we should become base and servile. God gives gifts that we may love him, and stripes that we may fear him.

Yes, often he mixes frowns with his favours, when they make us impudent, and kind speeches with his rebukes and chastisements. This in order to show in the hating of our faults he loves our persons ... This, so that he may make us ... to give reverence to him, no less to fear him in his favours, than to love him in his chastisements.

— George Downame, *A Homiletic Encyclopedia*, p. 183 (H.E.)

The smoking flax

We then that are strong ought to bear the infirmities of the weak, and not to please ourselves (Rom. 15:1).

C hrist will not quench the smoking flax. First, because this spark is from heaven, it is his own; it is kindled by his own Spirit. And secondly, it tends to glorify his powerful grace in his children, that he preserves light in the midst of darkness—a spark in the midst of the swelling waters of corruption.

There is a special blessing in that little spark ... We see how our Saviour Christ tolerated Thomas in his doubting (John 20:27); the two disciples that went to Emmaus, who staggered whether he came to redeem Israel or no (Luke 24:21). He did not quench that little light in Peter, which was smothered: Peter denied him, but he didn't deny Peter. 'If thou wilt, thou canst', said one poor man in the gospel (Matt. 8:2); 'If thou canst' said another (Mark 9:22); both were this smoking flax, neither of them were quenched.

If Christ had been concerned only with his own greatness, he would have rejected him that came with his *if*, but Christ answers *if* with a gracious and absolute grant, 'I will, be thou clean.'

The woman that was diseased with an issue did but touch, and that with a trembling hand, and even then but the hem of his garment, and yet she went away both healed and comforted ... Because the disciples slept from infirmity, being oppressed with grief, our Saviour Christ frames a comfortable excuse for them, 'The Spirit indeed is willing, but the flesh is weak' (Matt. 26:41) ...

Weak Christians are like glasses which are hurt with the least violent usage, but if gently handled will continue a long time. This honour of gentle use we are to give to the weaker vessels (1 Pet. 3:7) ...

— Richard Sibbes, *Works of Richard Sibbes*, pp. 51-53 (B.T.)

Union

Neither pray I for these alone, but for them also which shall believe on me through their word; that they all may be one; as thou, Father, art in me, and I in thee, that they also may be one in us ... (John 17:20-21).

H e (Christ) prays for union. This union is a mystery, a great depth ... It is a union of believers with God, with the Father and the Son; not an union of believers among themselves, at least not this only. For the union expressed in those first words, 'That they all may be one', is declared or illustrated in these following, 'As thou, Father, art in me, and I in thee'; and so is the same union with that in the last words, which is taken to be a union with the Father and the Son: 'That they also may be one in' or *with* 'us'.

'That they also may be one.' How? 'As thou, Father, art one in me, and I in thee' so 'they also may be one in us.'

This union has some resemblance to that between the Father and the Son. 'As' denotes not any thing of *equality*, but only something of *likeness*. That we may know what resemblance there is, we must inquire how the Father is said to be in the Son, and the Son in the Father ...

The Father and the Son are one and the same in nature and essence ... There is an essential union between the Father and Son, as he is God. No such union must be imagined between them and believers: the distance is no less than infinite; and if there can be any resemblance, it must be very remote. The most intelligible way of expressing this union ... is this: Believers are said to be 'one with the Father', because that Spirit which proceeds from him, and is called his Spirit, is in them ... They are not one *essentially* ... nor one *personally* ... nor one *morally only*, but one *spiritually* ... because one and the same Spirit is in both.

— David Clarkson, *Puritan Sermons*, Vol. 3, pp. 614-615 (P.S.)

War of the wills

For who hath known the mind of the Lord? Or who hath been his counsellor? (Rom. 11:34).

W e cannot prescribe how God should be glorified ... How have men fooled themselves and dishonoured God in the matter of worship! They invent and prescribe forms and modes, when they have no ground to believe that he will accept them. Nothing pleases God but his own will ...

We must not determine these things ourselves, as to how, when, where, whom, we please, for this would dishonour rather than credit the cause of God, because this matter wholly depends upon his pleasure. He has laid the whole platform and design in his own counsels and purposes; and in it all the several aspects of the mystery fit together, and add beauty to each other. Now any thing of our will would deform the rest, and subtract from that divine symmetry and concord which encompasses the wisdom, holiness, power, and sovereign grace of God. And we might as well teach him how he should govern the world, as how he should dispose of us. Would it be for God's honour, if we should decide when it should rain, and when shine; when there should be a storm, and when a calm? He that does not understand the whole counsel of God, cannot direct any fragment of it: 'Who hath known the mind of the Lord? Or who hath been his counsellor?' No, is it not most dishonourable that his creatures should advise him? That dust and ashes should correct his will (Isa. 45:9-10)? ...

God is not glorified but in his own way. For our wills must be resigned to and resolved into his ...

It is vain to think of honouring God, and doing our own will: give him all but his will, and we give him nothing.

— John Singleton, *Puritan Sermons*, Vol. 4, pp. 67, 71 (P.S.)

The last piece of armour

Wherefore take unto you the whole armour of God ... and the sword of the Spirit, which is the word of God (Eph. 6:13, 17).

Observe the order and place wherein this piece of armour (the sword) stands. The apostle first gives the Christian all the former pieces, and when these are put on, he then girds this sword about him. The Spirit of God, in Holy writ, I confess, is not always anxious to observe method; yet I think, it should not be unpardonable if I venture to give a hint of a double significance in the very place and order that this sword stands in.

First, it may be brought in after all the rest, to let us know how necessary the graces of God's Spirit are to our right using of the Word. Nothing is more abused than the Word. And why? Because men come to it with unsound and unsanctified hearts. The heretic quotes it to prove his false doctrine, and dares be so impudent as to cite it to appear on his behalf. But how is it possible they should father their monstrous births on the pure chaste Word of God? Surely it is because they come to the Word and converse with it, but bring not the girdle of sincerity with them, and being ungirt, are unblest ... A sword in a madman's hand, and the Word of God in some wicked man's mouth, are used much alike—to hurt only themselves and their best friends.

Second, it may be commended after all the rest, to let us know that the Christian, when advanced to the highest attainments of grace possible in this life, is not above the use of the Word; no, he cannot be safe without it ... It is not only of use to make a Christian by conversion, but to make him perfect also. It is like the architect's rule and line—as necessary to lay the top-stone of the building at the end of his life as the foundation of his conversion.

— William Gurnall, *The Christian in Complete Armour*,
Vol. 2, pp. 195-196 (B.T.)

Death's younger brother

But I would not have you to be ignorant, brethren, concerning them which are asleep ... (1 Thess. 4:13).

W hat a great word of comfort, namely, that our gracious relations, over whose departure we stand mourning and weeping, are but fallen asleep ... We may say of departed saints, as our Saviour said concerning the damsel in Matthew 9:24, they are not dead, but sleep. The same phrase is also used to his disciples concerning Lazarus: 'Our friend Lazarus sleepeth' (John 11:11).

That which we call death is not death to the saints of God; it is but the image of death, the shadow and metaphor of death, death's younger brother, a mere sleep, and no more.

There are two main properties of death which carry in them a lively resemblance of sleep. The first is that sleep is nothing else but the binding up of sense for a little time; locking up the doors, and shutting the windows of the body for a season. Nature then takes a sweet rest and repose, freed from all disturbance and distractions. Sleep is mere parenthesis to the labours and travails of this present life.

Secondly, sleep is but a partial privation, a privation of the act only, not the habit of reason. They that sleep in the night, awaken again in the morning, and the soul returns to the discharge of all her offices ... So shall the saints of God do: their heaviness may endure for a night (the night of mortality), but joy cometh in the morning. In the morning of the resurrection they shall awake again.

— Thomas Case, 'Mount Pisgah', *The Select Works of Thomas Case*,
pp. 2-3 (S.D.G.)

Constant complainers

And the Lord saith unto Joshua, Get thee up; wherefore liest thou upon thy face? (Josh 7:10).

Fruitless and heartless complaints, bemoaning themselves and their condition, is the substance of the profession that some make ... I have known some who have spent a good part of their time in going up and down, from one to another, with their difficulties and complaints ...

Others act the same way in their thoughts, though they make no outward complaints. They are conversant, for the most part, with a heartless despondency; and in some cases these are compounded by their natural constitution, or bodily infirmity. Examples of this kind occur to us every day. Now what is the advantage of these things? ...

How did David rouse himself when he found his mind inclined to such a frame? For having said, 'Why hast thou forgotten me? Why go I mourning because of the oppression of the enemy?' David quickly rebukes himself, saying, 'Why art thou cast down, O my soul? And why art thou disquieted within me? Hope thou in God' (Ps. 42:9, 11).

We must say then, to such heartless complainers, as God did to Joshua, 'Get thee up, wherefore liest thou upon thy face?' Do you think you mend your condition by merely wishing it better, or complaining that it is so bad? ...

What is it the Scriptures call for in your condition? Is it not industry and activity of spirit? ... Our Saviour tells us that 'the kingdom of heaven suffereth violence, and the violent take it by force' (Matt. 11:12). Our Saviour is not referring to the outward violence of its enemies seeking to destroy it, but to the spiritual fervency and alertness of mind that is in those who intend to be partakers of it ...

— John Owen, *The Forgiveness of Sins*, pp. 306-309 (B.B.)

Lord, direct the arrow

Brethren, my heart's desire and prayer to God for Israel is, that they might be saved (Rom. 10:1).

The physician is most concerned for those patients whose case is most doubtful and hazardous; and the father's pity is especially turned toward his dying child. So unconverted souls call for earnest compassion and prompt diligence to pluck them as brands from the burning (Jude 23). Therefore it is to them I shall first apply myself ...

But from where shall I get my argument? With what shall I win them? O that I could tell! I would write to them in tears, I would weep out every argument, I would empty my veins for ink, I would petition them on my knees. O how thankful should I be if I could prevail with them to repent and turn ...

But, O Lord, how insufficient I am for this work. Alas, with what shall I pierce the scales of Leviathan, or make the heart feel that is hard like the nether millstone? Shall I go and speak to the grave, and expect the dead will obey me and come forth? Shall I make an oration to the rocks, or declamation to the mountains, and think to move them with arguments? ... But, O Lord, Thou canst pierce the heart of the sinner. I can only draw the bow at a venture, but thou canst direct the arrow between the joints of the harness. Slay the sin, and save the soul of the sinner that casts his eyes on these pages.

There is no entering into heaven but by the straight passage of the second birth; without holiness you shall never see God (Matt. 7:14). Therefore give yourselves to the Lord now. Set yourselves to seek him now. Set up the Lord Jesus in your hearts, and set him up in your houses ...

— Joseph Alleine, *An Alarm to the Unconverted*, pp. 1-2 (B.T.)

I can never hit the target!

I press toward the mark ... (Phil. 3:14).

I s any man able to do that which God requires? If not, why then does God command us that which we cannot perform?

Herein Almighty God deals with us, as a father deals with his children. If a man has a son seven years of age, he will furnish him with bow and arrows, and lead him into the fields. He sets him to shoot at a mark that is twelve score paces off promising to give him some good thing if he hits the mark. And though the father knows that the child cannot shoot that far, yet he will have him aim at a mark beyond his reach, in order to try the strength and eagerness of the child. And though he shoots short, yet the father will encourage him.

In the same way Almighty God has furnished us with judgement and reason, as it were with certain artillery, whereby we are able to distinguish between good and evil, and sent us into this world—as into the open fields and sets his law before us a mark, as David speaks, promising to give us the kingdom of heaven, if we hit the same. And all the time he knows that we cannot hit this mark, that is, keep the law which he has set before us. Yet for the exercise of our faith, and for the testing of our duty and obedience to him, he will always have us to aim at it. And although we come short of that duty and obedience which he requires at our hands, yet he will accept and reward our good endeavour.

— Henry Smith, *A Homiletic Encyclopedia*, p. 3186 (H.E.)

19 NOVEMBER

Two questions to clip the wings

But if ye will not hear it, my soul shall weep in secret places for your pride ... (Jer. 13:17).

A Christian, if he has not a care, may be proud of his very humility. It is hard starving this sin, because it can live on almost nothing ... Be much in meditation on death and judgement. A serious and frequent meditation on death will be a means to kill pride. Ask yourself: What is man, but a little living lump of clay? And what is his life, but 'a vapour, that appeareth for a little time, and then vanisheth away?' Augustine doubted whether to call it 'a dying life, or a living death.' ...

Now you differ, it may be, from other men, and are superior to them in riches and greatness, in parts and privileges; but two questions may clip your wings ...

Who made you to differ? I suppose, none of you will say (as one once did) that you made yourselves to differ: you will confess, I hope, that you have nothing but what you have received; and so there is no room for pride or glorying. If you excel in any gift or grace, you must say of it, as he of his hatchet, 'Alas, master! For it was borrowed' (2 Kings 6:5).

How long will there be this difference? Death is at hand; it stands at the door; and that will level you with those that are the lowest. In the grave, whither we are all hastening, there is no difference of skulls; there the rich and the poor, the learned and the unlearned, all meet together (Prov. 2:22).

— Richard Mayo, *Puritan Sermons*, Vol. 3, pp. 387-388 (P.S.)

Lord, be pleased to shake my clay cottage before thou throwest it down. Make it totter a while before it tumbles. Let me be summoned before I am surprised.

— Thomas Fuller

Worse than heathens

But I say unto you, It shall be more tolerable for Tyre and Sidon at the day of judgement, than for you (Matt. 11:22).

I question whether there ever was, or can be in the world, an uninterrupted and internal denial of the being of God, or that men (unless we can suppose conscience utterly dead) can arrive at such a degree of impiety; for before they can stifle such sentiments within them they must be utter strangers to the common conceptions of reason, and deprive themselves of their humanity ...

Are they not worse than heathens? They worshipped many gods, these none; they preserved a notion of God under a disguise of images, these would banish him from both earth and heaven, and demolish the statues of him in their own consciences. They degraded him, these would destroy him. They coupled creatures with him (Rom. 1:25), 'Who worshipped the creature with the Creator' (as it may quite correctly be rendered)—and these would make him worse than the creature, a mere nothing.

Earth in this way becomes worse than hell. Atheism is a persuasion which finds no footing anywhere else. Hell, that receives such persons, in this point reforms them: they can never deny or doubt his being, while they feel his strokes ... Atheism is point blank against all the glory of God in creation, and against all the glory of God in redemption, and pronounces in one breath, both the Creator, and all acts of religion and divine institutions, useless and insignificant.

— Stephen Charnock, *The Evidence and Attributes of God*,
Vol. 1, p. 80 (B.B.)

Strange apparel

And it shall come to pass in the day of the Lord's sacrifice, that I will punish the princes, and the king's children, and all such as are clothed with strange apparel (Zeph. 1:8).

The crime: to be 'clothed with strange apparel.' The Septuagint renders it as 'exotic and foreign apparel'. Such come from afar, and very dear in price, but they will pay much dearer in their punishment, when justice calls them to account ...

The strange apparel (whether native or foreign) may apply to the material, or to the cut. Shallow minds, constant in nothing but inconstancy, are always altering either the stuff or the shape, the style or the trimming. It would be as easy to make a coat for the moon, as to fit the fickle humour of that unstable generation.

The punishment ... is indefinitely expressed: 'I will punish': but how, or in what way, degree, or measure he will punish, he reserves to himself ...

We should keep our distance from the strange fashions of apparel which are worn in the days we live! Here are some guidelines:

♦ Charity supplies us with one safe rule—that we impose a more severe law upon ourselves, and allow a larger indulgence to others ...

♦ In dubious cases we should take the safer side; we ought not to venture too near the brink of a precipice, when we have room enough to walk secure at a greater distance.

♦ A humble heart, crucified to the world, and conscientiously keeping its baptismal covenant, to renounce the pomps and vanities of a wicked world ... will be the best course.

— Vincent Alsop, *Puritan Sermons*, Vol. 3, pp. 488-491 (P.S.)

A tale of two cities

And thou, Capernaum, which art exalted unto heaven, shalt be brought down to hell: for if the mighty works, which have been done in thee, had been done in Sodom, it would have remained until this day (Matt. 11:23).

Capernaum and Sodom. Both were sinful cities, but their sins were of a distinct kind ... The sins of Sodom were sins against the law more directly, and against the light of nature, and of the highest scandal. Capernaum's sins were more against the new light of the Gospel, breaking forth upon them from Christ's ministry, and the mighty works whereby his doctrine was confirmed among them.

Now Christ, considering both these cities, and the sin of both, gives the decision: 'That it shall be more tolerable in that day for Sodom, than for that city.'

Does this not seem strange and amazing? Sodom was a city that was wicked to a prodigy and to a proverb. It is said, that 'the men of Sodom were wicked and sinners before the Lord exceedingly' (Gen. 13:13) ... Yet notwithstanding all this, it will be more tolerable for Sodom than Capernaum in the day of judgement.

Capernaum was 'lifted up to heaven' by many favours and privileges ... Christ himself, the Son of God, had been present in Capernaum, preaching, and doing many wonderful works in it, which Sodom never had ... After all this, Capernaum did not receive him nor his doctrine, but 'murmured' at both, and turned not to God with true repentance, this was the sin of that city ...

The worst of the heathen, who never had Christ preached to them, and salvation offered by him, shall fare better in the day of judgement, than those that continue impenitent under the Gospel. A tremendous doctrine.

— Matthew Barker, *Puritan Sermons*, Vol. 4, pp. 201-202 (P.S.)

The old paths

Thus saith the Lord, Stand ye in the ways, and see, and ask for the old paths, where is the good way, and walk therein, and ye shall find rest for your souls ... (Jer. 6:16).

All men in this world, having for their constituent parts a mortal body and an immortal soul, are passing out of this life into another: out of this, because of the mortality of the body; into another, because of the immortality of the soul. And all, both good and bad, are daily and hourly travelling to an everlasting and unchangeable state; whose bodies shall be quickly turned into lifeless dust, and their souls enter into heaven or hell, and be with God or devil, in joy or torment, when they come to their journey's end: and according to the way they now walk in, so it will be with them forever ...

The duties that are enjoined:

1. To ask and inquire after the right way that leads to rest and happiness ... It is 'the old way'. Seek not new paths to heaven: keep in the old way, that all the millions of saints, now happy in the enjoyment of their God, went in. If you would get to the place where they are, you must go the same way they did ...

It is 'the good way', as well as 'old'. For though goodness was before wickedness, yet every way that is old is not good ... See that your way be the good and the old way.

2. To walk in this way both old and good, when you have found it. For if man has the most exact knowledge of his way, and shall sit down or stand still, and not walk in it, he will never come to the place (which) that way leads unto. The way is pointed out by God himself to you: get up, then; arise, and walk therein; and that with hastened speed. Your way is to a long eternity; the night of death is coming upon you: be daily jogging on; do not loiter in your way. Time goes on; therefore so do you.

— Thomas Doolittle, *Puritan Sermons*, Vol. 6, pp. 560-561 (P.S.)

False peace

They have healed also the hurt of the daughter of my people slightly, saying, Peace, peace; when there is no peace (Jer. 6:14).

Some think that because God made them, surely he will not damn them. This is true, if they had continued good, as he made them. God made the devil good, yes an excellent creature, yet we know how that he shall be damned (Matt. 25:41). If God spared not his holy angels (Jude 6), after they became sinful, shall man think that God will spare him? A sinful man shall be judged at the last day, not according to what he was by God's first making; but as he shall be found defiled and corrupted by the devil, and by his own lusts ...

Some say their afflictions have been so many, so great, and so lasting, that they hope they have had their hell in this life; and so they have lulled their hearts to be quiet in respect of any fear of wrath at the last day.

I would ask such, whether they, being thus afflicted, have returned to the God who smote them (Isa. 9:13), and whether their afflictions have made them better, or whether, like Solomon's fool grinded in a mortar (Prov. 27:22), their sin and folly is still not departed from them? ...

There are many who compare their sins with the notorious sins of God's people committed before their conversion, and with the gross sins of Noah, Abraham, Lot, Peter, and other godly men, after conversion. They hence conclude, that since such are saved, they can entertain a good opinion of themselves, and hope they shall be saved ...

It is not safe to follow even the best men in all their actions, for in many things they all sin (Jam. 3:2), not only before, but after conversion.

— Henry Scudder, *The Christian's Daily Walk*, pp. 207-210 (S.P.)

The worms are in it

Yea, they despised the pleasant land, they believed not his word: But murmured in their tents ... (Ps. 106:24-25).

D iscontent and murmuring eats out the good and sweetness of a mercy before it comes ... Discontent is like a worm that eats the meat out of a nut, and then when the meat is eaten out of it, you have just the shell. If a child were to cry for a nut of which the meat has been eaten out, and is all worm-eaten, what good would the nut be to the child? So you would desire to have a certain outward comfort and you are troubled for the want of it, but the very trouble of your spirits is the worm that eats the blessing out of the mercy. Then perhaps God will give it to you, but with a curse mixed with it, so that you would be better if you never had it.

If a man or woman is discontented for want of some good thing, and God gives them that very thing before they are first humbled for their discontent, it will be no comfort to them, and more evil than a good to them ...

There are many things which you desire ... and think you would be happy if you had them, yet when they come you do not find such happiness in them. Instead they prove to be the greatest crosses and afflictions that you ever had. The reason was that your hearts were immoderately set upon them before you had them ...

Someone observes concerning manna, 'When the people were contented with the allowance that God allowed them, then it was very good, but when they were not content with God's allowance, but gathered more than God would have them, then, says the text, there were worms in it.'

— Jeremiah Burroughs, *Rare Jewel of Christian Contentment*,
pp. 67-68 (S.G.)

Trumpets of praise

Give us this day our daily bread (Matt. 6:11).

W hy is it called 'our bread', when it is not ours, but God's? We must understand it in a qualified sense; it is our bread, being gotten by honest industry. There are two sorts of bread that cannot properly be called our bread: the bread of idleness and the bread of violence.

God is the giver; he gives daily bread; he gives riches.

We often ascribe praise to second causes and forget God. If friends have bequeathed an estate, we look at them and admire them, but not God who is the great giver; as if one should be thankful to the steward, and never take notice of the master of the family that provides it all. Oh, if God gives all—our eyesight, our food, our clothing—let us sacrifice the chief praise to him; let not God be a loser by his mercies. Praise is a most illustrious part of God's worship. Our wants may send us to pray, nature may make us beg for daily bread; but a heart full of gratitude and grace renders praises to God. In petition we act like men, in praise we act like angels ...

God gives us daily bread, let us give him daily praise. Thankfulness to our donor is the best policy; there is nothing lost by it. To be thankful for one mercy is the way to have more ... God gives us an estate, and we honour the lord with our substance (Prov. 3:9) ... That we may be thankful, let us be humble. Pride stops the current of gratitude. A proud man will never be thankful; he looks upon all he has either to be of his own procuring or deserving. Let us see that all we have is God's gift, and how unworthy we are to receive the least favour; and this will make us much in doxology and gratitude; we shall be silver trumpets sounding forth God's praise.

— Thomas Watson, *The Lord's Prayer*, pp. 143-147 (B.T.)

Thanksgiving

And Jesus answering said, Were there not ten cleansed? But where are the nine? (Luke 17:17).

Ten lepers are here met. Those that are excluded from all other society seek the company of each other. Fellowship is what we all naturally need, even in leprosy; even lepers will flock to their fellows. Where will you find one spiritual leper alone? Drunkards, profane persons, heretics, will be sure to consort with their matches. Why should not God's saints delight in a holy communion? ...

The miracle, indifferently wrought upon all, is differently taken. All went forward according to the appointment, towards the priests; all were obedient; one only was thankful. All were cured; all saw themselves cured; their senses were alike; their hearts were not alike. What could make the difference but grace? And who could make the difference of grace, but he that gave it? He that wrought the cure in all, wrought the grace not in all, but in one ... We all pray, all hear; one goes away better, another criticises. The will makes the difference; but who makes the difference of wills, but he that made them? ... 'It is not of him that willeth, nor of him that runneth, but of God that sheweth mercy' ...

This one man breaks away from his fellows to seek Christ. While he was a leper he consorted with lepers: now that he is healed, he will be free ...

Full well did Jesus count the steps of those absent lepers: he knew where they were; he reproves their ingratitude, that they were not where they should have been.

— Stephen Charnock, *The Ten Lepers*, pp. 503-507 (B.B.)

And obey

Let every soul be subject unto the higher powers ... (Rom. 13:1).

The holy apostle Paul ... announces his precept; from which it appears that Christ is no enemy to Caesar, and the principles of the Christian religion are not inconsistent with those of loyalty. The best Christians will be found to be the best subjects. There are none so true to their prince as those that are most faithful to their God For what says our apostle? 'Let every soul be subject unto the highest powers.'

Every man, woman and child, that is capable of understanding what subjection means, be he of what rank or station he will, high or low, noble or base, rich or poor, of the clergy or of the laity (as some love to speak), let him be subject, not above, not 'exalt himself over that which is called God', but 'be subject unto the higher powers'. Who are they? The civil magistrates, kings ... and 'all that are in authority' (1 Tim. 2:2). These we are to pray for; to these we ought to be subject; to these we must pay tribute; these we must honour, support, and assist; these we are bound to obey ...

The end of their office ... is singularly good and greatly necessary, being designed for ... the preventing of vice, and the promoting of virtue.

— Samuel Slater, *Puritan Sermons*, Vol. 4, pp. 482-483 (P.S.)

He that seems righteous toward men, and is irreligious toward God, is but an honest heathen; and he that seems religious toward God, and is unrighteous toward men, is but a fake Christian.

— George Swinnock

Fit and meet

Giving thanks unto the Father, which hath made us meet to be partakers of the inheritance of the saints in the light (Col. 1:12).

Though by faith we are entitled to that inheritance, because we are the children of God by faith in Jesus Christ (Gal. 3:26), 'and if children, then heirs' (Rom. 8:17); yet, over and above our title to it, there is required in us a suitableness to and fitness for it. The father of the prodigal first embraces and kisses his poor returning son, and then puts the robe upon him, the ring on his hand, and shoes on his feet. He first pardons him, and then adorns him, and at last brings him into his house and feasts him. He fits him for his entertainment before he brings him to it (Luke 15:20-24). God pardoning a sinner is one thing, God fully saving him is another; his receiving him into favour, and receiving him into heaven; his giving him a right to the inheritance, and giving him the actual possession of it. The first is done in a sinner's justification, the other in his final salvation. Between these two, however, comes a third, which is God's working in him a fitness and meetness for that salvation ...

Indeed, if we look into it, we shall find that there is not only a congruity that they who are to be made happy should first be made holy ... but a necessity too, in that unholy souls have no capacity for true happiness. Mere natural hearts are not suited to a supernatural good. Heavenly enjoyments are above the reach of sensual creatures ... Now grace or holiness in the heart is that very temper I speak of, which makes a man capable of and fit for glory—a supernatural principle for a supernatural happiness.

— Edward Veal, *Puritan Sermons*, Vol. 6, pp. 214-215 (P.S.)

A traitor's end

I have nourished and brought up children, and they have rebelled against me (Isa. 1:2).

The same God that raised enmity to David from his own loins, procured him favour from foreigners. Strangers relieved him, whom his own son persecuted. Here is not a loss, but an exchange of love ...

He [David] that formerly was forced to employ his arms for his defence against a tyrannous father-in-law, must now buckle them on against an unnatural son. Now, therefore, he musters his men, delegates his commanders, and marshals his troops; and since their loyal importunity will not allow the hazard of his person, he at once encourages them by his eye, and restrains them with his tongue: 'Deal gently with the young man Absolom for my sake.' How unreasonably favourable are the wars of a father! ... Deal gently with a traitor! But of all traitors a son! And of all sons an Absalom, the graceless darling of so good a father! ...

David was not sure of his success: there was great inequality in the number. Absalom's forces were more than double those of David. It might have come to a contrary result, and David would have been forced to say, 'Deal gently with the father of Absalom.' ...

Let no man think he'll prosper by rebellion: the very thickets, and stakes, and pits, and wild beats of the wood, shall conspire to the punishment of traitors. Read on and see how a fatal oak has singled out the ringleader of this hateful insurrection, and will at once serve for his hangman and gallows ... as if God meant to prescribe this punishment for traitors: Absalom, Ahithophel, and Judas, died all one death ...

— Joseph Hall, *Contemplations*, pp. 236-237 (T.N.)

DECEMBER

The benediction

The grace of the Lord Jesus Christ, and the love of God, and the communion of the Holy Ghost, be with you all ... (2 Cor. 13:14).

The apostle tells us: 'There are three that bear record in heaven, the Father, the Word, and the Holy Ghost' (1 John 5:7). In heaven they are to bear witness to us ... Now this is done distinctly. The Father bears witness, the Son bears witness, and the Holy Spirit bears witness; for they are three distinct witnesses. So then are we to receive their respective testimonies: and in doing so we have communion with them individually; for in this *giving* and *receiving* of testimony consists no small part of our fellowship with God ...

Since there is such a distinct communication of grace from the respective persons of the Deity, the saints need to have distinct communion with them.

It remains only to intimate, in a word, *wherein this distinction* lies, and what is the ground of it. Now, this is that the Father does it by way of *original authority*; the Son by way of communicating from a *purchased treasury*; the Holy Spirit by way of *immediate efficacy*.

The Father communicates all grace by way of *original authority*: ' ... the Father raiseth up the dead, and quickeneth them ... ' (John 5:21) ... The Son, by way of making out a *purchased treasury*: 'Of his fullness have all we received, and grace for grace' (John 1:16) ... The Spirit does it by way of *immediate efficacy*: 'But if the Spirit of him that raised up Jesus from the dead dwell in you, he that raised up Christ from the dead shall also quicken your mortal bodies by his Spirit that dwelleth in you' (Rom. 8:11). Here are all three comprised, with their distinct concurrence for our quickening.

— John Owen, *Communion With God*, pp. 10, 16-17 (A.P.)

The eternal God

The eternal God is thy refuge, and underneath are the everlasting arms ... (Deut. 33:27).

*S*ome things have both beginning and end: as beasts and other corruptible creatures. And their duration is *time*, which has both beginning and end.

Some things have a beginning and no end: as angels and the souls of men, and the state of both in the other world ... Though by the absolute power of God there might be a period put into their being once begun, yet there is no principle of corruption in their own nature which should cause a cessation of their existing essence; nor is it in the power of any created power or second cause to take that being from them, which was given to them by the first cause. And these things, because they have no end, are eternal.

Only one being has neither beginning nor end, nor can have: and that is God. And his duration is eternity ... 'Eternity' in the most proper acceptance of the term excludes not only actual beginning and end, but all possibility of both ...

If you look backward, you cannot think of any one moment when God was not; if you look forward, you cannot think of any one moment when God shall not be. For if there had been one moment when God was not, nothing could ever have been—neither God nor creature: unless that which is nothing could make itself something; which is an impossibility, because working supposes being; and a contradiction, because it infers the being of a thing before it was; for, in the order of time or nature, the cause must be before the effect. Neither can you conceive of any one moment beyond which God should cease to be; because you cannot imagine anything in God, or distinct from him, that should be the cause of his ceasing to be.

— Thomas Doolittle, *Puritan Sermons*, Vol. 4, p. 5 (P.S.)

353

The faithful Creator

... let them that suffer according to the will of God commit the keeping of their souls to him in well doing, as unto a faithful Creator (1 Pet. 4:19).

*K*ing is a great title, and God is sometimes called a King; but he is not set forth by this title here, but by the title of Creator ...

Father is a sweet title, a title that carries an intimation of a great deal of love and compassion ... but a father, a compassionate father, cannot always help, succour, or relieve his children ... O, but a Creator can!

A Creator! Nothing can die under a Creator's hands. A Creator can sustain all. A Creator can, as a Creator, do what he pleases ...

The cause of God, for which his people suffer, would have been dead and buried a thousand years ago, had it not been in the hand of a Creator. The people that have stood by his cause, would have been out of the world both as to persons, name, and remembrance, had they not been in the hand of a Creator ...

Who could have thought that the three children could have lived in a fiery furnace; that Daniel could have been safe among the lions; that Jonah could have come home to his country ... or that our Lord should have risen again from the dead? But what is impossible to a Creator?

This, therefore, is a rare consideration for those that suffer according to the will of God ... They have a *Creator* to maintain and uphold their cause, a *Creator* to oppose their opposers ... A Creator can not only support a dying cause, but also *fainting spirits*. For as he fainteth not, nor is weary; so 'He giveth power to the faint ... ' (Isa. 40:29).

— John Bunyan, *Advice to Sufferers*, pp. 102-104 (A.B.P.)

The younger, the better

Rejoice, O young man, in thy youth; and let thy heart cheer thee in the days of thy youth, and walk in the ways of thine heart, and in the sight of thine eyes: but know thou, that for all these things God will bring thee into judgement (Eccl. 11:9).

Your greatest danger is of delaying your conversion ... Why does God require you to convert in your youth, before you are old? And just now, before you are a minute older? Death stands before old men's faces; and one would think they should not venture to put it off. It is somewhat farther out of your sight, indeed; but so swiftly it often comes, that it is a matter of wonder that you yourselves should be so daring as to do it. But, alas! Both of you are daily seen full of delays.

Full often in my pulpit I think, 'What number should I convert this time? My old folk think they may as well convert next week, and my young ones think they may convert next year! Both think they may convert another time.' And what says my trembling heart? Plainly thus: 'O delay, delay! thou bond of iniquity, thou bane of piety, thou bar of conversion, Satan's great barge into "the lake of fire and brimstone!" begone, and destroy not this congregation!'

Sirs, remember it; downright denial of conversion is nothing near so likely to ruin you as deferring and delaying it. Delay is the element of unregeneracy, as unregeneracy is the element of hell ...

Sirs, your young days are but days, and of short continuance; yes, and dubious. Some are old, as we speak, sooner than others. Their flowers sooner fade, and their grass more quickly withers. But whenever your evening falls, you shall wish it again to be morning with you. If nothing else will do it, old age will convince you of the excellence of youth.

— Henry Hurst, *Puritan Sermons*, Vol. 4, pp. 576-578 (P.S.)

Answering a fool according to ...

Having predestinated us unto the adoption of children by Jesus Christ to himself, according to the good pleasure of his will (Eph. 1:5).

A temptation which Satan inserts into the minds of carnal men is something like this: God's decree of predestination is as unchangeable as himself; therefore, if you are elected of God, you may go on in your sins, for you will certainly be saved, and he will give you repentance, although it may be deferred to your last gasp. But if you have been rejected of God in his eternal counsel, then do whatever you will, it is all in vain, for those whom he has reprobated shall be condemned. Therefore, it is much better to take your pleasure now in this life, for the punishments of the life to come will be enough in themselves without adding the torments of this life to them.

If we consider this temptation correctly, it is foolish and false. *Foolish*, as if a man should say: Your time is appointed ... If, therefore, it has been ordained that your time shall be short, use whatever vitamins and diet you will, you will not prolong your life one day. But if God has decreed that you shall live to old age, take any risks you like, run into any danger, overindulge at every meal, be a glutton—or eat nothing at all—and you will still live to be an old man ...

Now, who would not laugh at such absurd reasoning. Every man knows that just as God has decreed the length of our life, he has also decreed that we should use the means by which our lives can be preserved that long ... avoiding dangers, a good diet, medicine and exercise ...

For those whom God has elected, he has also ordained, that they should attain it, and use all the good means necessary ... For the ends and the means are inseparably joined in God's decree.

— George Downame, *A Homiletic Encyclopedia*, p. 1780 (H.E.)

A kingdom within

... the kingdom of God is within you (Luke 17:21).

When grace comes, there is a kingly government set up in the soul. Grace rules the will and affections, and brings the whole man into subjection to Christ; it kings it in the soul, sways the sceptre, subdues mutinous lusts, and keeps the soul in a spiritual decorum ...

Till the kingdom of grace comes, we have no right to the covenant of grace. The covenant of grace is sweetened with love, adorned with promises; it is our magna carta, by virtue of which God comes to be our God. Who are the heirs of the covenant of grace? Only such as have the kingdom of grace in their hearts. 'A new heart also will I give you, and a new spirit will I put within you' (Ezek. 36:26).

Unless the kingdom of grace is set up in our hearts, our purest offerings are defiled. They may be good as to their matter, but not as to their manner; they want that which should cultivate and sweeten them. Under the law, if a man who was unclean by a dead body, carried a piece of holy flesh in his lower garment, the holy flesh could not cleanse him, but he polluted it (Hag. 2:12-13). Till the kingdom of grace is in our hearts, ordinances will not purify us, but we will pollute them. Even the prayer of an ungracious person becomes sin (Prov. 15:8). In what a sad condition is a man before God's kingdom of grace is set up in his heart! Whether he comes or comes not to the ordinance, he sins. If he does not come to the ordinance, he is a condemner of it; if he does come, he is a polluter of it. A sinner's works are *opera mortua*, dead works which are dead cannot please God. A dead flower has no sweetness.

— Thomas Watson, *The Lord's Prayer*, pp. 45-46 (B.T.)

The two 'calls'

... The hour is coming, and now is, when the dead shall hear the voice of the Son of God: and they that hear shall live (John 5:25).

God's call sometimes is ineffectual, and sometimes effectual. So the same apostle plainly declares in 1 Thessalonians 2:13: 'For this cause also thank we God without ceasing, because, when ye received the word of God which ye heard of us, ye received it not as the word of men, but as it is in truth, the word of God, which effectually worketh also in you that believe.' Observe that it is the work of God's Spirit in the heart, superadded to the Word of the Gospel, as spoken by men, that makes any call effectual. Without this inward work, God may call, and the soul will never answer ...

It is this effectual work of God's Spirit, in regenerating the soul by infusing of habits of grace, which distinguishes an internal effectual call of God from a mere external and ineffectual one ... The text makes sure that it might be known whether or not God has so called you by his Word, as that also he has worked in you by his Spirit; whether God has illuminated your understanding, and inclined your will, so that you have complied with God's will, and have answered his call. Whether, when God drew you, you ran after him (Canticles 1:4); whether, when God entreated and persuaded you to be reconciled to him you consented (2 Cor. 5:20); whether, when he wooed you, he also won you; whether, when he invited you to the wedding supper of his Son, you made no excuse or delay, but accepted and welcomed the offer of the Gospel with faith and love (Luke 14:18). All which if you did do, it arose from the power of an inward call, being superadded to the outward call of the word ...

— Richard Fairclough, *Puritan Sermons*, Vol. 6, pp. 377-378 (P.S.)

Joy

Let them shout for joy, and be glad ... (Ps. 35:27).

I desire the dejected Christian to consider, that by his heavy and uncomfortable life, he seems to the world to accuse God and his service. He seems as if he had openly called him a rigorous, hard, unacceptable Master, and his work a sad, unpleasant thing. I know this is not your thought: I know it is yourselves, and not God and his service, that offends you. You walk heavily not because you are holy, but because you fear you are not holy, and because you are not more holy. I know it is not of grace, but for grace that you complain.

Don't you give too great an occasion for ignorant spectators to judge otherwise? If you see a servant always sad, that used to be merry when he served another master, will you not think that he has now a master that displeases him? If you see a woman live in continual oppressiveness ever since she was married, that used to live merrily before, will you not think that she has made an unpleasing match?

You are born and new born for God's honour; and will you thus dishonour him before the world? What do you (in their eyes) but disparage him by your very countenance and carriage, while you walk before him in so much oppressiveness? The child that still cries when you put on his shoes signifies that they pinch him, and he disparages his meat when he makes a sour face at it, and he disparages his friend when he is always sad and troubled in his company. He that says of God, 'Thou art bad, or cruel, and unmerciful', blasphemes. And so does he who says of holiness, 'It is a bad, unpleasant, hurtful state.' How then dare you do that which is so like to blasphemy, when you should be abstaining from all appearance of evil?

— Richard Baxter, *A Homiletic Encyclopedia*, p. 3038 (H.E.)

Read the records

But let a man examine himself ... (1 Cor. 11:28).

Till men are weary and heavy laden, and pricked at the heart, and quite sick of sin, they will not come to Christ for cure, nor sincerely enquire, 'What shall we do?' They must see themselves as dead men, before they will come to Christ that they may live. Labour, therefore, to set all your sins in order before you; do not be afraid to look upon them, but let your spirit make diligent search. Enquire into your heart, and into your life; enter into a thorough examination of yourself and all your ways, that you may make a full discovery; and call in ... the help of God's Spirit, out of a sense of your own inability to do this by yourself ... It is his proper work to convince of sin ...

Meditate on the number of your sins. David's heart failed when he thought of this, and considered that he had more sins than the hairs on his head. This made him cry out for the multitude of God's tender mercies. The loathsome carcass does not more hatefully swarm with crawling maggots, than an unsanctified soul with filthy lusts. Look backward; where was ever the place, what was ever the time, in which you did not sin? Look inward; what part or power can you find in your soul or body which is not poisoned with sin ...

O how great is the sum of your debts, who have been all your life running upon trust, and never did or can pay off one penny! ... Call to mind your omissions and commissions; the sins of your thoughts, words, and actions; the sins of your youth, and the sins of your riper years. Do not be like a desperate bankrupt that is afraid to look over his books. Read the records of conscience carefully. These books must be opened sooner or later.

— Joseph Alleine, *An Alarm to the Unconverted*, pp. 71-72 (B.T.)

The delights of the soul

... whatsoever ye do, do all to the glory of God (1 Cor. 10:31).

A man when he is weary may be refreshed ... by a variety of duties in his particular and general calling. And the best recreation to a spiritual mind, when it is weary of worldly employments, is to walk in Christ's garden (Canticles 4:12-15; and 5:1). There, by reading and meditation, singing psalms and holy conference, he will console himself with the sweet comforts of the Holy Spirit ...

In order that you may innocently enjoy recreation, follow these directions:

1. The matter of your recreation must be of a common nature, and of things of indifferent use. Things holy are too good, and things vicious are too bad, to be sported or played with.
2. Recreations must be seasonable regarding time; not on the Lord's day, in which time God forbids all men to seek their own pleasures.
3. Recreations must always be inoffensive, such as do no harm to yourself, or to your neighbour.
4. Recreations must be moderate, not sensual or brutish; looking at no higher or further end than earthly delights.
5. Whatsoever your diversion is, you must so recreate the outward man, that you are no worse, but rather better in the inward man.
6. In all recreations you must purpose the right end. The nearest and immediate end is to revive your weary body, and to quicken your dull mind; but your highest and principal end is that ... you may better serve and glorify God.

— Henry Scudder, *The Christian's Daily Walk*, pp. 47-49 (S.P.)

A consistent walk

For our conversation is in heaven ... (Phil. 3:20).

I t is not one or two good actions, but a consistent conduct, that tells whether a man is a true Christian. A true believer, like the heavenly orbs, is constant and unwearied in his motions and actions. Enoch '*walked* with God.' It is not taking a step or two in a way which demonstrates that a man is a *walker*, but a continued motion. No man is judged to be healthy by flushing a colour in his face, but by a good complexion. God considers no one holy for one particular act, but for a general course.

A sinner in some few things may be very good: Judas repents, Cain sacrifices, the scribes pray and fast; and yet all were very false.

In the most deadly diseases, there may be some intermissions, and some good symptoms. A saint in some few acts may be very bad: Noah was drunk, David defiled his neighbour's wife, and Peter denied his best friend; yet these persons were heaven's favourites. The best gold may have some grains of alloy. Sheep may fall into the mire, but swine love day and night to wallow in it.

A Christian may stumble, he may even fall, but he gets up and walks on in the way of God's commandments; the bent of his heart is right, and the scope of his life is straight, and thus he is considered sincere.

— George Swinnock, *A Homiletic Encyclopedia*, p. 3971 (H.E.)

Time-redemption

Redeeming the time, because the days are evil (Eph. 5:16).

Time-redemption is one of the lessons which God teaches those whom he corrects. In our tranquillity, how many golden hours do we throw down the stream, which we are likely never to see again ... It was the complaint of a well-known moralist, and may be our complaint: Who is there among us, that knows how to value time, and prize a day at a due rate?

Most men study rather how to pass away their time than to redeem it; being prodigal of their precious hours as if they had more than they could tell what to do with it. Our season is short, but we make it shorter. How sad it is to hear men complain, O what shall we do to pass away the time?

And think of Sabbath-time. It is the purest, the most refined part of time, a creation out of a creation, consecrated by divine sanction, and yet how cheap and common it is in most men's eyes. While many sin away their time, even more idle away those hallowed hours. Seneca used to jeer at the Jews for their ill husbandry, in that they lost one day in seven, meaning their Sabbath. It is, too, true of most Christians that they lose one day in seven, whatever else; the Sabbath for the most part is but a lost day. Some spend it on their lusts, and more with idleness and vanity. But O, when trouble comes, and danger comes, and death comes ... how precious would one of those despised hours be! Evil days will cry with a loud voice in our ears, 'Redeem the time.' ... And the day will come when God from heaven will announce that time shall be no more ... Will we have redeemed it?

— Thomas Case, 'The Rod and the Word',
The Select Works of Thomas Case, pp. 71-73 (S.D.G.)

The power of God's remnant

But yet in it shall be a tenth, and it shall return, and shall be eaten: as a teil tree, and as an oak, whose substance is in them, when they cast their leaves: so the holy seed shall be the substance thereof (Isa. 6:13).

A definite number for an indefinite: 'a tenth', that is, a small remnant, a few in comparison to the whole body of the inhabitants ... You don't realise to what extent you prevail with God for the prevention of national judgements. When other means fail, prayer may yet prevail. Human strength and human wisdom may be able to do a little; the power and policy of enemies may be too hard for the wisdom and strength of the godly: but when you can do least yourselves, you may engage God, by prayer, to do most. If he takes your part, he can turn the hearts of enemies, disappoint their devices, confuse their politics, or, if need be, break their power. Enemies are commonly the instruments of evil brought upon a land; yet they are but instruments; God himself is the principal agent (Amos 3:6). They are the rods in his hand, the scourges, which he uses or lays aside when he pleases ...

Think, how many times the prayers of the saints have prevailed with God in like cases. Moses' prayer prevailed to deliver Israel, when the Egyptians so closely pursued them ... Asa's prayer prevailed against Zerah and his Ethiopian army, and Jehoshaphat's against the Ammonites. And if prayer has been so prevalent, why may it not be so still? It is an old, proven means, which has not used to fail ...

You pray with the same kind of faith that they did, and your faith is grounded in the same promises; they are still the same: and the Mediator, who is to present your petitions to God, is still the same; and his interest in those that fear him, and his concern for them, is still the same ...

— John Collins, *Puritan Sermons*, Vol. 4, pp. 125, 149-150 (P.S.)

Keep the old receipts

Sing unto the Lord, O ye saints of his, and give thanks at the remembrance of his holiness (Ps. 30:4).

Be careful to keep your old receipts which you have had from God for the pardon of your sins. There are some display days, and Jubilee-like festivals, when God comes forth clothed with the robes of his mercy, and holds forth the sceptre of his grace more familiarly to his children than ordinary ... And then the firmament is clear, not a cloud to be seen to darken the Christian's comfort. Love and joy are the soul's repast and pastimes, while this feast lasts.

Now when God withdraws, and this cheer is taken off, Satan's work is how he may deface and wear off the remembrance of this testimony, which is so important for a believer's spiritual standing. Satan wants to deprive him of this evidence, so that when he accuses him again the believer will have nothing with which to defend himself.

It will benefit you, therefore, to lay them up safely: such a testimony may serve to non-suit your accuser many years hence. One affirmative from God's mouth for your pardoned state, carries more weight (though of old date) than a thousand negatives from Satan's.

— William Gurnall, *A Homiletic Encyclopedia*, p. 347 (H.E.)

God knows his grace in us, and will own it, when we doubt of it or deny it.

— Richard Baxter

The gift of memory

All the ends of the world shall remember and turn unto the Lord ...
(Ps. 22:27).

T he sanctification of the memory ... is the restoring of this faculty to its former integrity ... For when a man's corrupt nature is changed, all the faculties are renewed, there is a new creation of him. This is done:

By purging the faculty ... As the Holy Spirit of God burns up the dross of the powers of the soul, so of the memory with the rest, and erases out of it many sinful impressions which were there.

By strengthening it. For, as sin weakens, so grace strengthens the faculty. This effect it has on the understanding and the will, so it has upon the memory. It is apparent that many, who, before their conversion to God, would forget whole chapters and sermons, yet, after their new birth, they would carry away a great deal of them. God's Spirit helps them, and, according to our Saviour's promise, 'brings all things to your remembrance' (John 14:26). Grace stops the leak in that vessel, which sin has made.

By filling it with good things. When the new creature is born again, no newborn child desires and longs more for milk, than the soul does for knowledge and wisdom. Consequently the memory is stored with Scripture truths, promises, rules, and helps. Then the substance of all that is apprehended by the sanctified understanding, is conveyed to the memory, and lodged there.

— Richard Steele, *Puritan Sermons*, Vol. 3, p. 352 (P.S.)

Ready for the audit?

... Give an account of thy stewardship ... (Luke 16:2).

Those that propose a good end, must call themselves to a strict and severe account, how that end is to be obtained or lost. A superficial account is in some respects worse than none at all; for by shuffling the account you are only bribing God's officer (natural conscience) to delay the inevitable, till one day death surprises you with a summons to present your account to Christ himself. I will name four metaphors which will illustrate and prove this:

1. We must give such an account *as a scholar to his teacher*, of what he learns. 'And he said unto them, Know ye not this parable? And how then will ye know all parables?' (Mark 4:13).
2. You must give an account *as a steward to his master.* 'Give an account of thy stewardship; for thou mayest be no longer steward' (Luke 16:2). But here is the difference between being stewards to our *heavenly* and to an *earthly* master: Christ and his servants have but one and the same interest ...
3. We must give an account *as a debtor to his creditor.* 'The kingdom of heaven [is] likened unto a certain king, which would take account of his servants ... ' (Matt. 18:23). We are so sinfully indebted to the justice of God, that unless we are discharged upon our Surety's payment, we must be imprisoned with devils to all eternity.
4. We must give an account *as a malefactor to his judge.* 'Every idle word that men shall speak, they shall give account thereof in the day of judgement' (Matt. 12:36). Unprofitable words cannot escape being accounted for. Let us fulfil all these metaphors in calling ourselves to account; and when we have done that, we still have not done all.

— Samuel Annesley, *Puritan Sermons*, Vol. 4, pp. 176-177 (P.S.)

Bleeding the vine?

And thou shalt remember all the way which the Lord thy God led thee
these forty years in the wilderness, to humble thee, and to prove thee ...
(Deut. 8:2).

God afflicts us for our profit, that we might be partakers of his holiness. The flowers smell sweetest after a shower; vines bear better after bleeding; the walnut tree is most fruitful when most beaten; saints spring and thrive most internally, when they are most externally afflicted.

Manasseh's chain was more profitable to him than his crown. Luther could not understand some Scriptures till he was in affliction ... God's house of correction is his school of instruction. All the stones that came about Stephen's ears did but knock him closer to Christ, the cornerstone. The waves did but lift Noah's ark nearer to heaven; and the higher the waters grew, the more the ark was lifted up the heaven. Afflictions lift up the soul to more rich, clear, and full enjoyments of God.

'Behold, I will allure her, and bring her into the wilderness, and speak comfortably unto her' (Hos. 2:14), or rather, as the Hebrew has it, 'I will earnestly or vehemently speak to her heart.' God makes afflictions to be but inlets to the soul's more sweet and full enjoyment of his blessed self. When was it that Stephen saw the heavens open, and Christ standing at the right hand of God, but when the stones were about his ears, and there was but a short step between him and eternity? And when did God appear in glory to Jacob, but in the day of his troubles, when the stones were his pillows, and the ground his bed, and the hedges his curtains, and the heavens his canopy? Then he saw the angels ...

— Thomas Brooks, *A Homiletic Encyclopedia*, p. 119 (H.E.)

Now or never

... behold, now is the accepted time ... (2 Cor. 6:2).

I t is an undeniable truth that the day of life and the day of grace are not always of the same length. And even if they were, that could be no warrant for delaying the work of your salvation. But, one would think, your life's uncertainty itself, if considered, should be of weight enough to press you to haste, and make your wilful delay as impossible as it is impious. For even those who pray for the dead do not hold it lawful to pray for any after their death, that have not repented or been converted in their lifetime. If you die unconverted, your fathers and mothers are taught to consent to your being damned; and the best friends you have are forbidden to pray for you to be taken out of hell, or to be cooled in it.

You do not imagine, I hope, that a soul crying, 'God be merciful', just before his death, is a saving conversion. If it were, we might well say, 'Heaven is the receptacle of the most and worst of men; and a great part of the Scriptures is taken up in requiring our needless labour.' But we are well sure of the contrary: though you ought to be told, that if it were really so, yet your delay would still be an enormous folly; since your ability to utter these words at your death are as uncertain as anything. You have little reason to think that your present obstinacy shall not then be punished with at least impotency ...

But who has bewitched hearers of the Gospel? Neither law nor Gospel knows any way to heaven by a delayed conversion. The law requires continuing, the Gospel requires beginning and persevering; neither admits of delaying.

— Daniel Burgess, *Puritan Sermons*, Vol. 4, p. 562 (P.S.)

Probationers for eternity

... behold now is the accepted time ... (2 Cor. 6:2).

*D*o something every day in preparing for your eternal state. If anything of importance confronts you, this is it. If I could prevail with you in anything, O that it might be in this! ... If in anything I should be serious in preaching, and you in hearing; this is it. The longer your abode shall be, the greater preparation you should make. When we exhort you to prepare for other duties, it is done in order that you might be prepared for the eternal world ...

God has set you in this world for this very work—to make ready for eternity. Consider, I beseech you, and demand an answer from yourself: why has God brought you out of nothing and given you a being more noble than all his visible works? ... Do you think, it was that you should go for riches, and not grace; things temporal, not eternal; to buy and sell, and eat and drink and sleep? Do you in your conscience think that God has appointed you no higher things to think about, no more permanent things to get? Reason will convince you, conscience will prove it to your face, and the immortality of your own souls will undeniably argue, that God has made you for nobler ends, higher functions, and greater concerns ...

As you go out of time, so you must in the same state go into eternity. If you die in your sin you must in your sin go down to hell. This is a life of trial. Here in time you are probationers for eternity; and as you are found at the end of time, so your state shall be determined for an eternity of happiness, or misery without end.

If you go out of time unfitted for eternity, better you had never been in time.

— Thomas Doolittle, *Puritan Sermons*, Vol. 4, pp. 32-33 (P.S.)

Long life?

With long life will I satsify him, and shew him my salvation (Ps. 91:16).

L ong life and length of days is the blessing and gift of God, that which he promises and performs to all those who fear him and walk in his ways. But many of the children of God die untimely, and live not long; how, then, is this true?

This is not simply a blessing, as if he were happy who lives long, but as a symbol or sign of God's good favour and love. If, then, he shows his love to some rather by taking them out of this life, than by prolonging their days, he does actually perform his promise rather than break it. If a man promises ten acres of ground in one field, and instead gives him a hundred in another, he has not broken his promise.

So if God has promised long life, let's say, a hundred years here, and then not give it to him, but gives him instead eternity in the heavens, he has not broken his promise. For long life is not promised as a blessing and a happy thing in itself, but as a sign of his goodwill, and which is greater sometimes to be taken out of this life. Just as Jeroboam's good son was taken out, so that he might not be infected with the sins of his father's house, and inflicted with the sight of those horrible judgements that fell upon that graceless family. It was no bad bargain to be taken from earth to heaven, from the conflict to the triumph, from the battle to the victory, from men to God, and to the company of his angels and saints.

— Richard Stock, *A Homiletic Encyclopedia*, p. 3257 (H.E.)

Life is to be measured by action, not by time; a man may die old at thirty, and young at eighty; nay, the one lives after death, and the other perished before he died.

— Thomas Fuller

371

God's footsteps

O the depth of the riches both of the wisdom and knowledge of God! How unsearchable are his judgements, and his ways past finding out! (Rom. 11:33).

I t is true, there are some doctrines so plainly revealed in Scripture that he that runs may read them, especially such as concern salvation ... But then there are other truths which, as they are not very clearly revealed, but are so deep and profound, that fully comprehending them is beyond our reach. Though we may be satisfied that it is truth, yet we cannot comprehend *how* it should be; there is something that lies deep, out of our view, which, after the utmost study, cannot be found out. Not that Gospel truths contradict our soundest reasonings, but transcend them.

There is a great difference between these two, namely, a contradicting and a transcending of our reason. What *contradicts* our reason is not, *and cannot be,* received by us; but what *transcends* our reason may, and in many cases must, be entertained and embraced. That which contradicts our reason is not to be received, nor can it be a part of true religion, in that if it has nothing of reason in it, it is unreasonable ... What is contrary to reason must be rejected, and by no means embraced ... God lays no man under the obligation of believing what cannot possibly be true ... But though what is contrary to reason must not be received as an article of our creed, yet what transcends it may ...

Even in these transcendent doctrines and providences, we may behold the footsteps of God's transcendency and incomprehensible greatness, whereby we are forced to conclude that they are of God ... When I consider the transcendency of God, the infinity of him in every perfection, I cannot but be abundantly satisfied to behold his footsteps in the things that are before me.

— Stephen Lobb, *Puritan Sermons*, Vol. 3, pp. 417-418, 433 (P.S.)

Repair to the covenant

Although my house be not so with God; yet he hath made with me an everlasting covenant, ordered in all things, and sure ... (2 Sam. 23:5).

This Scripture is very striking. It is a wonderful statement by David, who did not have the covenant of grace revealed as full as we have. Mark what he says: 'Although I do not find my house so', that is, so comfortable in every way as I would wish. Since it is not so, what has he got to console his spirit? He says, 'He has made an everlasting covenant with me.' This is what helps in everything. Some men will say, I am not thus and thus with God ... or it is not with my house and family as I hoped it might be; perhaps there is this or that affliction on my house ... Can you read this Scripture and say, Although my house is not so blessed with health as other men's houses are, although my house is not so, yet he has made an everlasting covenant with me ...

We can be sure of nothing here, especially in these times. A man can be sure of very little that he has, and who can be sure of his wealth? Perhaps some of you here have lived well and comfortably, all was well with you, and you thought your mountain was strong, but within a day or two you see everything taken away from you. There is no certainty in the things of this world; but he says, the covenant is sure ...

Thus you see how a godly heart finds contentment in the covenant. Many of you speak of the covenant of God, and of the covenant of grace; but have you found it as effectual as this to your souls? Have you sucked sweetness from the covenant, and contentment to your hearts in your sad conditions? It is a special sign of true grace in any soul, that when any affliction comes, he kind of naturally repairs immediately to the covenant.

— Jeremiah Burroughs, *Rare Jewel of Christian Contentment*,
pp. 70-71 (S.G.)

The news from heaven

... behold, I bring you good tidings of great joy ... (Luke 2:10).

W hat is meant by the Gospel? According to the original word, it signifies any good news or joyful message ... But usually in Scripture it is restrained, by way of excellency, to signify the doctrine of Christ, and salvation by him to poor sinners ...

The revelation of Christ, and the grace of God through him, is without comparison the *best news* and the *joyfulest tidings* that poor sinners can hear. It is such a message as no good news can come before it, nor no ill news follow it. No good news can come before it, no, not from God himself to the creature. He cannot issue any blessing to poor sinners until he has shown mercy to their souls in Christ ... God *forgives* and then he *gives* ... Again no ill news can come after the glad tidings of the Gospel, where it is believingly embraced. God's mercy in Christ alters the very property of all evils to the believer ...

Five ingredients are desirable in a message ... First, for a message to be joyful it must be *good*. No one rejoices to hear evil news ... Second, it must be some *great good*, or else it has but little effect ... Third, this great good must *intimately concern them that hear it* ... Although we often rejoice to hear of some great good that has come to another, it affects us much more when it comes to us ... Fourth, it adds to the joyfulness of the news if the tidings come to us as *a surprise* ... Fifth, to complete the joy of all these, it is most necessary that the news be *true* and *certain*. Otherwise all the joy will be over ... All these ingredients happily meet together in the Gospel, and makes the joy of the believing soul touch the highest point that his affections can possibly bear.

— William Gurnall, *The Christian in Complete Armour*,
Vol. 1, pp. 479-481 (B.T.)

The city of David

For unto you is born this day in the city of David a Saviour, which is Christ the Lord (Luke 2:11).

All the actions of men, especially the public actions of public men, are ordered by God to other ends than their own. The edict of Caesar went out not so much from Augustus, as from the court of heaven. What did Caesar know of Joseph and Mary? His charge was universal to all his subjects through all the Roman empire. God intended this census only for the blessed virgin and her Son, that Christ might be born where he should. Caesar meant to fill his coffers; God meant to fulfil his prophecies ...

O the infinite wisdom of God in casting all his designs! There needs to be no other proof of Christ than Caesar and Bethlehem; and of Caesar than Augustus. His government, his edict, pleads the truth of the Messiah. His government was now in peace throughout all the world, under that quiet sceptre which made way for him who was the Prince of Peace. If wars will be the sign of the time of his second coming, peace was the sign of his first ...

Whither must Joseph and Mary come to be taxed, but unto Bethlehem, David's city? The very place proves their descent. He that succeeded David on his throne must succeed him in the place of his birth. So clearly was Bethlehem designed to this honour by the prophets, that even the priests and the scribes could point Herod to it, and assured him that the King of the Jews could nowhere else be born. Bethlehem, justly, the house of bread; the bread that came down from heaven is there given to the world. Whence should we have the bread of life, but form the house of bread? ...

— Joseph Hall, *Contemplations*, pp. 410-412 (T.N.)

Mild he lays his glory by ...

And being found in fashion as a man, he humbled himself ... (Phil. 2:8).

He came not in the majesty of a king, attended with his body-guard, but he came poor; not like the heir of heaven, but like one of an inferior descent. The place he was born in was poor; not the royal city of Jerusalem, but Bethlehem, a poor obscure place. He was born in an inn, and a manger was his cradle, the cobwebs his curtains, the beasts his companions. He descended of poor parents ... That they were poor appears by their offerings, 'a pair of turtledoves' (Luke 2:24), which was the usual offering of the poor. Christ was so poor that when he wanted money, he was forced to work a miracle for it (Matt. 17:27). When he died he made no will. He came into the world poor.

Why did he come? That he might take our flesh, and redeem us; that he might induct us into a kingdom. He was poor, that he might make us rich. He was born of a virgin, that we might be born of God. He took our flesh, that he might give us his Spirit. He lay in the manger that we might lie in paradise. He came down from heaven, that he might bring us to heaven ...

Christ's taking our flesh was one of the lowest steps of his humiliation. He humbled himself more in lying in the virgin's womb than in hanging upon the cross. It was not so much for man to die, but for God to become man was the wonder of humility. He 'was made in the likeness of men' (Phil. 2:7). For Christ to be made flesh was more humility than for the angels to be made worms ... He stripped himself of the robes of his glory, and covered himself with the rags of our humanity.

— Thomas Watson, *A Body of Divinity*, pp. 136-137 (B.T.)

A plot of free grace

And without controversy great is the mystery of godliness: God was manifest in the flesh ... (1 Tim. 3:16).

In the creation, man was made in God's image; in the incarnation God was made in man's image ... Why was Jesus made flesh?

1. The *causa prima*, and impulsive cause, was free grace. It was love in God the Father to send Christ, and love in Christ that he came to be incarnate. Love was the intrinsic motive. Christ is God-man, because he is a lover of man ... Christ's taking flesh was a plot of free grace, and a pure design of love. Christ incarnate is nothing but love covered with flesh. As Christ's assuming our human nature was a masterpiece of wisdom, so it was a monument of free grace.

2. Christ took our flesh upon him, that he might take our sins upon him. He was, says Luther, *maximus peccator*, the greatest sinner, having the weight of the sins of the whole world lying upon him. He took our flesh that he might take our sins, and so appease God's wrath.

3. Christ took our flesh that he might make the human nature appear lovely to God, and the divine nature appear lovely to man ...

The pure Godhead is terrible to behold, we could not see it and live; but Christ clothing himself with our flesh makes the divine nature more amiable and delightful to us. We need not be afraid to look upon God through Christ's human nature. It was a custom of old among shepherds to clothe themselves with sheepskins, to be more pleasing to the sheep. So Christ clothed himself with our flesh, that the divine nature may be more pleasing to us ...

Through the lantern of Christ's humanity we may behold the light of the Deity.

— Thomas Watson, *A Body of Divinity*, pp. 134-136 (B.T.)

The sages and the star

... for we have seen his star in the east, and are come to worship him (Matt. 2:2).

The east saw that which Bethlehem might have seen: often those which are nearest in place are farthest off in affection. Large objects, when they are too close to the eye, do so overfill the sense that they are not discerned. What a shame is this to Bethlehem! The sages came out of the east to worship him whom the village refused. The Bethlehemites were Jews; the wise men Gentiles. The first entertainment of Christ was a prediction of the sequel: the Gentiles shall come from far to adore Christ, while the Jews reject him.

Those easterlings were great searchers of the depths of nature, professed philosophers; them had God singled out to the honour of manifestation of Christ ... It is an ignorant conceit, that inquiry into nature should make men atheistical. No man is so apt to see the star of Christ, as a diligent disciple of philosophy. Doubtless this light was visible to more but only they followed it; they who knew that it signified more than nature. He is truly wise that is wise for his own soul ...

These sages were in a mean between the angels and the shepherds. God would, in all the ranks of intelligent creatures, have some to be witnesses of his Son. The angels direct the shepherds; the star guides the sages. The wisdom of our God proportions the means to the disposition of the persons. Their astronomy had taught them this star was not ordinary, whether in sight, or in brightness, or in motion. The eyes of nature might well see that some strange news was portended to the world by it: but that this star designed the birth of the Messiah, needed yet another light. If the star had not had a commentary of a revelation from God, it could only have led the wise men into a fruitless wonder.

— Joseph Hall, *Contemplations*, pp. 410-413 (T.N.)

Goodbye, old world!

For what shall it profit a man, if he shall gain the whole world, and lose his own soul? (Mark 8:36).

T he millstone which turns about all day, grinding corn for others and not for itself, at night stands in the same place where it was in the morning. After a great volume of grain has passed by, it is now emptied of all, having received nothing in the bargain but wearing itself out for the profit of others. In the same way, worldly men engrossed in the pursuit of earthly vanities toil throughout the day, and when the night of death comes they are in the same position as they were when they began. All they have is the labour for their pains; they retain nothing of the things which have passed through their hands, and are ultimately forced to leave them to the world, from which they first had them ...

Let us not foolishly imagine that our minds can be satisfied with worldly vanities; nor should we greedily seek for a greater measure of them, when we are not satisfied with a less. The hunger in our hearts proceeds not from want of earthly abundance, but from the unnatural nourishment they offer to the mind of man. It can no more satisfy our soul's hunger, than it can satisfy our bodies to feed on the wind ...

If, therefore, we would have such sufficiency of these worldly things to bring us contentment, we must attain it by moderating our affections, rather than by multiplying these vanities. If we would have our thirst slaked and abated, it must not be by larger drinking of these unsatisfying drinks, which will only increase our appetite, but by purging away worldly lust and concupiscence, which are the true cause of our insatiableness.

— George Downame, *A Homiletic Encyclopedia*,
pp. 4969, 5009 (H.E.)

Times are bad, God is good.

— Richard Sibbes

Grace and glory

Thy kingdom come ... (Matt. 6:10).

W hat kingdom then is meant when we say, 'Thy kingdom come'? Positively a twofold kingdom is meant.

1. The kingdom of grace, which God exercises in the consciences of his people. This is ... God's lesser kingdom ... We pray that the kingdom of grace may be set up in our hearts and increased.
2. We pray also that the kingdom of glory may hasten, and that we may, in God's good time, be translated into it.

These two kingdoms of grace and glory differ not specifically, but gradually; they differ not in nature, but in degree only. The kingdom of grace is nothing but the beginning of the kingdom of glory. The kingdom of grace is glory in the seed, and the kingdom of glory is grace in the flower. The kingdom of grace is glory in the daybreak, and the kingdom of glory is grace in the full meridian. The kingdom of grace is glory militant, and the kingdom of glory is grace triumphant. There is such an inseparable connection between these two kingdoms, grace and glory, that there is no way of passing into the one but by the other. At Athens there were two temples, a temple of virtue and a temple of honour; and there was no going into the temple of honour, but through the temple of virtue. So the kingdoms of grace and glory are so closely joined together, that we cannot go into the kingdom of glory but through the kingdom of grace. Many people aspire after the kingdom of glory, but never look after grace; but these two, which God has joined together, may not be put asunder.

— Thomas Watson, *The Lord's Prayer*, p. 43 (B.T.)

Grace is young glory.

— Alexander Peden

A letter from prison

Cast thy burden upon the Lord, and he shall sustain thee ... (Ps. 55:22).

R everend and Dear Brother:
Grace, mercy, and peace be to you. I am well. My Lord Jesus is kinder to me than ever he was. It pleases him to dine and sup with his afflicted prisoner ... Put Christ's love to the trial, and put upon it our burdens, and then it will appear love indeed. We employ not his love, and therefore we know it not ... I dare not say but my Lord Jesus has fully recompensed my sadness with his joys, my losses with his own presence. I find it a sweet and rich thing to exchange my sorrows with himself.

Brother, this is his own truth I now suffer for. He has sealed my sufferings with his own comforts, and I know that he will not put his seal upon blank paper. His seals are not dumb nor delusive, to confirm imaginations and lies. Go on, my dear brother, in the strength of the Lord, not fearing man who is a worm, or the son of man that shall die. Providence has a thousand keys, to open sundry doors for the deliverance of his own, even when all is over.

Let us be faithful, and care for our own part, which is to do and suffer for him, and lay Christ's part on himself, and leave it there. Duties are ours, events are the Lord's ... It is our part to let the Almighty exercise his own office, and steer his own helm. There is nothing left to us, but to see how we may be approved of him ... who is God Omnipotent.

— Samuel Rutherford, *Letters of Samuel Rutherford*, p. 238 (B.T.)

To be a pilgrim

Who would true valour see,
Let him come hither;
One here will constant be,
Come wind, come weather.
There's no discouragement;
Shall make him once relent
His first avow'd intent
To be a Pilgrim.

Who so beset him round,
With dismal stories,
Do but themselves confound;
His strength the more is.
No lion can him fright;
He'll with a giant fight,
But he will have a right
To be a Pilgrim.

Hobgoblin, nor foul fiend,
Can daunt his spirit;
He knows he at the end,
Shall Life inherit.
Then fancies fly away;
He'll fear not what men say;
He'll labour night and day
To be a Pilgrim.

— John Bunyan, *Pilgrims Progress*, Part 11.

Abbreviations

A.B.P. — American Baptist Publications Society, Philadelphia, Pennsylvania, U.S.A.

A.P. — Associated Publishers, Grand Rapids, Michigan, U.S.A.

B.B. — Baker Book House Co., Grand Rapids, Michigan, U.S.A.

B & S — Blackie & Son, Glasgow, Scotland, U.K.

B.T. — Banner of Truth Trust, Edinburgh, Scotland, U.K.

B.T.M. — *Banner of Truth Magazine*, Edinburgh, Scotland, U.K.

G.A.M.— Grace Abounding Ministries.

H.E. — *A Homiletic Encyclopedia,* selected and arranged by R.A. Bertram, Funk and Wagnalls Publishers, New York, U.S.A.

J.O. — Printed for J. Ogle, Edinburgh, Scotland, U.K.

P.S. — *Puritan Sermons*, 6 volumes. Richard Owen Roberts Publishers, Wheaton, Illinois, U.S.A.

R.P. — Reiner Publications, Swengel, Pennsylvania, U.S.A.

R.&R. — *Reformation and Revival Journal*, Carol Stream, Illinois, U.S.A.

S.D.G. — Soli Deo Gloria, Ligonier, Pennsylvania, U.S.A.

S.G. — Sovereign Grace Book Club, Evansville, Indiana, U.S.A.

S.G.P. — Sovereign Grace Publishers, Grand Rapids, Michigan, U.S.A.

S.P. — Sprinkle Publications, Harrisonburg, Virginia, U.S.A.

T.N. — Printed for Thomas Nelson, in Edinburgh, Scotland, U.K.

20 C. — *Twenty Centuries of Great Preaching*, Word Books, Waco, Texas, U.S.A.